Juana Mora, PhD
David R. Diaz, PHD
Editors

Latino Social Policy
A Participatory Research Model

The Haworth Press®
New York • London • Oxford

Latino Social Policy
A Participatory Research Model

THE HAWORTH PRESS

New, Recent, and Forthcoming Titles of Related Interest

Latino Social Policy
A Participatory Research Model

Juana Mora, PhD
David R. Diaz, PhD
Editors

The Haworth Press®
New York • London • Oxford

The Haworth Press, Inc., 10 Alice Street, Binghamton, NY 13904-1580.

Cover design by Lora Wiggins.

Library of Congress Cataloging-in-Publication Data

Latino social policy : a participatory research model / Juana Mora, David R. Diaz, editors.
    p. cm.
    Includes bibliographical references and index.
    ISBN 0-7890-1759-8 (hard : alk. paper) — ISBN 0-7890-1760-1 (soft : alk. paper)
    1. Latin Americans—Research—California—Los Angeles. 2. Latin Americans—California—Los Angeles—Social conditions. 3. Latin Americans—Research—Mexico. 4. Latin Americans—Mexico—Social conditions. 5. Action research—California—Los Angeles. 6. Action research—Mexico. 7. Los Angeles (Calif.)—Social policy. 8. Mexico—Social policy. I. Mora, Juana M. II. Diaz, David R., 1951-

E184.S75L3637 2003
305.868'079494'072—dc21

2003001811

Dedication and Acknowledgments

Dr. Mora

I would like to dedicate this book to all the community workers and *promotoras* whom I have met over the years. Your grassroots efforts are my hope for the future.

I would also like to acknowledge the tremendous support and assistance from my co-editor, Dr. David Diaz, and my husband, Dr. Kent Kirkton who supports all my efforts.

Dr. Diaz

Finally, Bobby Rider, you will forever be spending those wonderful afternoons sailing over the skies of Laguna Beach with Francine Marie, sharing laughs, those bright smiles, intense liberation discussions, memories, and love for us all.

Jimbo, you are with Russell, two Bioleys in life's full circle, traversing the universe with our spiritual leader, *Tio* Walter.

CONTENTS

SECTION III: RESEARCH TO POLICY AND PRACTICE—INFLUENCING LATINO POLICY AND PROGRAM DEVELOPMENT

Chapter 8. Community Action Research with Census Data: The Latino Coalition for a New Los Angeles, 1992-1993

ABOUT THE EDITORS

Juana Mora, PhD, is Professor in the Chicana/o Studies Department at California State University in Northridge. She is a nationally recognized expert on Latina/o culturally focused substance abuse treatment and prevention and has taught courses on Latino health, families, and women. Dr. Mora has been named an American Council of Education Fellow, has received the Hero of the Year Award during Hispanic Heritage Month from KCET public television and the Union Bank of California in Los Angeles, and is a former member of the Center for Substance Abuse Prevention National Advisory Council. She has published numerous journal articles and co-edited a special issue on substance abuse prevention and treatment for Latinas for the *International Journal of the Addictions.*

David R. Diaz, PhD, is Assistant Professor in the Chicana/o Studies Department at California State University in Northridge. He is an expert on urban planning and environmental impact analysis and works with community-based nonprofit groups in relation to urban policy and gang intervention programs. Dr. Diaz is a contributing editor to *La Opinion,* the leading Spanish-language newspaper in Los Angeles.

CONTRIBUTORS

Teresa Córdova, PhD, is Associate Professor of Community and Regional Planning. She teaches foundations of community development, community planning methods, political economy of urban development, community economics, planning and organizing, and the seminar on thesis and professional project. Dr. Córdova is Director of the Resource Center for Raza Planning, a center within the School of Architecture and Planning that enables students to engage in research and policy analysis on issues affecting traditional communities in New Mexico. She sits on numerous boards and steering committees of community development corporations, planning organizations, and campus committees. She is the president of the Rio Grande Community Development Corporation, which serves the South Valley near Albuquerque. She works closely with the environmental justice movement and publishes on global/local relations, grassroots activism, and issues of community development. Professor Córdova, who received her PhD from the University of California, Berkeley, also publishes in the field of Chicana Studies.

Claudia Dorrington, PhD, MSW, is Associate Professor of Social Work in the Department of Sociology, Anthropology, and Social Work at Whittier College, Whittier, California. Her master's in social work and PhD in social welfare are from the University of California, Los Angeles, School of Public Policy. Her areas of interest are the provision of health and social welfare services to Latinos, immigrants, and refugees, particularly with regard to health promotion, service access, and the development of community-based organizations. Her current research is focused on HIV/AIDS prevention, Latino women's health prevention and health access, and Latino persistence and access to higher education. Her practice activities center on health promotion and early childhood and family literacy program planning and evaluation.

Víctor García is a cultural anthropologist at Indiana University in Pennsylvania, where he teaches courses on Latin America, peasant societies and economies, and Latinos and Latin American diasporas.

Besides teaching, he is also the assistant director of ethnic and cultural studies at the Mid-Atlantic Addiction Training Institute on campus. His research interests include transnational labor migrations, political economy of industrial agriculture and farm work in the United States, and lately, alcohol abuse among transnational migrants in farming communities. Dr. Garcia's research experience on Mexican farmworker populations and rural enclaves in California and Pennsylvania has brought him recognition as a leading researcher on these subjects. His findings have been published in book chapters and research reports, put forth in working papers, and presented in numerous papers given at national and international conferences.

David E. Hayes-Bautista is currently Professor of Medicine and Director of the Center for the Study of Latino Health and Culture at the School of Medicine, University of California, Los Angeles. He graduated from the University of California, Berkeley, and completed his MA and PhD in medical sociology at the University of California Medical Center, San Francisco. His research focuses on the dynamics and processes of the health of the Latino population using both quantitative data sets and qualitative observations. The Center for the Study of Latino Health combines these research interests with teaching of medical students, residents, and practicing providers to manage the care of a Latino base effectively, efficiently, and economically. His publications appear in *Family Medicine*, the *American Journal of Public Health, Family Practice, Medical Care,* and *Salud Pública de México.*

Juan Munoz, PhD, is Assistant Professor in the Department of Secondary Education at California State University, Fullerton. He received his PhD from the Graduate School of Education and Information Studies at the University of California, Los Angeles (UCLA). After returning from military service during the Persian Gulf War, he attended California State University, Los Angeles, where he earned a master's degree in Mexican-American studies with an emphasis in literature and literary theory. Prior to attending UCLA, he was a high school English teacher. He also graduated from the University of California, Santa Barbara, where he received a baccalaureate in psychology. His current academic work targets the educational experiences of inner-city students, with a special interest in the education of ethnic minority students. His work professionally and personally has sought to lessen the misunderstandings surrounding ethnicity and poverty, and to illuminate the multivariate structures that maintain inequity and compromise the promise of American democracy.

Beatriz Solís is Director of Culture and Linguistic Services for L.A. Care Health Plan, the largest Medicaid plan in the country. Beatriz developed the first department dedicated to addressing cultural and linguistic issues in a managed care setting. Prior to her working at L.A. Care, she was a research associate and project manager with the Center for Health Policy Research at UCLA. Beatriz is currently a doctoral student in the School of Public Health at UCLA, where she also earned her master's degree. She has focused her research efforts on HIV/AIDS and the impact of this disease on women of color; Latina sexual health; access to health care coverage for low-income women; and welfare reform. She has co-authored articles and reports on the aforementioned topics. She serves as a board member for the California Pan Ethnic Health Network. She also serves as a board member to the California State Department of Health Services, Department of Women's Health. She has recently received a grant from The California Endowment to further her work in the area of addressing systemic barriers to health care access for culturally and linguistically diverse populations in Los Angeles County.

Olga A. Vásquez, PhD, is an ethnographer of education in the Department of Communication at the University of California, San Diego. Professor Vásquez is the lead author of *Pushing Boundaries: Language and Culture in a Mexicano Community* (1994) and sole author of *La Clase Mágica: Imagining Optimal Possibilities in a Bilingual Community of Learners* (2002). Her research examines the role the native language and culture play in intellectual development, the model systems of collaboration that must be in place to provide the needed resources, and the impact that specially designed educational activities have on both individuals and institutions. Vásquez's research also extends into areas of collaboration with other linguistic minority groups, including several local Native American groups. She received her PhD from Stanford University.

María Teresa Vázquez Castillo was born and grew up in Mexico City, where she completed her BA in economics at the National Autonomous University of Mexico (UNAM). At the University of California, Berkeley, she obtained her master's in city and regional planning with a concentration in regional and environmental planning. Her PhD studies at Cornell University focused on international planning with an emphasis on Latin American studies (Mexico-United States), gender studies, and community development. Her research includes both domestic and international topics in planning policy, theory and history, qualitative methods, and planning for diverse and immigrant communities.

James Diego Vigil, PhD, is Professor of Social Ecology (Department of Criminology, Law, and Society) at the University of California, Irvine. He received his PhD in anthropology from UCLA and has held various teaching and administrative positions. As an urban anthropologist focusing on Mexican Americans, he has conducted research on ethnohistory, education, culture change and acculturation, and adolescent and youth issues, especially street gangs. This work has resulted in such publications as *From Indians to Chicanos: The Dynamics of Mexican American Culture,* Second Edition (1998), *Personas Mexicanas: Chicano Highschoolers in a Changing Los Angeles* (1997), *Barrio Gangs* (1988), and articles in journals such as *Harvard Educational Review, Hispanic Journal of Behavioral Sciences, Human Organization, Social Problems, Aztlan,* and *Ethos,* the journal of the Society for Psychological Anthropology. His new book, A *Rainbow of Gangs: Street Cultures in the Mega-City* (2002) addresses cross-cultural themes among the street gangs of Los Angeles. Current research activities include fieldwork in Chiapas, Mexico, tracing peasant adaptation to the city, and continuing data collection concerning schooling and academic achievement among high school students in East Los Angeles.

Introduction

Participatory Action Research: A New Vision and Practice in Latino Communities

Juana Mora
David R. Diaz

We need to respect people who do things with their hands; farmworkers, carpenters, mechanics. We tell people, "you are on a deserted island and you can only take one person with you, would you rather have an attorney or a farmworker?" Professional people get those degrees to serve people who work with their hands. The people who create the world work with their hands.

Dolores Huerta
El Andar, 2001

INTRODUCTION

Traditional research methods have generally not succeeded in producing socially meaningful knowledge for and about Latinos. Part of the reason for this is a lack of trust of "researchers" in Latino communities based on a history of exploitation by researchers who often did not have the best interests of the community in mind when conducting their studies. In fact, many gathered information and later utilized it to advance their careers. Data gathered under these circumstances seldom had a positive effect on or benefited those studied (Baca-Zinn, 1979; Marin and Marin, 1991). In fact, this type of research often had a negative effect on the studied communities because the findings portrayed residents and families as dysfunctional or pathological (Vaca, 1970; Casas, 1992).

Previous experience with researchers has resulted in the current guarded and mistrustful relationships between Latino residents and community leaders and those who attempt to conduct research on communities. Many community gatekeepers are reluctant to cooperate with researchers unless there is some evidence that the research project and findings will benefit and remain within the community (Corbett et al., 1991). The unfortunate result has been that Latino communities have suffered from a lack of research attention as well as a lack of community-oriented researchers who understand their communities and have the ability to work in partnership with community groups and organizations.

A key problem is that traditional research has failed to address major social needs in Latino communities; thus it is important to reconsider both how traditional research is conducted and how it can be reconstructed to produce knowledge that addresses social concerns and problems in Latino communities. Research that is conducted on behalf of communities and addresses important social policy concerns will significantly improve the current strained relations between researchers and Latinos as well as inform community leaders and practitioners about the resources and needs of each community.

A reconsideration of the vision and practice of research on issues that are current, relevant, and important for Latinos has never been as critical as it is in the current era. Latinos represent 35.3 million or 12.5 percent of the total U.S. population (U.S. Census Bureau, 2001). According to the 2000 U.S. Census, the Latino population increased by 57.9 percent from 22.4 million in 1990 to 35.3 million in 2000, compared with a 13.2 percent increase for the total U.S. population (U.S. Census Bureau, 2001). It is expected that this growth will continue and that Latinos will constitute 25 percent of the U.S. population by the year 2050 (U.S. Census Bureau, 1996).

In some states, such as California and Texas, Latinos represent a substantial portion of the population. For example, according to a recent report by the Public Policy Institute of California, 33 percent of the state population is Latino (PPIC, 2002). In Texas, Latinos comprise 19 percent of the population (U.S. Census Bureau, 2001).

For policy and program development considerations, it is also important to note the youthful nature of the U.S. Latino population and its future involvement in the workforce and in educational and other U.S. institutions. The 2000 U.S. Census reports that while 25.7 percent of the U.S. population is under eighteen years of age, 35 percent of Latinos are under age eighteen. The median age for Latinos is 25.9 years compared to 35.3 in the overall population (U.S. Census Bureau, 2001).

Although the Latino populace continues to increase, it is underrepresented in major social and educational institutions. Disparities in health and education between Latinos and the general population continue to exist in alarming proportions. For example, Latinos twenty-five years of age and older are still less likely than non-Latinos to have graduated from high school (54.7 versus 85 percent) (U.S. Census Bureau, 1997) and are more likely to die prematurely from certain diseases, such as diabetes (U.S. Department of Health and Human Services, 2000).

The visible demographic changes in some regions of the nation have produced increased interest in this population from politicians, community leaders, the media, and major corporations. It is not uncommon in places such as Los Angeles to view advertising in Spanish by major communications corporations, marketers, and the food industry, all of which are attempting to gain the Latino market share. There is an awareness, at least among some segments in society, that Latinos are becoming a major social and cultural force in many urban centers of the United States (Davila, 2001).

In health, education, employment, and criminal justice the institutional response to Latino growth has been less enthusiastic—partly because of the challenges and increased demands on these institutions that comes with a changing consumer profile. Those individuals who are in positions of leadership and are aware of the impact of changing demographics in their institutions want to understand this community. However, although there is a desire to understand a range of issues, the resources, information, and data necessary to properly serve this population are often not available. Administrators in positions of power and leadership desperately require accurate information about Latinos but do not know where to find the information. In fact, there is no central repository of accurate health, education, and cultural information about Latinos. Such a body of information needs to be established, and it is strongly suggested that in order for accurate data, resources, and information to be compiled, it must be done so in conjunction with those who are affected by the problems identified. There has never been a greater need or a better time for community leaders, policymakers, researchers, and community residents to jointly build new avenues for improving conditions in their communities.

In the past decade, researchers frustrated by traditional research methods have adopted nontraditional research strategies to engage community residents in the development of community surveys and social policy analysis. Many of these scholars were influenced by the emergence of ethnic and women's studies in the 1960s, both of which emphasized giving voice in the academy to those who had previously been marginal (Rosaldo, 1989; Garcia, 1997).

The major purpose of this book is to promote a new vision and practice of research design and production that incorporates the "subjects" as integral participants in the development of social policy fieldwork. In addition, the ideals of ethnic and feminist studies for scholars to engage in community struggles are also advanced. In this new vision, the "subject" is important not just to the research process but also to the success of the research.

In a number of projects analyzed in this book, the subject assumes multiple roles in a range of social policy environments and is empowered in the process. The subject community is invested with power over the research process and has authority in the management and implementation of the research, including the review and critique of the validity of survey instruments and the interpretation of findings.

Research on Latinos that is exploitive in nature can be subject to serious methodological flaws and questionable findings. Anthropologists have advocated arguments identifying the benefits of incorporating subjective views in the production of knowledge (Rosaldo, 1989). This book will argue that the entire research endeavor must be participatory in nature in order to produce qualitatively different research that is based on community-identified problems and needs. In designing research within this framework, familiar cultural concepts and language are utilized to collect data with the input of community residents and leaders. Data produced in this fashion will more accurately reflect local issues and also strengthen the relationship between the researcher and community members.

A CRITIQUE OF TRADITIONAL RESEARCH STRATEGIES: OBJECTIVITY, SUBJECTIVITY, AND POWER

Participatory action research (PAR) is defined by Green et al., cited in Minkler as "systematic inquiry, with the collaboration of those affected by the issue being studied, for purposes of education and taking action or effecting social change" (Minkler, 2000, p. 192). A participatory approach to research challenges several basic tenets of traditional social science. It questions the notion of objectivity and distance between researcher and subject, it expands the notion of knowledge (including who has knowledge and who can produce knowledge), and it recognizes that there are multiple ways of acquiring knowledge. From this perspective, community members are viewed as active and knowledgeable agents. They understand the issues and needs in their neighborhoods and possess the capability to collaborate with the researcher to select appropriate research methods, develop meaningful research questions, and collaborate in data collection, analysis, and interpretation. In turn, the role of the researcher also changes from that of an external "expert" to that of a facilitator and someone who is also open to gaining cultural knowledge about and from the "subject" community (Padilla and Salgado de Snyder, 1992; Gomez and Goldstein, 1996).

A major issue confronting researchers concerned with conducting research in Latino social environments is the professional demand of the technical superiority of the researcher that is embedded in institutional training and culture (Darder, 1991). Most social science disciplines continue to promote the notion that the universe of the "subject" is superfluous to the social science research process. The observer (researcher), in training and perspective, diminishes the contributions from the subject (those studied). In the past, subject communities have been perceived as marginalized "others" with limited technical value and knowledge (Pollner and Emerson, 1983).

Latino scholars and others who are interested in conducting research in Latino settings do not receive adequate preparation in graduate school to engage in the challenges associated with community-based research partnerships. Many scholars do not develop an understanding of how skills they have gained through their education can be useful to community groups. Often, researchers are trained in methods, philosophies, or paradigms that have limited relevance to issues or problems confronting community groups. Thus, they are not trained to build a link between their knowledge and the needs of community groups. A major challenge to implementing participatory action research is that due to isolated and elitist academic training, researchers often need to adjust their attitudes and understanding of their role in conducting community-based research. They will need to view themselves as facilitators of a community process of inquiry rather than assuming the principal investigator roles that traditionally give the researchers much power over the entire research enterprise. Under these new circumstances, the researcher facilitates a process, engages many voices into the process, and assists in developing a group consensus about the goals, process, and interpretation of studies. University scholars/researchers, as supportive as they may be, may feel challenged in the process of building community-researcher partnerships.

The relationship between "observer" and "subject" is not the only difference between traditional research approaches and PAR. Another difference is the purpose of the research. In most traditional research endeavors, the purpose of research is to advance knowledge in some area and the science surrounding the study of the topic. While PAR has similar goals—to advance new methods and science—the main purpose is to utilize data to create social change. With this orientation, PAR methods serve to advance not only academic careers but also the social conditions of residents and communities (Andrews, 1996).

In conducting PAR, traditional concepts of knowledge, who has knowledge, and who can produce knowledge are also challenged (Myrdal, 1969). For example, within a PAR framework, the cultural knowledge, such as cultural definitions of health and oral traditions of community groups, are important sources of knowledge in addition to other forms of empirical data. In this context, the subjects "come to consider as their central value the recognition and the experience of themselves as subjects and of others as similar to themselves only by their capacity to be subjects" (Touraine, 1988, pp. 11-12).

One of the main lessons from the case studies presented in this book is that the relationship between subject and observer, ideas about who has and can produce knowledge, and the hierarchical power relations between research and the studied must change in order to better address major social, economic, environmental, health, and educational problems in contemporary U.S. society.

PARTICIPATORY ACTION RESEARCH:
PHILOSOPHY AND PRINCIPLES

Research defined as participatory is conducted by, for, or with the participation of community members and it should result in some form of policy or social change. Research that is conducted from this perspective values the knowledge implicit in community settings, not universities. It is research that studies problems identified by the community and not only from the vantage point of the researcher. In addition, it is research that is disseminated widely in the community, not solely for research publications, which are generally not accessed by nonpractitioners. Participatory research includes communities in significant aspects of research, from the planning stages to the dissemination and utilization of findings.

Participatory action research concepts and ideas began as a result of researchers questioning the ability of "top-down" research methods to solve major social problems (Minkler, 2000). In the 1960s, the establishment of ethnic and women's studies programs which produced feminist and ethnic scholarship also influenced the development of research that is inclusive and for the purpose of social change (Rosaldo, 1989; Acuna, 1992).

The philosophy and principles of the PAR approach are based on three key integrated elements in PAR: *research, education,* and *action.* Participatory action research is based on social science methods of systematic inquiry and data collection, but it diverges from traditional research by including *education* and *action.* PAR does not end at the data collection phase but includes the utilization of social data to educate those affected by the data and to stir people, programs, and communities to action. In ideal forms, this is a cyclical process that begins with fact finding (with community involvement), action, reflection, and further fact finding and inquiry.

Research and evaluation that is based on a PAR philosophy and approach

- involves community residents in the design, implementation, interpretation, and dissemination of data;
- keeps the locus of the research in communities, not universities;
- studies problems identified by the community, not the researcher;

- disseminates knowledge and information widely in the community;
- recognizes that there are multiple ways of knowing and acquiring knowledge; and
- acknowledges that community members are most knowledgeable about their community needs and conditions.

The orientation of participatory research is to utilize research to assist people to improve their lives, programs, and circumstances. Given the increasing percentage of Latinos in the United States and the unsolved social problems facing this population, a participatory model has promise for advancing research as well as positive solutions to address social problems. A participatory model has several benefits for Latinos, including professional training for local residents, enhancing the services of community programs, and the advancement of data-driven policies for the benefit of Latino residents.

Although this model has not been consistently applied in Latino settings, it has been applied in various degrees to the study of HIV/AIDS (Gomez et al., 1999), substance abuse, mental health, community development, environmental health, and education. Beginning in the mid-1980s, several Latino social science researchers throughout the country began work in community settings designing important research projects developed to benefit community groups directly. The knowledge that is gained in conducting this type of field work has not been widely documented and disseminated to broader audiences. We hope that this book will address this deficiency in the literature. The important work and lessons learned in the field by prominent researchers who are attempting to partner with community groups for the purpose of addressing important social, urban, and health problems constitutes an important arena of practical and theoretical discourse in the social sciences.

The Challenge of Applying PAR in Latino Barrios

While the ideas, principles, and philosophy of PAR are appropriate and have the potential to significantly change how research is perceived and conducted in Latino communities, some challenges arise in the implementation of participatory research. Among Latinos the major challenges are related to access and trust building, identifying specific research needs, working with community groups that may have low literacy levels, and identifying researchers who have the interpersonal and cultural skills needed to build important community alliances.

All of the researchers selected for this book have confronted challenges and contradictions between their personal knowledge, training and expertise, and the new knowledge and roles they have gained as a result of their work in community settings. Community-based, participatory action research is a difficult and tedious experience, questioning theory and practice in a manner that demands placing trust and value in those who are knowledgeable about their social environments and needs. However, when theory and practice collide new synergies evolve which change the conceptualization of the relationship between the researcher and the community. This book not only recognizes a benefit to this engagement of contradictions within the field but also offers that this process is essential to the development of local knowledge and social action.

STRUCTURE OF THE BOOK

The primary purpose of this book is to promote action/participatory research methods, approaches, and philosophies in the study of Latino communities. A secondary purpose is to bring together in one collection case studies of projects that have attempted to apply these methods in the study of important social, health, and education issues in Latino communities throughout the United States.

The value of this book, we believe, is that it brings together critical, recent thinking and practice in participatory research methodologies in one book of projects that are critical and innovative in their application of participatory methodologies.

Many of the case studies included here begin by addressing a duality of conflict, preserving a staid professional distance while attempting to obtain information and data in demanding social environments. These environments are often resistant to "professional intervention" (Chanan, 1992), in which the value of that relationship has historically resulted in minimalist or meaningless policy in relation to the problem being addressed in the research design (Moore, 1967). This crisis, revolving within the credibility and value of social research, as is apparent throughout the book, has become the initial stage of discovery in the evolution of devising different strategies in the field.

Redefining strategies, both at the conceptual stage and in the field, is an essential aspect of the participatory research approach advocated in these case studies (Stevenson et al., 1996). Expanding boundaries and incorporating nontraditional knowledge are deemed important components from a philosophical position that is concerned about both process and technical proficiency. This perspective, placing emphasis on the accumulative knowledge of subject and observer, forms the foundational strategy for obtaining data and opening access to reluctant individuals who frequently view professional logic with disdain and resistance (Rosaldo, 1989). In most instances, the development of a sense of power sharing in relation to information and the transfer of knowledge at the inception constitutes an essential methodological strategy that is also an avenue for engendering trust and fostering active participation in the project.

Engaging community residents within the framework of a particular project occurs on a range of levels. In some case studies, the researcher hires and trains community residents to collect door-to-door survey data. This strategy, advocating direct empowerment, acknowledges the benefit of local knowledge in terms of access to information. It also challenges preconceived stereotypes that assume local knowledge implies professional inferiority. Other authors strive to integrate themselves into the community and to engage community residents as a first stage in the determination of whether data gathering is either feasible or appropriate. Thus, even at this earlier stage, residents can have a central role in the determination of whether research assumptions are practical and whether the researcher has a valid role within that universe. In placing the "subject" and its corresponding community in a position of central importance, the observer/researcher is also willing to acknowledge his or her own limitations in relation to community knowledge.

The value of developing knowledge from different vantage points requires engaging in a fluid, collaborative exercise in information gathering and sharing with the goal of mutual trust in the establishment of future knowledge. It is a collective experience that cannot be achieved when the observer follows a strict regime of domination over the subject (Darder, 1991).

Developing this series of case studies is designed to inform, change, and invigorate future projects in Latino communities. Although most of these projects were implemented in the 1990s, the participatory and locally based strategies evolved over a period of time through trial and error, acknowledging that limitations related to the strict adherence to professional neutrality, the preservation of professional objectivity, and maintaining distance from the subject in reality created artificial boundaries and barriers to accessing meaningful and accurate information in community settings.

Challenging the reified position of the subject has generated a new Latino research agenda that has replaced distance between researcher and community residents with strategies designed to share power over research. The goal of obtaining local knowledge in its most qualitative context has benefited tremendously from the integration of the subject into the process of field research. In this instance, the power of local knowledge, which constitutes the center of the subject and the core rationale for observers to engage in this arena, begins to assume its proper role in the development of research methodology.

Section I: Creating a New Vision and Role for Research in Latino Communities

Creating a new vision involves assuming chance in hope of opportunity. The participatory research agenda documented in this book occurred mainly due to a new generation of researchers who questioned both training and their own role as professional investigators. Conducting research in conjunction with community groups or residents is a task fraught with unanticipated technical and practical problems. Although this challenge has placed additional burdens on the researcher, both professional and practical, it is an essential component in how they have strived to improve the conceptual framework of knowledge within a barrio social logic.

Chicana/o academics are confronted with a challenge: How can they transfer knowledge developed within academic institutions into specific, community-oriented research that beneficially influences government policy and programs? In Chapter 1 Córdova addresses the "brain drain" in which Chicana/o scholars in academic settings are not supported and have difficulties developing research that addresses a range of social and urban issues impacting barrios. She also points to the conflict between a professional culture within academia that undermines the concept of community research in relation to what is considered "professional scholarship" by peers who have control over careers in the institution. Furthermore, Córdova challenges the perception that scholarship should perpetuate "regimes of truth" (Michel Foucault) for the university rather than critically evaluate these constructs.

Córdova promotes strategies that articulate avenues to support problem-solving research addressing the social crises of the barrio. She advocates a return of professionally trained academics to barrio settings, where they can design projects that have relevance to the barrio residents. This requires a reassessment of the types of research agendas that will have a direct impact of everyday life in *colonias* and barrios in the United States. In addition, this goal is important in relation to how the next generation of Chicana/o academics will view and value their social experience and how that vantage point will influence Chicana/o research agendas in the future.

Section II: Latino Community and Research Partnerships in Practice

All of the researchers involved in the projects highlighted in Section II have confronted contradictions, conflictive power relations, and dilemmas in the field that forced them to reconceptualize traditional approaches to methodological strategies in community environments. The commonality of these histories is centered on how practitioners, through a range of strategies, incorporated local knowledge and the community of subjects directly into the research process. The fear of the unknown, both in terms of how "nonprofessionals" could perform in a demanding investigative situation and abandoning claims to intellectual primacy, created an uncertainty that would be resolved only through a process of negotiation and trust. Adopting a philosophy advocating a participatory research agenda validated a perspective that demanded a rethinking of academic training. The disjunction between two realities, institutionally oriented practice and the subject community, contributed to a tension concerning reconciling status and power within the arena of community research. The establishment of what essentially are research partnerships has evolved into a new Latino agenda in the social sciences.

In Chapter 2, Olga Vásquez advocates a comprehensive, integrated model of a culturally relevant pedagogy that extends beyond a school-based learning environment into the community and home. The goal is to prepare Latino parents to become active partners in education and to critically and successfully participate in different cultural domains that acknowledge their bicultural educational demands. In particular, this strategy assists lower-income parents to encourage, facilitate, and enhance the learning experience with their children, thus reinforcing academic goals. In this perspective, the concept of parental involvement is reconstructed to include both community-based and school-oriented interventions.

The research project was developed to address how differing cultural realities influence academic achievement and qualitative parental participation. Vásquez places particular importance on the communication styles and values of parents in relation to the class distinctions that exist between themselves and teachers. The role of parents is reevaluated in relation to the significant contributions they can make and roles they can assume to reduce barriers to educational access, and methods of interacting with their children during learning exercises is the major focus of a holistic, community-based strategy. This model also recognizes the impact of the household economy on learning as a central aspect of changing the relationships between the educational environment and the community.

The Central American community in Los Angeles has evolved into a major interest group since the early 1980s, when political refugees began seeking asylum and respite from the brutal civil wars in that region. This immigrant community is burdened by a lack of services and social support in Pico-Union and Westlake, which are the highest density and most violent neighborhoods of Los Angeles. Dorrington and Solís, in Chapter 3, have developed a research methodology designed to build community capacity and empowerment in relation to public health delivery systems in this area. Their goal is to develop community-based leadership that will effectively advocate for a marginalized immigrant social sector that has not received adequate resources to meet the demand for affordable health care.

Dorrington and Solís have an extensive history of analyzing community health initiatives and programs oriented to the Central American community. They have engaged area residents to participate directly in a range of public health programs and advocacy. In conducting field research and designing survey instruments, the concept of empowerment is translated directly into this technical process. Local knowledge is considered an essential element in the research methodology and review of research strategies prior to implementation in a field environment. Both authors utilize residents in the field survey process. They recruit, train, and mentor community members with the objective of transferring knowledge to the community.

The benefits of this approach are related to obtaining qualitative data and democratizing research inquiry through participatory evaluation of research projects. The partnerships that they have developed in the past have enhanced service delivery and the expansion of health education programs in a bilingual and bicultural community. An important consideration is how this participatory approach has assisted Central Americans to confront their marginalization in the politics of the city. Local government has viewed this community as a small sector within the context of a major urban metropolis. Thus, beginning in the 1980s to date, Central American concerns have not been adequately addressed in the intervening two decades. Dorrington and Solís have utilized empowerment research as an avenue to improve the delivery of public health services and generate a political voice for a community that has major unmet demands on the social service delivery systems in the region.

Research that focuses on migrant communities and substance abuse within this population is a monumental challenge. In his experience conducting ethnographic research with transnational Mexican migrants, Víctor García argues in Chapter 4 that in addressing this issue, a binational context is essential in determining causes and consequences related to this problem. The culture of the immigrant experience, both in relation to the alienation of comprehending a different society and the expectations that are projected on social networks, impact factors related to substance abuse. Linking social problems to economic, social, or personal stresses related to the immigrant experience absent a binational focus is, in this perspective, inadequate in capturing the universe of influences related to this issue.

A major consideration in developing research methods focused on transnational migrants is gaining access to subjects at the site of employment, in this case the agriculture industry. Since a significant percentage of laborers are undocumented, both employers and employees are reluctant to participate in projects that could potentially expose them to sanctions in the future. Often, the first obstacle is convincing the migrant workers that it is an important arena of research and that the documentation and analysis of their life experiences has value. Another problem is developing a comprehensive understanding of migrant networks of social relationships that have a direct influence on both the issue and obtaining data.

García emphasizes the central importance of utilizing critical ethnography in field research, especially in relation to difficult study populations such as migrant workers. Critical ethnography enhances how researchers access the subject and develop qualitative data by developing a trust that often eludes conventional practitioners.

García advocates the establishment of a collaborative binational research strategy to enhance understanding of the substance abuse issue in this population. This requires linkages with institutions located in regions of origin and the implementation of bicultural methodological perspectives that facilitate the comprehensive gathering of data and qualitative information. This agenda also demands the involvement of employers and their understanding of the function of research analysis in relation to the labor pool. Thus, in designing a methodology that can incorporate migrant workers, García advocates the establishment of a series of partnerships to capture the totality of the social networks, personal behavioral patterns, and social constructs that influence substance abuse among migrant workers in the Midwest.

Gang violence, youth alienation, and ex-offender status are linked to poverty and marginalization in a society that places high value on materialism. The association of barrio gang culture in lower-income Chicano communities is reflective of the failure of public education, underdevelopment, and historic racism in this society. Gang culture in the nation's major urban barrio, East Los Angeles, has an influential and historical lineage in relation to the evolution of urban experience in this community. James Diego Vigil, who co-authors Chapter 5 with Juan Munoz, has an extensive and impressive personal investment in research related to the gang phenomenon in the Southwest. He has refined how he views gang members and strategies to gain qualitative data and information from a social sector that values secrecy, manifests strong internal social controls, and actively shuns intrusion into the gang dynamic. One of his methods, developed through extensive interaction, has been to recruit, train, and empower gang members as direct participants in the research team. In this perspective, the subjects are also transformed into observers while maintaining their identity within local culture.

One of the most transformative results of this strategy is gaining the trust of gang members. Vigil, in acknowledging his outsider status, also recognized the serious limitations that that status posed in obtaining qualitative data while conducting field research in some of the most violent neighborhoods in the United States. The transfer of knowledge embedded in training gang members indicated to the extended gang network that their social context would be respected and that they had a tangible linkage to the research process. Another factor was the reality that their marginalization was not a barrier to how Vigil approached his role as observer. In essence, by directly engaging gang members—in the field research—selected gang members were empowered to have a direct, participatory role in research methodology, design, and knowledge.

Engaging gang members presents a series of issues and problems to the research profession. They often have limited educational achievement, there is a distinct social distance and distrust in the relationship, they have to address internal gang dynamics which tend to discourage any open discourse with outsiders, and they have to develop a sense of confidence in their capability to conduct field research. In spite of these issues, which are all potentially insurmountable in terms of successfully transitioning into the role of research associate, there are important benefits to field research. The fact that Vigil has been able to work through a series of problems and effectively utilize gang members in his research projects is also a reaffirmation of the importance of working with the community to better understand the issues encountered in the field. His leadership in this field has influenced others interested in gang-related sociological challenges who have also utilized a strategy of transfer of knowledge in incorporating marginalized social actors into the research process.

One of the major internal conflicts that María Teresa Vázquez Castillo encountered while conducting field research was whether her training and role was a valid rationale for actually being in the specific field situation she had identified. She questioned the basis of her institutional perspective in truly comprehending the social and cultural networks situated in an *ejido* in Mexico. This identity crisis was not solely based on positions of power but rather on the credibility of observing indigenous society in a manner that would accurately reflect reality, a reality that she knew could only be experienced by living in the society for an extended period of time. This approach, she hypothesized, would create a period of internalizing everyday life as a method to reduce professional distance, which is discussed in Chapter 6.

In challenging the rationality of the project, Vázquez Castillo strove to immerse herself with the *ejido* community as a methodological strategy in relation to her project. Her struggle with distance, while not totally resolved, afforded her the opportunity to establish a synergism within the social network she deemed essential in conducting field research. Vázquez Castillo's experience bridged her identity of an urban Mexicana educated in the United States with a rural society that has maintained traditions and histories central to the cultural values of the southwest United States and Mexico. Broadening her personal worldview and reducing intellectual hierarchy was her solution to issues confronting field research in indigenous communities.

The Pico Aliso development in Los Angeles is the largest single concentration of public housing in the western United States. The Department of Housing and Urban Development (HUD), under the leadership of former Secretary Henry Cisneros, advocated the redevelopment of an aging and deteriorating housing stock. The City of Los Angeles Housing Authority targeted Pico Aliso for major renovations. David Diaz led a research team in a comprehensive needs assessment of residents in a community that contained numerous gangs, a high level of urban violence, entrenched territoriality, and a historically significant social culture. One of the main goals of the project was to transfer power to area residents in relation to the implementation of the study. Thus, the research team was committed to recruit, train, and mentor public housing residents in the conduct of a professional research project. In this context, empowerment translated into direct participation in virtually all facets of research development, design, and implementation.

A major issue was to educate a resident-dominated team on the function and importance of research. Another important consideration was to elicit local knowledge throughout the process. The participation of public housing residents proved invaluable on a number of levels. Their knowledge was pivotal in relation to maneuvering through episodes of gang violence, traversing conflictive gang territory, and gaining the trust of various sociopolitical factions within the resident community. Diaz, who wrote Chapter 7, had another goal, instilling a sense of confidence in the professional capabilities of residents in administering the field survey of the study. An important aspect of training residents for the study was to create an environment of equals in a team setting. Their understanding of the power of their responsibilities was essential toward implementing the study in a timely and professional manner. This project is an example of how professionals can break barriers and shatter stereotypes that situate marginalized public housing residents as a social sector with extremely limited intellectual skills. The negativity of marginalization was the first issue that the research team addressed by encouraging resident staff to express issues, problems, and solutions throughout the process. Empowerment within this case study translated into self-esteem and confidence that residents could implement a demanding research project in a relatively short time frame. These residents performed admirably and proved crucial in addressing a range of issues that were essential to the success of the entire research project.

Section III: Research to Policy and Practice— Influencing Latino Policy and Program Development

Field research, developing primary data and qualitative knowledge, is critical to the creation of social programs that address the social crises of the barrio. How research is translated in the political and administrative arenas is fundamental to the social construction of government policy and programs addressing a broad range of urban sociological issues.

In Section III, the linkage between funding, research, program development, and public policy in barrios is addressed. Within the arena of research and program development, although the level of resources has improved since the 1980s, this support remains meager in relation to the demographic changes and opportunities that exist, mainly in the Southwest. Conversely, the 2000 census indicates that sociological issues concerning the Latino community will be prominent considerations in numerous regions of the country: the Midwest, the South, and rural European-American communities, which historically had not experienced significant Latino migration until the 1990s. The politics of public and private funding is a critical issue for

Latina/o researchers and practitioners, an issue not without its own controversies. The contributors in this section propose new avenues for funding community/research collaborations as well as discuss the politics of funding.

In the aftermath of the infamous Rodney King beating by members of the Los Angeles Police Department and the incomprehensible "not guilty" verdict by a European-American jury in Simi Valley, the city erupted into the most destructive urban social and economic insurrection in the nation's history (Diaz, 1993). A fact that the national media curiously failed to cover was that the highest level of economic destruction occurred in Latino barrios. David E. Hayes-Bautista assisted a Latino community coalition to develop a policy response to a range of social and urban problems correlated to important issues confronting the city during that era. The officially sanctioned Rebuild L.A. organization had minimal Chicano representation and placed limited attention to barrio considerations in relation to the organization's weak efforts to assist the city's recovery. This group essentially recycled the problem because they constituted the very leadership that watched the city decline prior to the King events (Diaz, 1993).

Hayes-Bautista was among a few Chicanos that attempted to force the city's elite to address the crises in urban barrios. He assisted the hastily developed coalition in establishing a policy agenda, identifying key data requirements, and assessing the limited effectiveness of past city policies and programs, and he worked collectively in developing findings and recommendations. This research process, discussed in Chapter 8, evolving in the midst of crisis, incorporated an activist approach to community research. Hayes-Bautista designed a process and methodology that fostered broad participation in designing a research agenda. This strategy trained nonprofessionals in an important aspect of urban policy and assisted in leading a collective in a jointly directed policy report submitted to city leaders.

Juana Mora is one of the most successful researchers in the field of Chicana/o studies and has developed extensive professional networks with federal agencies and major foundations in the United States. Her focus of inquiry is related to substance abuse and public health. Her experience in grant writing and negotiations with foundations and government provides a unique perspective on current issues confronting Latina/o researchers and community groups. Mora is familiar with how funding sources view the Latino community, difficulties in gaining the attention of funding administrators, and how proposals oriented to social policy in barrios are reviewed. In Chapter 9 she discusses the gaps in funding between those community groups who have the technical expertise to compete for private and public funding and those that do not have this skill. She addresses the critical need to fund Latino community capacity development initiatives to assist Latino grassroots groups to develop the skills and infrastructures to sustain viable service programs in the community.

REFERENCES

Acuna, R. (1992). Chicano studies: A public trust. In Córdova, T. (Ed.), *Chicano studies: Critical connection between research and community* (pp. 2-13). The National Association for Chicana/o Studies.

Andrews, A.B. (1996). Realizing participant empowerment in the evaluation of nonprofit women's services organizations: Notes from the front line. In D.M. Fetterman, S.J. Kaftarian, and A.Wandersman (Eds.), *Empowerment evaluation* (pp. 141-158). Thousand Oaks, CA: Sage Publications.

Baca-Zinn, M. (1979). Field Research in minority communities: Ethical, methodological and political observations by an insider. *Social Problems, 27,* 209-219.

Casas, J.M. (1992). A culturally sensitive model for evaluating alcohol and other drug abuse prevention programs: A Hispanic perspective. In M.A. Orlandi (Ed.), *Cultural competence for evaluators: A guide for alcohol and other drug abuse prevention practitioners working with ethnic/racial communities* (pp. 75-116). Rockville, MD: U.S. Department of Health and Human Services.

Chanan, G. (1992). *Out of the shadows: Local community action and the European Union.* Dublin, Ireland: Loughlinstown House, Shankill Comp.

Corbett, K., Mora, J., and Ames, J. (1991). Drinking patterns and drinking related problems of Mexican American husbands and wives. *Journal of Studies on Alcohol, 52,* 215-223.

Darder, A. (1991). *Culture and power in the classroom.* New York: Bergin and Garvey.

Davila, A. (2001). *Latinos Inc.* Berkeley: University of California Press.

Diaz, D. (1993). *Another failure of black regime politics: Political inertia and corporate power in Los Angeles.* California Studies Conference V: Reassembling California, February 4-6. Sacramento, CA: The Center for California Studies.

Garcia, A. (1997). *Chicana feminist thought: The basic historical writings.* New York: Routledge.

Gomez, C. and Goldstein, E. (1996). The HIV prevention evaluation initiative: A model for collaborative and empowerment evaluation. In D.M. Fetterman, S.J. Kaftarian, and A. Wandersman (Eds.), *Empowerment evaluation* (pp. 100-122). Thousand Oaks, CA: Sage Publications.

Gomez, C., Hernandez, M., and Faigeles, B. (1999). Sex in the new world: An empowerment model for HIV prevention in Latina immigrant women. *Health Education and Behavior,* 26 (2): 200-212.

Marin, G. and Marin, B. (1991). *Research with Hispanic populations.* Newbury Park, CA: Sage Publications.

Minkler, M. (2000). Using participatory action research to build healthy communities. *Public Health Reports,* 115: 191-197.

Moore, J.W. (1967). Political and ethical problems in a large-scale study of a minority population. In G. Sjoberg (Ed.), *Ethics, politics and social research* (pp. 225-244). Cambridge: Schenkman Publishing.

Myrdal, G. (1969). *Objectivity in social research.* New York: Pantheon Books.

Padilla, A.M. and Salgado de Snyder, V.N. (1992). Hispanics: What the culturally informed evaluator needs to know. In M.A. Orlandi (Ed.), *Cultural competence for evaluators* (pp. 117-146). DHHS Publication No. (ADM) 92-1884. Washington, DC: U.S. Department of Health and Human Services.

Pollner, M. and Emerson, R.M. (1983). The dynamics of inclusion and distance in fieldwork relations. In R.M. Emerson (Ed.), *Contemporary field research* (pp. 235-252). Prospect Heights, IL: Waveland Press.

Public Policy Institute of California (2002). A state of diversity: Demographic trends in California's regions. *California Counts Population Trends and Profiles,* 3 (5): 1-15.

Rosaldo, R. (1989). *Culture and truth.* Boston: Beacon Press.

Stevenson, J.F., Mitchell, R.E., and Florin, P. (1996). Evaluation and self-direction in community prevention coalitions. In D.M. Fetterman, S.J. Kaftarian, and A. Wandersman (Eds.), *Empowerment evaluation* (pp. 208-233). Thousand Oaks, CA: Sage Publications.

Touraine, A. (1988). *The return of the actor.* Minneapolis: University of Minnesota Press.

U.S. Census Bureau (1996). *Resident population of the United States: Middle Series Projections, 2015-2030, by sex, race, and Hispanic origin, with median age.* Washington, DC: Department of Commerce.

U.S. Census Bureau (1997). *Statistical abstracts of the United States.* Washington, DC: U.S. Department of Commerce.

U.S. Census Bureau (2001). *The Hispanic population: Census 2000 brief.* Washington, DC: Department of Commerce.

U.S. Department of Health and Human Services (2000). *Healthy people 2010: Understanding and improving health.* Washington, DC: Government Printing Office.

Vaca, N. (1970). The Mexican American in the social sciences: 1912-1970. *El Grito,* 3(3): 25-47.

SECTION I:
CREATING A NEW VISION
AND ROLE FOR RESEARCH
IN LATINO COMMUNITIES

Chapter 1

Plugging the Brain Drain:
Bringing Our Education Back Home

Teresa Córdova

PREAMBLE
National Association for Chicana and Chicano Studies, 1972

The National Association for Chicana and Chicano Studies (NACCS) arose in 1972 in order to encourage a type of research which it felt could play a key part in the political actualization of the total Chicano community. The Association called for Chicano research that was committed, critical, and rigorous. As such, an association of Chicano scholars was envisioned not as an academic embellishment, but as a structure rooted in Chicano political life.

The Association has, from the beginning, presupposed a divergence from mainstream academic research. We recognize that mainstream research, based on an integrationist perspective which emphasized consensus, assimilation, and the legitimacy of societal institutions, has obscured and distorted the significant historical role which class conflict and group interests have taken in shaping our existence as a people to the present moment. Our research efforts are aimed at directly confronting such tenuous images and interpretations and challenging the structures of inequality based on class, racial, and sexist privileges in this society.

I wish to acknowledge the researchers with the Resource Center for Raza Planning. I also wish to thank the many friends and allies who support my community-based work. I especially thank Miguel Angel Acosta for his utmost integrity and commitment to the connection between university and community.

25

In shaping the form of this challenge, the Association holds that our research should generate information that can lead to effective problem-solving action. Our research should address itself to the pressing problems and issues affecting our communities. It is clear, however, that problem-solving cannot be detached from an understanding of our position in this society. Solutions, in order to be meaningful, must go beyond uncoordinated concrete efforts; they must be organized and guided through study and analysis which suggest possible directions for our communities. Our concern with immediate problems of our people, then, is not separated from a critical assessment of our relatively communal situation.

Accordingly, the Association also recognizes and emphasizes the broader scope and significance of Chicano research. We must not overlook the crucial political role of ideas in the construction and legitimization of social reality. Dominant theories, ideologies, and perspectives play a significant part in maintaining structures of inequality. It is imperative that Chicano scholars struggle against these structures on a theoretical as well as on a policy level. Thus it is urgent that we construct theories and perspectives which explain the basic dynamics of the Chicano past, present, and future. Since ideas can point to possible directions for our people, they are of fundamental importance in defining and shaping our future.

PREAMBLE
Mujeres Activas en Letras y Cambio Social, 1984

We are the daughters of Chicano working class families involved in higher education. We were raised in labor camps and urban barrios, where sharing our resources was the basis of survival. Our values, our strength, derive from where we came. Our history is the story of working people—their struggles, commitments, strengths, and the problems they faced. We document, analyze, and interpret the Chicano/Mexicano experience in the United States. We are particularly concerned with the conditions women face at work, in and out of the home. We continue our mothers' struggle for social and economic justice.

The scarcity of Chicanas in institutions of higher education requires that we join together to identify our common problems, to support each other and to define collective solutions. Our purpose is to fight the race, class and gender oppression we have experienced in the universities. Further we reject the separation of academic scholarship our communities. We draw upon a tradition of political struggle. We see ourselves developing strategies for social change—a change emanating from our communities. We declare our commitment to seek social, economic, and political change through our work and collective action. We welcome Chicanas who share these goals and invite them to join us.

Chicana/o Studies was founded upon *ideals of connectedness* between university and community, whereby we pledged to apply the products of our education toward addressing the issues and problems facing Chicana/o communities. For the sons and daughters of working-class laborers, our education was inseparable from our commitment to our communities. Numerous educated Chicanas/os have dedicated their lives to serving their communities. In visits to campuses across the country, I meet Chicanas/os and other students of color who want an education that is relevant to their communities. In their curricular searches, they seek analytical and technical tools to help them understand and address the conditions in their communities.

Despite the legacy of these ideals and commitment within practice, students frequently express disappointment. Race and ethnic studies programs, which may arouse curiosity and commitment, do not always adequately provide the instruction that satisfies students' need to return home equipped to add to their communities. Some professors of color feel it is "inappropriate" to taint research with subjective (or subversive) influences such as seeking change or training agents of change. Others believe they *are* effecting change simply by writing. This is sometimes the case. More often, we read journal articles and ask, "And? So what? What do we know, now that we know this?"

Many scholars, as they are being trained, strive to replicate the rules of "good research" without thinking about those rules, who created them, and what *really* constitutes "good research." Finally, others struggle with the dilemma of wanting to write relevant articles that come from their *corazones* (hearts) and their communities, but do not necessarily know how, particularly in the face of the pressures of their disciplines' formulas. Professors are not adequately employing or conveying tools to address conditions in Latina/o communities. As a result, rather than adding brain power to our communities, Latinas/os are losing many of the beneficiaries of higher education to conventional assumptions of what constitutes legitimate research. How can we stop the "brain drain" and bring educated practitioners back home?

Plugging the brain drain begins by identifying the sources of the leakage. What are some of the reasons that so many Chicanas and Chicanos in higher education are not effectively redirecting research activities back to their communities? This chapter begins by reaffirming the value of *problem-solving research,* then noting some of the political pitfalls that trap many Chicana/o scholars, leaving them unable to effectively concern themselves with community interests. Next, aspects of higher education that undermine relevant education are examined, particularly the underlying epistemological and methodological assumptions that serve as the basis for what academia considers "good scholarship." I conclude with an analytical tool and examples of problem-solving research.

My purpose in writing this critical analysis is to contribute to dialogues on how we can more effectively tie our university work to the challenges encountered in our working-class communities. The chapter is preliminary, not exhaustive. How can we redefine our concepts of research? I share some of my strategies to suggest exciting possibilities for community-based education in a university setting. These ideals for Chicana and Chicano Studies are as alive and relevant today as they have ever been. Because of the many students who desire an education that equips them to serve their communities (or at least the communities or traditional homelands of their grandparents), the ideas in this chapter are dedicated toward encouragement and support. Despite the particular focus on Chicana and Chicano Studies, interactions with numerous students of color assure me that these points are relevant to their experiences as well.

CONNECTING UNIVERSITY AND COMMUNITY
THROUGH PROBLEM-SOLVING RESEARCH

The ideals expressed in the NACCS and MALCS preambles suggest the importance for Chicana and Chicano scholars to seek problem-solving research. The immediate question arises: What does it mean when we say "Our research should generate information which can lead to effective problem-solving action"? It seems to be a very simple concept: the outcome of a research effort should have direct applicability to solving problems. Will problem-solving action automatically follow from descriptions of the problem or ideological statements about the problem? What about an analysis of dynamics of the situation or assessments of the actors engaged in confronting that problem? Are these necessary *and* sufficient elements of problem-solving research? Do we need to do more than focus on problems but think also about solutions? How can we formulate recommendations that can be implemented and directly impact the outcome of a particular set of dynamics? How do we ensure that we are not simply reproducing relations of inequality through the research process and through the implications of our results? These questions, and a host of others, stimulate a discussion about the use of research and the value of Chicana/o Studies for the "political actualization" of Chicana/o communities.

We do not seem to have many in-depth discussions about *how* to create a research agenda that will make a difference in the lives of people in communities and develop effective problem-solving research. Those who have these interests must share examples of their work, assess what is effective and/or lacks influence, confront and resolve issues, and inspire and support one another. Sharing this commitment provides the critical space to address obstacles and ascertain the basis of this brain-drain leakage.

Before I share examples from my efforts to add problem-solving goals into research, the contentious discourse regarding what constitutes legitimate research is addressed. The dichotomous divisions over what is "good scholarship" do, in fact, have implications for whether we as Chicana/o scholars are perpetuating or challenging the "truth regimes" (Foucault) of the university. Challenging the truth regime and creating alternatives is necessary for us to develop the problem-solving research that is part of our obligations as faculty and students who were educated as a result of a social movement.

Faculty in the university who promote counterhegemonic ideals and practices often find that they are in a "war zone," engaged in the ongoing battle about what constitutes legitimate knowledge and action. These battles against "the powers that be" are not surprising; unfortunately we spend endless hours in battles against those who function as agents of colonial power—the overseer.[1] It is the overseer who protects the interest of the "master" and, in this case, helps reify and enforce the use of the master's tools for legitimate research. Once we recognize and name their interference without letting it stop us, we can proceed with the production of positive action and problem-solving research.

The confrontation begins the moment we raise the importance of community presence and consideration in academia. The ideals of Chicano and Chicana Studies call for the integral connection between university and community, although faculty have battled over the extent of its importance. Many opponents frame our community involvement in dichotomous terms—as a matter of Chicana/o Studies being either activism *or* scholarship. Critics immediately construe any discussion of community as outdated rhetoric. Within Chicano and Chicana Studies, different positions on this issue result in major internal divisions, which are reflected in debates within the NACCS and some debates about local Chicana/o Studies programs.

The Vibrancy of and Challenges to Chicana/o Studies

The fervor that generated Chicana/o Studies led to exciting, vibrant work. Chicana/o scholars replaced racist stereotypes about Mexican Americans, which were pervasive in nearly every piece of written work up to that time, with proud articulations of Chicana/o life and history. Continuing the few pioneering works that preceded us, Chicana/o scholars analyzed mythic heroes, transformations of culture and economy, labor organizing efforts, immigration patterns, social conditions, and power relations (e.g., sexism and homophobia). Writers and artists created literature, poetry, art, and critical analysis. Scholars continue to produce exciting, well-documented research, creative works, and critical analyses.

The scholars creating this literature, which is evolving from the movement to establish Chicana/o Studies departments and programs, are significant for a multitude of reasons:

1. They provide curricular material.
2. They resurrect and reflect the world from the point of view of the Chicanas and Chicanos who live it.
3. They provide a source of history, pride, and commitment.
4. They provide insights on the politics of power relations.
5. "Speaking for ourselves" is a critical aspect of liberation.

The works of Chicana/o Studies established a vehicle for generations of students and professors to use to formulate and perpetuate identities of *chicanismo* (a consciousness of our interdependence rooted in our culture and history) and to develop a permanent legacy. We have more work to do, however, as we stretch the boundaries of our education to make our work more directly useful to confronting the exacerbated issues that global restructuring has brought to our communities.

DYNAMICS OF DICHOTOMOUS DIVISIONS: THE DEBATE OVER WHAT CONSTITUTES LEGITIMATE RESEARCH

I attended my first NACCS conference in 1981. A critical mass of feminist Chicanas organized for several years to promote the presence and respect of Chicanas within the association. Later, I worked with others of like mind to organize a political action committee that later took the name Committee for Political Action and Strategy (COMPAS). The main purpose of COMPAS was strict adherence of the NACCS to its preamble. When this committee attempted to address the ideals articulated in the document, I was astounded to encounter such hostility and anger at the thought that Chicana/o professors should be held accountable for any kind of effort that could be construed as "activism." Contorted faces screamed at me, "Not all of us want to be activists!" and "Not all of us have time to do work in the community!"

It was amazing that this initial effort—to set aside one half-day of a three-day conference to reflect on the preamble—was met with such incredible resistance. Critics offered elaborate and contrived excuses for why this would interfere with the "normal" activities of the conference, and "What about the scholars who were waiting to present their academic papers?" When the successful half-day meeting occurred, several participants' rancor was so intense that they never returned to the NACCS. In their perspective, a political agenda would compromise the quality of their scholarship and the standing of the NACCS as a scholarly organization. In a recent effort to revive a Chicana/o Studies Program, a Chicana colleague turned to me with anger and said, "Chicano Studies is not about community activism.

Some people want to study history for the sake of it!" It was her anger that was most striking, as though, somehow, she felt threatened.

It is interesting that they dismissed efforts to address "the problems and issues facing our communities" as activism—as though they had spoken of a taboo subject. Some go so far as to assert, in newspaper editorials, that the outdated focus on activism is the source of the problems of Chicana/o Studies. These critics believe that activism is incongruous with good scholarship and that researchers must choose between the two. Nonetheless, the task of developing counterhegemonic actions and maintaining a focus on community-centered projects remains a critical task within academia.

In relation to Chicanas/os who are firm in their sense of obligation, discussions on how to effectively engage in problem-solving research are sparse. Consequently, even those who would like to engage in such research sometimes proceed in ways which fail to produce research that tangibly improves the lives of people who are the focus of this research agenda. Often, the pressures of tenure or disciplinary formulas limit the vision for possible strategies for both surviving in academia and producing work that will better the lives of people around us. Chicana/o researchers need to develop forums to discuss these issues and share mutual concerns and strategies to maneuver through this professional reality.

The purpose of this chapter is to promote more discussion toward articulating mechanisms for producing more problem-solving research so that we might *plug the brain drain, and bring educated Latinas/os back home.* I ask how the brain drain occurs due to epistemological and methodological dynamics that function as part of a truth regime. Second, I propose some suggestions for plugging the leaks, supplemented with brief case studies. Finally, I conclude that our solution lies in closing the dichotomous division that defines scholarship and activism as mutually exclusive.

EPISTEMOLOGICAL AND METHODOLOGICAL LIMITATIONS

The university is a central location for establishing knowledge as a discourse of power, where the power to decide what is considered truth or not is tied to the power to legitimate that truth (or nontruth). As Michel Foucault reminds us,

> Each society has its régime of truth, its "general politics" of truth: that is, the types of discourse which it accepts and makes function as true; the mechanisms and instances which enable one to distinguish true and false statements, the means by which each is sanctioned; the techniques and procedures accorded value in the acquisition of truth; the status of those who are charged with saying what counts as true.[2]

This regime of truth is connected to class interests, where knowledge serves a legitimation function to maintain those interests, particularly those tied to the logic of capital. Enforcing a particular concept of truth, therefore, is intended to reinforce particular class interests. The university as an institution is a key arena where "legitimate" knowledge is established. Although discourses of power may have qualities of constraint and repression, they are not, nor have they ever been, uncontested. Indeed, the process of determining what is "legitimate knowledge" and for what purpose that knowledge should be produced is a political debate that rages in the university. Through the knowledge that is produced and distributed, we can either reinforce the class interests of elites or we can represent working-class interests. We may choose, or we may act unknowingly. Regardless, our actions have implications.

Within the university, there are canons in relation to what constitutes legitimate research, established reasons for conducting research, and formulas for how questions are framed. Similarly, methodological tenets prescribe how to obtain information and how to view the subjects of research. Protectors of the canon view rationalism, objectivity, and detachment as a superior method to yield a "truth" protected from the biases of passion and subjectivity. Academic rebels have long rallied for the perspective of the actor and the legitimacy of the "subjective" voice. The very premise of Chicano/Boricua/Native American/black studies was a challenge to Eurocentric definitions of what constitutes legitimate knowledge. A positive outcome of postmodernist contentions is the advancement of the critique of modernist claims of rationality and universalism. In the following section, I suggest that academics also need to critique the manner in which we conceptualize the reasons why we do research and the ways in which we formulate our questions.

Social science methodology texts typically state that three major reasons exist for conducting research: exploration, description, and explanation. We may conduct exploratory research in anticipation of a larger project, conduct descriptive research because we want to characterize situations or events, and conduct explanatory research because we want to know why something occurred. Of course, most research contains elements of all three. Each of these research objectives is an avenue toward a larger goal—that of advancing knowledge. A legitimate research project uses the particular relevant literature as its starting and ending point. Researchers, through training and experience, learn to develop hypotheses or questions that are central to the production of knowledge. Subsequently they collect and assess empirical data in terms of how they advance the knowledge within the conventions of the literature.

Good scholarship advances knowledge by building the literature within a respective discipline. A poignant moment in my graduate education occurred when a professor I was considering as a thesis advisor told me that the community I was studying—my community—was not important except to the extent that it "informed the literature." Of course, he was stating that this community's value as a research topic would occur only if the literature was advanced by studying it. Some might say, "Of course. Isn't that why we do research?" Conversely, I ask, "Why do we do research?" Is it to inform the literature? What does the literature actually accomplish in relation to community empowerment and development? This professor's position evaded the question of value and how academic literature addresses issues confronting Chicana/o communities.

It is not that advancing the literature in disciplines is not valuable; it is just that reifying it can be a distraction for those interested in producing knowledge that directly benefits barrios and *colonias* (neighborhoods). From this perspective, Latinas/os are trapped in a process whereby questions emerge from written words laden with Eurocentric starting points, elitist assumptions, and culturally inferior constructions of those who are not engaged in the research or who are excluded from it. A critical point is that acceptance of this logic translates into placing the demands of academia as superior—and more legitimate—than knowledge derived outside academic circles.

Consequently, we define our results in terms that academics create and less so in terms of the issues and perspectives of the people who are subjects of that literature. If the starting point is an often racist and classist set of studies, we are always in a reactive mode, and one of reproducing the dominant epistemological paradigm. Although not shy about critiquing the literatures within various disciplines for tenure reviews and publication goals, we find ourselves situating our research within the framework established by that very literature.

Again, the question arises, "Why are Chicanas/os conducting research?" When consciously and competently produced, advancing the literature by incorporating previously disenfranchised perspectives is most definitely an important enterprise. This does, in itself, enhance the experience of future minority academics who seek relevance within the literature and express a willingness to challenge the regime of truth. This project, however, must be focused for it to be effective in relation to community empowerment. This is notably different from addressing the literature simply to advance oneself in the university.

The ideals of Chicano Studies advocate research that effects change which leads to a positive difference in the lives of people in our communities. A colleague once stated, "If you are not making people's lives better, then what's the point?" If I am going to study *my* community, shouldn't it be for the purpose of addressing issues facing that community? How can I possibly ignore those issues solely for the sake of advancing the mandates of a discipline that may not reflect the interests or produce recommendations on how to address the social crises of the barrio? We can then address and change the parameters of the debates within the literature with a different starting point than the literature itself. In doing so, our contributions to the literature are most significant and useful.

Is there an effective way to resolve the seeming contradiction between doing academic work and working for social change to improve our communities? Is there a way that we can address the literature without always making it our starting point and the only purpose for our research? Are there ways of doing academic writing that allow us to break from the limitations of reifying the literature while still benefiting from what is useful? Are there more effective ways to advance the literature without perpetuating the assumptions that deny the importance of the subjects of that literature? I suggest that freeing ourselves from the constraints of the literature is an important step in developing research that effectively addresses the needs of Chicana/o communities. We can do so, and still fall within the realm of acceptable standards, enough to allow us to remain in the university. In other words, I suggest that though confronting a perennial dilemma of choosing between "their" standards and "our" ideals, we should continue our research in terms of the questions most relevant to our communities. This approach not only increases the possibilities for effective problem-solving research and the development of a critical literature, but also creates a sociopolitical environment within academia that will be of substantial assistance to future minority researchers.

REFRAMING OUR RESEARCH QUESTIONS

In this endeavor, bridging the schizophrenic feeling of being in the "research field," contemplating the issues facing the community, and the experience in the university remains problematic. Geographic separation exacerbates this sense of distance. I can remember, for example, conducting research on military expansion into southern Colorado and then returning to Berkeley to ask, "What literature should be the focus to frame this research project?" The trips back and forth left me feeling as if I were a Ping-Pong ball but I still was unable to resolve the dilemma of disconnection. Although I knew better, it took me awhile to break away from the search to make my community relevant in terms of the literature. I did so by instead asking, "What is my analytical object?" From this perspective, I have developed, over the years, an outline that I use in my own work and deliberately use in my advice to thesis students. This outline offers a vehicle to break from having to define community research in terms of a constricting literature while demonstrating that Latinas/os are conversant in current debates and, more important, draw upon its useful elements. This approach bridges a divide, indicating how field research and literature review "fits" into mainstream academic conventions without being rigidly bounded. It also enables Chicanas/os to draw upon the most useful and relevant studies that were previously published. This outline-driven process is an effective mechanism for directly framing research questions in terms of issues; thus it is more likely to create problem-solving research.

An Outline for Framing a Research Project

When conducting research, the first criterion is that the research be useful in addressing a concrete issue or set of issues. The ability to determine the contours of an issue requires familiarity with a specific community, which demands direct interaction with the people impacted by that issue—those who have something at stake in its resolution. Reviewing pertinent demographic data, local government reports, and other documents also enhances an understanding of major community issues. Framing a research project with a key issue prior to proceeding into field research increases the likelihood of producing useful, problem-solving research.

This outline is a tool, a methodology, and a process. As such, it has several characteristics and purposes. First, it is fluid, dynamic. A researcher can enter the outline at any point and move back and forth through its various parts. For example, even though data collection is addressed at a particular point in the outline, one may be collecting data all along to inform the research design. Second, it allows the researcher to more effectively integrate various aspects of the research, crystallizing how each section relates to other areas. Third, this process provides clarity and motivation because in the middle of the research, when questions such as "Why am I doing this?" arise, one may return to the articulation of the issue or problem, the need to answer "So what?" Fourth, it provides a vehicle to work with community groups to determine what is important and what might be useful through the research process. This outline is useful whether working individually or in the context of a research team. After repeated use, it almost becomes automatic and seems to follow an underlying logic. Utilizing an outline is a method that allows framing the research in the context of stakeholder perspectives and needs. (Figure 1.1 graphically depicts the outline process.)

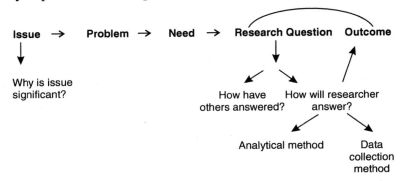

FIGURE 1.1. Outlining Problem-Solving Research

An Outline for Problem-Solving Research

I. Introduction
- A. What is the *issue* (as defined by the people affected by the issue)?
- B. Why is the issue *important?* (What is at stake for those affected by the issue?)
- C. What is the *problem* (which stems from the issue) that will be addressed?
- D. Why is addressing this problem *significant?* (What difference will addressing the problem make to those affected by the problem?)
- E. What are the *assets* (of the community) that can be built upon to address this problem?
- F. What is the unmet *need* (which stems from the problem) that will be encountered through the research process?
- G. What *questions* are you or your team asking about the issue? (What research questions will enable the project to address the need?)
- H. Why are these questions *significant* to the stakeholders?
- I. *How* are you or your team proposing to *answer* the questions? (What is the analytical approach? What methods of obtaining information will you use?)
- J. How have *others* answered the questions? (What do other books, articles, documents, or sources indicate?)
- K. What *outcome* will be produced from this research that meets the need and, in turn, addresses the problem?

II. The Body of the Paper
- A. Use information gathered to answer questions.
- B. Organize the information to address questions in a logical way.
- C. Use information as evidence.
- D. Only use information that directly addresses questions.
- E. Be precise in language. (Say what you mean.)
- F. Back up what you say. (Provide references for sources of information.)

III. Conclusion
- A. Summarize answers to questions. Use information as evidence to build your analysis.

   B. Articulate how your answers build on assets to address the established need.

   C. Suggest implications of the answers for the issue.

   D. Determine how your answers shed light on the issue.

   E. Describe how your answers contribute to and/or change the parameters of the debate in the literature.

   F. Provide recommendations. Use the answers to your questions to make recommendations to address the problem and the larger issue.

   G. Suggest questions for further research. Suggest next steps to further the research on the issue.

The first step in using this outline to design a research project is to ask, "What is the issue?" This question is more difficult than it first appears. Clearly and precisely articulating *the issue* is a tedious and complex task. Researches are not generally used to framing the starting point in this way. "What topic should be addressed?" and/or "What questions do I want to ask?" are common starting points. But it is not unusual for the topic to be stated broadly or for the questions to be detached from a larger issue. The question should be viewed from different perspectives. "What concerns the researcher?" "What is *at issue?*" Thus, one may ask, "What is the key issue that matters to the communities which are the focus of field research? The process of phrasing the starting point this way forces the analyst to think in terms of an issue that the subsequent research will address.

Formulation of an issue should not be conducted in a vacuum. This requires an informed perspective and direct engagement. Although this engagement will be influenced by the literature, relevant studies, and documents, it can, and often should, evolve directly from the perspective of the social sectors that are directly affected that have an understanding based on their knowledge in relation to its effects or resolution.

The next question is, "Why is this issue significant?" If an issue is in dispute, what are the ramifications of its resolution? What difference does the outcome make to the community confronting the issue? What is at stake? Asking these questions forces researchers to articulate the relevance of their projects, and thus imbues their activities with a sense of meaningful motivation.

When the answers to these questions are articulated, the following challenge emerges: "What is important about this issue and the challenges that it generates?" What problem stems from this issue that can be addressed through field research? A multitude of possible answers exists, but the important deciding factor is what problems do *researchers and/or the community* want to address in the research? This problem should be manageable, and one that is within a reasonable time frame. Not every aspect of an issue will be addressed; therefore, focusing on a particular problem set is essential. Each problem generates a set of needs that, if addressed, can in turn assist in resolving the problem. It is then important to determine which assets within a community can assist in defining *the problem.* Building from those assets, what are the unmet needs? The researcher's task, then, is to identify, generally with stakeholders, a set of specific issues that will be addressed in the research. Rephrasing *the need* statement as a question becomes *the research question.*

The research question is a coherent statement of the questions, surprisingly absent from many studies, which provides focus and direction for the project. A key consideration is, "What is the significance of this question?" What new knowledge will be gained when data purport to answer a particular issue? Will the answer illuminate the issue and how can its major components be confronted? Most important, a fundamental conflict in relation to field research is "So what?" What difference will the project make and to whom? The significance of that question forces researchers to address the need stakeholders have articulated. This need arises from a problem that is directly connected to a larger issue.

It is then helpful to specify the anticipated outcome of field research. What is the end product of the project? For example, will policy recommendations, an impact analysis, or some other research result from the activity? How will this outcome be significant in addressing the main issues that generated the project?

For example, several students in a recent thesis preparation seminar articulated their issue as the declining agricultural land in the South Valley (contiguous to Albuquerque) and the implications for the survival of land-based cultures and local food supply. Based on his interaction with stakeholders and his familiarity with the issues, one student defined the problem as land-use decisions that promulgated the decline. The *need* was defined as a restructuring of subdivision regulations to allow for easier transfer between generations. His research question, therefore, was a rephrasing of this need: "How can alternative subdivision regulations be created to facilitate the passing of land between generations without contributing to the increasing decline of agricultural land?" The *outcome* of this project would be a set of recommendations for changes in the subdivision regulations. This approach provides an analytical vehicle to organize the conceptualization of the project.

Another student who was also concerned with the decline of agriculture defined the problem as a decrease in the economic feasibility of agricultural production and therefore a need to demonstrate avenues for improving the economical feasibility of the industry. The main research question was, "How can agriculture in the South Valley be made more economically feasible?" The conclusion of the report is a strategy for increasing the economic feasibility of agricultural activities on the urban fringe of Albuquerque.

The next step in the outline is to examine the ways that other researchers, policy analysts, or communities have answered the research questions posed. Often, depending on the issue, previous policy documents and reports exist that are directly relevant to the issue. Stories from community members are key, particularly to give a previous history that is knowable only through oral accounts. This is also the point at which the researcher can turn to whatever literature may be relevant and accessible to consider how the products of that literature may contribute to an understanding of the issue at hand. This search for relevant literature does not necessarily bind the researcher to one literature or even one discipline. I remember with amusement a comment that a sociologist once made to me: "You don't seem to be tied to one paradigm. Why is that?" My answer was easy: "To me, the issue at hand is significant. I use whatever previous literature may be relevant to help address that issue. I view the literature as a tool, not a paradigm within which I must function."

Once these research challenges have been met, the next phase is the articulation of methods to answer the research questions that have been developed. This requires an analytical design. That is, analytically, how will the answer to the larger research question be pursued? The researcher needs to specify the meaning of concepts and how to measure those concepts. What are the relationships among the concepts? For example, is the researcher asserting causation? Other decisions involve being clear on the parameters of the population and selecting a sample. Settling on an analytical design requires thinking through the relationship between the information the researcher will gather and how it will provide the answers to the questions posed. Again, this stage is more effectively conducted when stakeholders are involved in the design—particularly in identifying what concepts are relevant and how they are used.

In one of the examples, the student who was pursuing the question of how agriculture can be more economically feasible began by asking a series of what should be termed *operational questions*. For example, Would pursuing the "organic" market be a good strategy? What is the market for organic produce in the Albuquerque area? What are consumer patterns? What are the current production patterns and consumer needs? The articulation of these questions enabled the student to "get at" the major research question. By answering operational questions, the researcher can obtain answers to the larger research question.

Next, an assessment of data collection methods should be developed to gain information useful to the initial question set. The data collection design constitutes the work plan to develop information through interviews, archives, and other sources. Depending on how formal the research project is, the design will vary in relation to resources. Again, in the previous example, the student, in consultation with South Valley agricultural producers and community developers, proposed to design and implement a survey to assess consumer patterns and conduct interviews with organic retailers and agricultural producers. Thus a range of data-gathering strategies will allow the researcher to obtain the information and evidence required to answer the major research question(s). Once again, this is an essential entry point for involving stakeholders. Often data collection technique requires formally involving the stakeholders through surveys, interviews, and focus groups. Stakeholders assist researchers in developing appropriate sources of information including snowball samples, previous reports, and access to other data.

I use the introduction section of this outline as the proposal for the research project. It then serves as the introduction to the full thesis. In writing a paper it serves as an analytical starting point, which may be revised as the analysis is developed. While working with manuscripts or with students and stakeholders, an extensive time investment is required to articulate the thesis. Depending on the scope of the research project, it can also take months to complete. Students, when stating their main problem, should be prepared to revise it several times. Once the researcher articulates and internalizes this section, he or she feels empowered to proceed with the remainder of the project.

The report that identifies both the focus of the thesis and the results of the research effort should answer the major research questions. Generally, the data should be presented in a manner that clearly answers the questions posed. In addition, students should organize the information in a logical way. Rambling, illogic, or contradictory statements are a distraction to otherwise interesting information. Outlines assist in the organization of the information. The information should be used as evidence to address important issues. When conducting research, an extensive wealth of information is generated. Researchers become attached to specific data sets and find it difficult to limit their use in reports. Generally, the report should rely on only the information that directly addresses the main research questions. Language should be precise, and references should be provided as sources of information. Additional ideas and information can be developed as a section titled Questions for Further Research.

The conclusion provides an opportunity to consider the information gathered in terms of the major issues. How has the research addressed the need and contributed to meeting the challenges that were initially articulated? First, summarize the answers to the questions. Second, indicate the implications of these answers in terms of the issues. How should these issues be viewed in light of the analysis? Next, on the basis of the analysis, identify the main recommendations related to the issue. What might be the next set of action steps? Finally, what are the questions for future research? How might one further consider this issue? The conclusion captures the significance of the research project and states its usefulness as problem-solving research.

The power of this outline is in the process of thinking through the design and analysis of a research endeavor.[3] This proposed design uses formal methodological techniques selectively and sometimes informally, as tools to gather and analyze information. This effective mechanism guides research interests toward problem-solving research and increases the likelihood of fulfilling the goals stated in the NACCS and MALCS preambles.

INTERACTIVE RESEARCH

Whether we are able to apply research in a useful and effective way is partly a function of how we frame the research design. Articulating an issue that is significant to stakeholders involves interacting with them. Learning what is important to them, their opinions, and their ideas for solutions requires interaction. Unfortunately, researchers are not always properly trained to engage with communities. Epistemological and methodological decisions affect how to determine the issues/problems/needs of a community.

How we define ourselves in relation to the subjects of our research is an important decision that either separates us or connects us to community stakeholders. Again, research rules of objectivity and detachment place us at a critical distance that is a presumably superior position to produce a superior research outcome. Even when we stretch academic boundaries and venture into a community to conduct interviews or observe "the natives in their natural habitat," academia has instilled in us a sense that we are the experts and the subjects are inferior to our expertise. This underlying set of epistemological assumptions may be very subtle and we may not even realize that we have assumed those roles. There is to some degree an amount of appropriation, as we build careers by studying the subjects, while their lives go on, virtually unimproved by our direct presence. Other times, the research field proves frustrating, because we wish we could have made a difference.

The act of studying "subjects" transforms them into academic objects. Their existence is significant to the extent that they serve an academic pursuit of advancing the literature. Although most Chicanas/os articulate a love of their communities, the implicit operating assumptions set us up to detach our work from those communities. Onesided, in-depth interviews or randomly sampled surveys can, but do not automatically, generate the interactive quality that is necessary to adjust an understanding of a situation based upon the emergent product resulting from an interactive process. An *interactive element of research* usually is missing from both the literature and discussions of methodological design.

Distance and detachment preclude problem-solving research. Onesided perspectives increase inaccuracies while multiple perspectives provide greater insight regarding the complexities of an issue. The researcher can facilitate the consideration of several perspectives. It is only through interaction that we can understand and produce outcomes that directly address the needs of those being researched. Symbolic interactionists, beginning with George Herbert Mead, have understood the significance of interactive processes and the outcomes of those interactions as emergent products. Interaction shapes the "self" and the understanding that the self has of the world.

How can we say that we know or understand the community without direct interaction with it? Saying so does not make it so. Qualitative interaction is more substantial than just participant observation. Thus, I suggest the following guidelines for *interactive research:*

- Engage—do not make research "objects" out of people.
- Spend time.
- Do not position yourself or even think of yourself as the carrier of superior knowledge—assume that people have a base of knowledge that comes from their experience of the world.
- Learn to listen; listen to learn.
- Reflect on yourself and the meaning of your work—do not be disingenuous about your own potential contribution.

Interactive research is time-consuming and complex. By directly engaging the world, the researcher confronts the complexities of that world, such as the array of economic, political, ecological, cultural, and social factors. Researchers experience a loss of control and a realization that they do not always have the answers. This sense may lead researchers to find comfort in ideological certainties through preconceived concepts of how the world is supposed to be and how they are supposed to react to it. They then fit what they see in terms of that ideological formation. This form of deductive thinking is common yet problematic, because it significantly decreases the likelihood of hearing the voices of those with whom we speak. By filtering those voices through ideologically based versions of the truth, we also decrease the likelihood of proposing pragmatic solutions. By inductively building bases of knowledge, however, researchers create the foundation for directing that knowledge to community development. Inductively, they can develop the types of information that are relevant to address important issues. Thus community-generated data lead to the development of new theoretical constructs and emancipatory literature.

In advancing this logic, researchers can conceive the best empirical assessment inductively through a process of interaction with those who are "the focus of study." It is in direct interaction with those experiencing the "issue" that practitioners are able to determine the contours of that issue, the problems, the needs, and thus, the appropriate research questions. Interactively framing the research agenda and problems to be addressed in terms of the needs of people who are directly impacted ensures that the researcher does not impose an ideology on his or her subjects. Thus, the researcher is no longer studying *them* but studying *with them*. Similarly, the researcher is learning from the subject while, it is hoped, the subject is also learning from the professional. This orientation constitutes a critical basis for problem-solving research.

Problem-Solving Research

We can sit in the classroom and determine what to study or we can work directly with communities to develop a research agenda based on significant issues. Communities, of course, are not homogeneous, thus the realm of possibilities is enormous. We have participated far too long in a research approach that objectifies rather than empowers. What is important from the stakeholders' viewpoints?

Fortunately, in the field of planning, a number of approaches and techniques are available to use in working with communities. For example, strategic planning techniques articulate community goals and list activities to achieve those goals. What role can research play in attaining those desired outcomes? If we work with advocacy and community groups, we can ascertain, along with the organizers, the kinds of information that would be helpful to their efforts. Similarly, we can work with community development organizations or service providers to help determine what type of information and research would benefit their groups. We can also interact with policymakers and community members to know the parameters of an issue and which research might be useful to resolve those issues. In the role of "independent researchers" addressing policy or programmatic issues, we can conduct *strategic research*.

Whatever techniques are used to ascertain a research agenda, a number of important factors are related to this process. First, we are determinaing a research agenda *with* communities or organizations and our work should make a direct contribution to their efforts.

Second, communities and organizations have *assets,* and any work that we do should build on the talents, skills, and resources of others. Chicana/o communities have long insisted on not being treated as "inadequate" or "needy" by academics, service providers, or technical assistants. Asset-based strategies are more effective starting points when ascertaining fundamental issues/problems/needs in the design of a research agenda.

Third, building the research capacity of those who have historically been treated as research objects is an essential goal of field research. For example, while conducting a survey, researchers determine questions, use student interns to gather information, and then interpret the results. Conversely, a group from the community can jointly determine the questions, implement the survey, and interpret the results. Ideally, obtaining a grant to retain local residents will provide a mechanism to implement this type of project. It is also helpful to train residents in the techniques of questionnaire construction, administration, and analysis. This facilitates a transfer of knowledge in relation to how formal surveys are developed, thus ensuring that the data remain in the community. This enhances the capacity of residents to complete a survey project through their own internal resources in the future.

Finally, build community—or at least add to others' efforts to do so. Increasingly, in planning circles community building is an essential component of revitalization. A community-building process makes a difference in people's sense of belonging, connection, and commitment. A few years ago, in developing a grant proposal to build university capacity to work with communities, we connected with a local community development corporation. Together, the group convened area residents to discuss specific community concerns, how the project related to other efforts, and what the university could provide directly to the area. This series of meetings led to the development of specific objectives for the grant, generated some very successful brainstorming for integrating a range of activities related to economic development, and brought various sectors of the neighborhood together for the first time. The community-building role that we played was an important contribution to the overall revitalization effort in that community.

Admittedly, the field of planning facilitates and promotes these techniques and approaches as part of university work. Not all planners use these approaches and not all of those who do use them well. What is important to convey, however, is how the approach, the possibility, and the implications of research interests can be directly connected to issues facing our communities. Fundamentally, it is correlated with principles and perspectives regarding how Latinas/os view themselves in relation to who and what is researched.

Examples of Community-Based, Problem-Solving Research

The South Valley, near Albuquerque, New Mexico, is a predominantly Chicano/Mexicano semirural community that has a strong sense of history, a unique cultural landscape, strong family ties, but also problems with inadequate infrastructure, under- and unemployment, low per-capita income, and high dropout rates. Because of its proximity to Albuquerque, it also faces increasing urban encroachment and threats to its land-base and agricultural economy.

As a resident and president of the board of the Rio Grande Community Development Corporation, I am involved in community development issues and often attend a variety of community meetings. Through my involvement in the community, I am aware of many of the contemporary issues that concern local residents. As the director of the Resource Center for Raza Planning (RCRP) in the School of Architecture and Planning at the University of New Mexico, I have the capacity to bring university resources to address these community issues. More important, through RCRP and the Community and Regional Planning Program where I am a faculty member, I actively recruit community members into the master's program, which enables them to develop skills and expertise that they apply in their work with their own communities. While in the program, their experiences at RCRP provide opportunities to engage in real-world planning issues.

In the following section, I describe two instances of community-based research by the Resource Center for Raza Planning that involve a fourteen-acre parcel of land in a stable, but low-income neighborhood in the South Valley. The parcel of land is known as the Sanchez Farm and represents the legacy of the Sanchez family and the importance of agriculture in the area. Family members still live adjacent to the site. In 1997, Bernalillo County purchased the property with the intention of building a detention pond for storm water management in the area. Community members were very interested in seeing the detention pond be built in a way that enhanced rather than detracted from the neighborhood. Products of discussions for the site by the community and the county, however, lay dormant.

In fall 2000, we learned about "a business-led collaborative" sponsored by the local utility company. Its goal was to develop a "learning facility" to improve South Valley's labor force, with the aim of making Albuquerque a more cost-competitive area, thus facilitating the recruitment of companies into the area. This economic development strategy is complex and not without some merit. This particular nine-building, 35,000-square-foot facility, however, was planned for the Sanchez Farm in the middle of a residential, primarily Chicano neighborhood. Architectural designs were drawn and extensive politicking had already occurred, but no one had asked the neighbors how they viewed the project and what they considered to be the potential impacts of the facility on their neighborhood and quality of life.

The issue facing this community involved institutions and interests outside the neighborhood that were making plans for the area without involving residents or attempting to ascertain the potential impacts of the project on the community. The issue was significant because it had implications for the quality of life in the neighborhood and its ability to withstand this massive development project. The problem was the absence of an impact analysis of the project on the neighborhood. The assets available to address this problem were the opinions of the residents. A need existed, therefore, to know the possible impacts of the project from the viewpoint of the residents so that they could influence the decisions affecting the site. Our research question was "What are the potential impacts of this proposal on the neighborhood?" Our outcome was a community impact analysis.

There were numerous steps in the analytical method, beginning with an assessment of the actors and the parameters and plans for their project. University-based research could be an effective avenue in providing an "independent" impact analysis that began with the opinions of the neighborhood residents regarding both the programs and the facilities being proposed. Nine weeks were spent in the initial phase of gathering information, including developing a questionnaire. Through a door-to-door random sample survey, we came to know residents and what was important to them. We followed with a set of focus groups in which people freely expressed their opinions and concerns. In addition, a series of interviews with relevant stakeholders and local politicians was conducted.

On the basis of the survey and focus groups, we developed a set of impact variables that we used to analyze the proposal. These variables primarily included traffic, parking, displacement, and land use. We supplemented our analysis with historical and demographic information about the neighborhood. Choices for additional information were determined by what people in the neighborhood indicated was important to them. In addition, other variables were added that were known to be important from the perspective of those making the decision on use of the site, for example, compatibility with the drainage function of the site and compatibility with land-use regulations.

After five months of conducting community impact analysis, we hosted a community meeting on January 31, 2001, attended by neighborhood residents, local government officials (elected and appointed), and representatives of the group proposing the project. After our presentation and comments by local residents, the local county commissioner announced that the project would not go forward on this site. Residents were ecstatic and voiced their appreciation to the research team for helping to "save our neighborhood." As a result, we established a strong commitment to and connection with the residents. Our interest in the community continued in relation to future planning for this fourteen-acre site.

Several months later, in fall 2001, as the county and the local flood control authority proceeded with their plans for the detention pond (Sanchez Farm), they expanded in their plans the amount of flood plain that would drain into this property and from there to the river. Both neighbors and members of the Community Advisory Committee to the project were concerned that the drainage pond would become a "big hole" in the middle of the neighborhood. Public works and flood control authorities agreed to design a detention pond that would not be just a "big hole," but the issue remained of how to translate the desires of residents into a design that satisfied the engineers. Once again, the future of the neighborhood was at stake and once again we made ourselves available.

The problem was not in getting the engineers to agree to develop a neighborhood amenity associated with the pond. The engineers felt stuck, however, regarding *how* to connect the community ideas for the site with their engineering considerations and create a design for the pond. The assets available for this project were the residents' ideas of what they did and did not want for this site. There was a need, however, to facilitate a dialogue between the community and the engineers and then to represent these ideas in a design for the drainage pond. The research question was "What is the community vision, what are the engineering considerations, and how can they be represented in a site design?" Our outcome was a site design for the drainage detention pond that reflected this dialogue.

The analytical method consisted of gathering information and assessing existing conditions of the site, determining the community vision, identifying engineering considerations, establishing goals for our project, and developing a site design. The research team collected information through site assessments, maps, previous designs, relevant interviews, and previous documents. A community visioning meeting was held with residents using community-planning techniques. Residents were invited to attend the meeting through mailings, door-to-door invitations, and phone calls. Over the course of two and one-half months, beginning in January 2002, we completed the work and then presented the design to the community residents for review. On the basis of their comments, a new site design was developed. The county and regional flood control authorities are using this community plan and will incorporate the site design into their final documents for the contractor. Construction begins in fall 2003.

This brief description demonstrates various aspects of an effective and useful problem-solving approach to research. The field of planning, especially community-based planning, has a history of locally based citizen participation in the decision-making process. Nonetheless, our conscious and strategic research approach allowed us to work directly with and sometimes on behalf of communities. This is the philosophy of the mission of the Resource Center for Raza Planning, which is committed to the "survivability and sustainability of traditional communities in New Mexico":

> We promote integration between higher education and our traditional communities through the application of planning processes and techniques. RCRP conceives planning as multi-disciplinary,

intergenerational, directly responsive to community needs, and developed through ongoing, long-term relationships.[4]

CLOSING THE DICHOTOMOUS DIVISION

The era of global restructuring is ushering in new and increased forms of exploitative relations. Increased social inequality and polarization characterize the restructuring economy. This discussion, thus, is not purely academic, but suggests that the choices we make about how or whether to serve our communities has implications beyond ourselves. There is, therefore, more potential and urgency for community-oriented research conducted by educated Chicanos and other people of color.

In 1972 the NACCS preamble declared that "our research should address itself to the pressing problems and issues affecting our communities." Within the preamble, however, language suggests that we, as educated intellectuals, will offer "possible directions for our communities." Though idealism may drive scholars interested in developing solutions, it is essential that the location of that work be alongside communities to contribute to efforts to develop and implement solutions. The key for this concept of *connectedness* is not to view research as separate from community.

Within this argument, it is not claimed that every Latina/o must conduct field research, only that too few are engaged—and it is not enough. This chapter is for conscientious researchers who continue to endorse this perspective. In this manner, *we* define, along with communities, what constitutes good scholarship. Consequently, we challenge academic truth regimes that define activist research as not being legitimate. Rather than buy into the dichotomous division that separates research and activism, Latinas/os and others must assert the primacy of values and priorities centered on community empowerment.

Chicana/o researchers need to continue to develop criteria and standards for the types of research agendas that meet tangible community demands in relation to quality of life and socioeconomic revitalization. Research that is designed only to reinforce an ideology or theory based on unequal power relations does not foster that goal of community development. Although we can draw upon a rich legacy of epistemological and methodological approaches to research, it is the dialogue between academic researchers and communities, based on experiences and examples, that will yield the most helpful ideas on connecting research to our communities. A multitude of issues involving education, health, mental health, environmental justice, economic development, and community and regional planning can benefit from research. Numerous individuals and organizations would welcome useful contributions made by *plugging the brain drain and bringing our education back home.*

NOTES

1. See Córdova, Teresa, "Power and Knowledge: Colonialism in the Academy," in Trujillo, Carla (Ed.), *Living Chicana Theory.* Berkeley, CA: Third Woman Press, 1997, pp. 17-45.

2. Michel Foucault, *Power/Knowledge: Selected Interviews and Other Writings 1972-1977.* New York: Pantheon Books, 1977, p. 131.

3. For a workbook of this outline, contact the Resource Center for Raza Planning, School of Architecture and Planning, University of New Mexico, Albuquerque, NM 87131, or rcrp@unm.edu.

4. Mission Statement RCRP, School of Architecture and Planning, University of New Mexico, Albuquerque, New Mexico, 87131. RCRP can be contacted at rcrp@unm.edu.

SECTION II:
LATINO COMMUNITY AND RESEARCH
PARTNERSHIPS IN PRACTICE

Chapter 2

A Participatory Perspective on Parent Involvement

Olga A. Vásquez

This chapter focuses on an approach to parent involvement that is symbolically as well as materially participatory. It examines a community of learners in which low-income, Mexican-origin parents partner with members of a university research team in an after-school, computer-based activity that not only promotes the academic achievement of the children but also enhances the parents' intellectual skills. In assuming a critical role in the design, implementation, sustainability, and dissemination of resource-rich learning environments, these parents add a participatory dimension to a project that initially had been conceived as a mechanism for enhancing the cognitive development of elementary-school-aged children (see Cole, 1996; Cole and Nicolopoulou, 1991). The heightened level of participation among parents and community members expanded Rogoff's (1994) notion of a community of learners beyond individual transformation to a restructuring of institutional access and participation. Thus, as individual participants assume "transforming roles and understanding in the activities" (p. 209), they *also* acquire mainstream social and cultural capital that allows them to participate fully in the multiple worlds they traverse in everyday life. In the process, the parent-participants also transform the project, called *La Clase Mágica* (The magical class), into a social action endeavor.

Over a decade of ethnographic data—field notes, videotapes, audiotapes, and field-developed tools generated by the university team and the parent-participants—document the powerful role parents have played in the success of the program. Although typically these adults have had limited formal education, they nevertheless learned to deploy the project's core principles in the day-to-day management of the site, assumed responsibility for developing new curricular materials, and trained incoming staff members from the community. Parent participation at *La Clase Mágica* has not only sustained the project but also made possible its expansion to several other locations, thus providing ample evidence that involving individuals with minimal mainstream cultural and social capital at high organizational levels can be advantageous for both the sponsoring institution and the participants.

Involving parents in every aspect of the project—from the development of the initial vision to the assessment of the long-term impact—has been important for two reasons: First, discrete, unilinear approaches to the redistribution of educational resources to underserved populations have not proven successful (UC Black Eligibility Task Force, 1992). Second, minority parents themselves have a stake in the educational enterprise. The analysis in this chapter documents how they possess material and symbolic capital that can be effectively mobilized to support learners and help educational institutions carry out their missions (see also Moll et al., 1990; Vásquez, 2003). Excluding parents who are outside the reach of mainstream culture potentially strips them of their social and political voice. Wong-Fillmore (1991) has found that among Chinese Americans, leaving parents out also can estrange them from their children. Finally, because parent involvement is an expectation in American schools, including a broad spectrum of parents should be a high priority for teachers and school administrators.

The following two sections will discuss the role parents play in American classrooms and provide an overview of *La Clase Mágica*, an after-school project with much promise of serving as the transition between home and school. Next I will focus on two parents whose participation has had the dual benefit of supporting the program's success and broadening their own social and intellectual development. The conclusion will propose a new definition of parent involvement and principles to guide an effective partnership between parents and educators. This participatory framework has important public policy implications for education and social reform.

PARENT-SCHOOL INTERACTION
IN CONTEMPORARY SOCIETY

Parental involvement in school activities is a common expectation in the United States, especially when children are in the elementary years. Partnerships with parents have been found to benefit the children, the parents, the schools, and the community as a whole (National Education Goals Panel, 1995). Widespread awareness and support of parents' central role in schooling is evident in the National Education Goals set in 1990 by then-President George H. W. Bush and the nation's governors. The eighth goal states: "By the year 2000, every school will promote partnerships that will increase parental involvement and participation in promoting the social, emotional, and academic growth of children." The degree to which this goal was achieved nationwide is debatable. Research, however, indicates that schools continue to be ineffective in addressing the needs of Latino parents and their children (Sosa, 1996; Valdes, 1996). The beliefs and experiences of Latino parents often pose impossible challenges for school personnel who work within a model of the "standard family" (Valdes, 1996).

What constitutes parent involvement varies from supplying snacks and a helping hand in the classroom to supplying the appropriate attitudes, aspirations, and values in the home. Research suggests that socioeconomic and ethnic background plays a decisive role in whether parents participate physically or symbolically (Lareau, 1986; Stanton-Salazar, 2001; Nieto, 1996). Inside and outside the classroom, most parents who are actively involved in school activities are English speaking, Anglo, and middle class. Lareau (1986) has found that parent involvement draws heavily on "social and cultural resources of family life," which correspond closely to the backgrounds of a teacher workforce that is overwhelmingly white and monolingual (p. 2). Thus, whether involvement consists of the nonacademic role of "room mother" or the more cognitively oriented role of teacher's assistant, it is typically carried out by parents who share the classroom teacher's cultural and linguistic background (Lareau, 1986, 1989). The same is true at the institutional level: White, monolingual parents prove to be effective partners in site-based decision making and evaluation of major educational programs (Utterback and Kalin, 1989).

Low-income, minority parents' family values, expectations, and models for achievement, by contrast, shape their involvement in distinct ways, ones more symbolic of the natural resources of the home. Despite the nearly insurmountable cultural and structural barriers to involvement they confront, these parents, too, have been shown to be effective partners in school and classroom activities (see Sosa, 1996, for details on barriers seen by both teachers and parents). Griffith and collaborators (1997), for example, found that involving African-American and Latino parents in meaningful partnerships in school activities not only contributed to an increase in parent involvement, it also positively affected the children's academic achievement. Other, more conventional strategies of parent involvement also have shown relative success in bridging the gap between home and school. A particularly effective approach sends students (Heath, 1983; Wiggington, 1985) and teachers or researchers (Moll and González, 1994; Alvarez and Vásquez, 1994) into homes and neighborhoods in search of communities' "funds of knowledge" to harness and then integrate into the instructional curriculum. Inspired by Heath's (1983) work in the Carolinas and further developed by Moll and his collaborators at the University of Arizona, this "inquiry-based instruction" opens the curriculum to multiple forms of knowledge at the same time that it positions community representatives as valid and contributing partners in schooling. Parents are approached in the home or community for their specialized knowledge and are often asked to share their expertise directly with students during special visits to the classroom (Moll and González, 1994).

Literacy training has also proven a successful strategy for involving minority parents in their children's formal education. Some efforts focus on school forms of literacy as a means for training parents to actively scaffold their children's learning (Edwards, 1987); other efforts accomplish both objectives through the use of community literacy practices (Delgado-Gaitan 1990, 1996; Durán et al., 2000). Delgado-Gaitan, for example, found that among bilingual groups, providing literacy training in both languages empowered parents to actively pursue participation in school activities and to engage in career planning.

Recent research (Suarez-Orozco and Suarez-Orozco, 1995; Nieto, 1996) illustrates the methods in which the symbolic capital of the home—parents' communication styles, values, and models that lead to personal achievement—provides effective motivation for children's success in school. Symbolic messages, such as "Next time, you should do better" or "My mom says that they want me to go to school. . . . That way, I won't be stuck with a job like them" (Nieto, 1996, p. 296), are manifestations of what Gibson and Ogbu (1991) call "parents' cultural models for getting ahead." The influence of symbolic resources of the home is best captured by Carola Suarez-Orozco and Marcelo Suarez-Orozco (1995), who show the direct impact of the social conditions of the family on the achievement rates of children from war-torn countries in Central America. Feeling privileged, children who managed to escape and immigrate to the United States strive to succeed in order to compensate for the suffering of those less fortunate members of their families who stayed behind or who were lost in the war. According to these scholars, the children's symbolic capital can be mobilized through the content and interactional structure of culturally responsive classrooms. For example, using terms of endearment such as *mijo* (my son), *Teresita* (little Theresa), *queridita* (dear one), and *mí niñita* (my little girl) minimizes the youngsters' natural discomfort in the presence of an unfamiliar authority figure. This type of interpersonal sensitivity acts as an effective motivational device to compel children to behave in culturally appropriate ways.

As these previous studies suggest, evaluating academic achievement and parent involvement in light of diversity raises important questions. First, what exactly is meant by "involvement"? Second, what is the relationship of involvement to class, gender, language, and ethnicity? The historical shift that has occurred from expecting parents to help with nonacademic tasks in the classroom to expecting them to engage in more cognitively oriented tasks exposes some of the underlying distinctions that bolster forms of involvement. Financially strapped parents who work in jobs with little autonomy are often unable to participate in parent-teacher conferences, PTA meetings, and classroom events, since these activities usually take place during their work hours. Furthermore, these parents' resources stand worlds apart from those emphasized in the classroom (Gallego and Cole, 2000). There is no guarantee that the models for getting ahead which these parents support can, as Gibson and Ogbu (1991) argue, be harnessed and mobilized in the classroom unless the parents themselves actively participate. Incorporating the values and cultural forms of minority parents into the instructional program, as Nieto (1996) advocates, assumes a biculturalism on the part of a teacher workforce that is overwhelmingly monolingual and monocultural. It also assumes a sociopolitical shift away from the predominantly mainstream and English-dominant cultural knowledge that currently characterizes the typical classroom.

These concerns do not diminish the importance of the research that has uncovered the valuable social and cultural resources of minority populations. They do, however, highlight how vulnerable low-income, minority parents are to exclusion and/or isolation in mainstream educational contexts. Their low level of education, limited fluency in English, and working-class backgrounds frequently cast them as outsiders and unlikely intellectual partners. Teachers, bombarded by media misrepresentations of diverse populations, often subcribe to negative stereotypes of minority parents (e.g., believing that in certain ethnic groups parents are apathetic or that certain minorities lack "culture"). Ill-prepared for their students' cultural and linguistic diversity, teachers, too, experience fear and distrust along with difficulty in communicating with minority parents (Stanton-Salazar, 2001). Despite these many barriers, however, minority parents' cultural/symbolic capital has measurable influence on their children's academic success. These parents can and do rise to the occasion when asked to participate in developing the cognitive and social skills of their children; and, as experiences at *La Clase Mágica* make clear, this involvement produces impressive positive personal and organizational results.

CREATING A NEW CULTURAL ACTIVITY IN PARTICIPATION

La Clase Mágica has its roots in an after-school educational activity called the Fifth Dimension (5D) (see Cole, 1996; Cole and Nicolopoulou, 1991). Developed by collaborators at the Laboratory of Comparative Human Cognition (LCHC), at the University of California, San Diego (UCSD), 5D was initially designed for the study of cognitive and literacy development among middle-class Anglo children. The underlying model calls for a partnership between university students enrolled in an undergraduate practicum course and elementary-school-aged children; activities are based at a field site located at a local community institution. The undergraduates assist the children through a multitude of computer-based activities that are simultaneously academically oriented and entertaining. Children are encouraged to direct their own learning and development through a theoretically based system of artifacts that makes innovative use of computer and telecommunication technology. The engaging quality of the model arises from its grounding in a mixture of play and education: the children draw on their own imaginations as they conceive of a magical world where they are able to accomplish great feats of reasoning under the attentive guidance of an electronic entity called "the Wizard."*

The 5D model achieved great success locally and internationally, but initial efforts to adapt it to serve bilingual learners in a Mexicano community adjacent to the program's original site encountered a range of distinctly different challenges. The Fifth Dimension's goals, content, and tools were poor matches with the language and culture of the new target population. It proved difficult to recruit children from the community as well as difficult to retain those that the staff did manage to recruit. In addition, the multiple epistemologies and knowledge sources bilingual learners use for meaning making and problem solving were unaccounted for in both the theory and practice of the original model. A new model, with its own distinctive contour, was required. Fortunately, the malleability of 5D made it possible to quickly transform it into *La Clase Mágica*—an activity that would effectively address the material and intellectual needs and resources of the new target group.

The new project was designed to examine the bilingual and bicultural resources that Mexican-origin children deploy as they engage in a prearranged set of computer-based, cognitively oriented activities. Spanish and Mexicano culture was incorporated into every aspect of *La Clase Mágica*'s development. For instance, the magical entity became known as "el Maga" (a combination of masculine and feminine forms of the words "the Wizard") to avoid assigning masculine gender to the only authority in the system (as the word "wizard" does in English). All of the instruction guides were written in a mixture of Spanish and English, a style of language use found in the homes and community of bilingual speakers (Zentella, 1997). Within

---

*"The Wizard" is a staff member who communicates with the children via online written dialogues.

a span of six years, as parents and community members joined the implementation team as salaried participants, three additional sets of activities were added to the existing organizational structure. These activities—*Mi Clase Mágica* for preschool children, the Wizard Assistant Club for second-level participants of *La Clase Mágica,* and *La Gran Dimensión* for adults—not only positioned community members as managers of the day-to-day operations of the site but also as creators of a new cultural activity.

At the broad institutional level, *La Clase Mágica* represents a model system of collaboration among several institutions. At its core are UCSD; St. Leo's, a small Catholic mission in north San Diego County; and the Mexican-origin families who form the laity of the mission (see Vásquez, 2003). Although not central to the day-to-day operations of the site, two other supporting institutions—the local Head Start program and the local Boys and Girls Club—provided financial assistance for the project's activities. These two institutions each fund the salaries of project personnel who work directly with specific constituencies. *La Clase Mágica* enables these institutions to redistribute material and intellectual resources to a historically underserved population. Furthermore, the project's multiple lines of collaboration function as a catalyst for change in negotiating solutions at each point of contact where discoordinations between a marginalized group and mainstream institution occur. Since parent participation is evenly dispersed throughout the system, parents—particularly mothers—are situated where they can identify the specific points of discoordination as well as develop workable realignments.

La Clase Mágica's role as an agent of change is particularly important because of its unique location. Situated at the convergence of multiple boundaries, *La Clase Mágica* makes it possible for marginalized participants to acquire and/or maintain the languages, skills, and cultures of the multiple institutional partners that sustain the project. It is a space between school and community, English and Spanish, minority and mainstream cultures, and imagination and reality where participants gain access to and may involve themselves in multiple worlds. At this juncture, *La Clase Mágica* mediates Mexican-born residents' transition into mainstream culture and its institutions at the same time that it reinforces maintenance of the home culture. The program is designed to be a supportive environment in which parents and children are introduced to the English-speaking society of the United States, to computers and telecommunication, and to forms of inquiry associated with the critical-thinking practices that are privileged in the American classroom. Opportunities to acquire these experiences and competencies assist families to circumvent the "cultural schisms and synergisms" that result from intergenerational discontinuity (Buriel and Cardoza, 1988; Buriel, 1993). Instead of widening the gap between parents and children, the organizational and philosophical structures of *La Clase Mágica* facilitate a continuous recycling of accumulated knowledge. Thus, children learn from adults and adults learn from children in a continuous cycle that flows through generations and institutional contexts. As Rogoff (1994) points out, adults and children who work together in a community of learners "are active in structuring shared endeavors, with adults responsible for guiding the overall process and children learning to participate in the management of their own learning and involvement" (p. 213). This type of collaboration between children and adults in both formal and informal learning settings is particularly relevant to maintaining the continuity of experience between the generations that is often lost among immigrant groups (Dewey, 1938).

Participation Across Multiple Worlds

From its inception, *La Clase Mágica* has had a strong impact on parents as well as on children. The educational goals of the project and its focus on computer and telecommunication technology were important factors that interested parents. They knew the difficulties their children experienced in school and they were well aware of the factors that impeded academic success. Recent research indicates that Latino parents want their children to succeed in school, but they also realize that they lack the resources to help them (UC Latino Eligibility Task Force, 1997). In the community *La Clase Mágica* serves, parents knew that *las computadoras* (the computers), as they called the project for many years, could provide educational enhancements that are far beyond their financial capability. They also understood that computer skills and experience with information technology are key to high-paying professions. It was not unusual for parents to remark that "everyone needs to learn computers in this country." They frequently asked for advice on where to purchase reasonably priced computers or how to operate systems that they had purchased. Another factor that drew parents to the activities of *La Clase Mágica* was the ease with which they could negotiate the language, culture, and space of the project. *Las computadoras* was literally across the street from their homes, located on the mission grounds, a place most frequented nearly every day. And, because *La Clase Mágica*'s activities are conducted in Spanish, with many references to Mexicano culture, even parents who knew very little about computers and the Internet quickly felt at ease, realizing that they were both welcomed and valued.

Of course, not all parents achieved the same depth of understanding or involvement as the women who headed the site activities as coordinators. Conversely, even if they are not fully generalizable, the coordinators' achievements are important. For low-income, Spanish-dominant women who typically had no more than the equivalent of a junior high school education to develop such a strong knowledge base indicates the inherent potential of this type of involvement, both for the project and the adult participants. Moreover, the knowledge the coordinators acquired was passed on to those parents less integrally involved in the project. In monthly meetings, the coordinators urged other parents to become involved in their children's education. Later, in formal training sessions, they taught new staff the *la rason de acción* (theories of action) of various aspects of *La Clase Mágica* and explained how to negotiate the rules and norms of the local public school system. When at the urging of UCSD's Center for Research in Education Assessment and Teaching Excellence (CREATE) a new project site was opened in an underperforming school, parents felt that the school structure impeded their fluid and integral involvement. They developed an alternative, an approach to parent involvement that sustained the flow of accumulated knowledge out to the periphery of parents who were unable to participate fully in the activities at the new site. The group was called *los promotores* (parent trainers), after Friere's literacy cadres. Another example of the value and role that accumulated knowledge has played in the project is the development of a strategy called "under wing," in which each member of the staff is asked to pair up and train someone who could assume his or her role in the event that the individual is unable to fulfill his or her responsibilities. This strategy makes it possible to retain acquired knowledge as long as possible and to maintain the stability of the project.

For the most part, coordinators are special individuals—natural-born leaders who stand out in a group. They are recruited from among a larger group of parents who volunteer at the site, assisting the children with the computer-based activities. Their willingness and ability to follow through on tasks, their ease and comfort among individuals of all ages, and their obvious commitment to the community single these women out as potential candidates for the role of *cordinadora* (coordinator). These adult assistants, in turn, suggest other members of the community as potential staff. Initially, the coordinators' chief responsibility was to manage the day-to-day operations of the site. Eventually, they assumed the role of adapting the curricular materials, using their cultural and linguistic background as intellectual resources. Lourdes Durán and Angelina Torres are two coordinators who enrolled their young children in *La Clase Mágica* and later became indispensable as assistants on the community side of the project. More than a decade ago, when I first visited the mission to conduct a preliminary ethnographic study of the community, I identified Lourdes Durán as a possible candidate for a staff position. Later, she recommended Angelina Torres and then trained her in the theory and practice of *La Clase Mágica*.

IN THE ACT OF TRANSFORMATION

With very few exceptions, Lourdes Durán and Angelina Torres mirror the typical demographic profile of first-generation immigrants. They are young, Spanish speaking, and working class. Both were born in Mexico and had immigrated to the United States less than twenty years before. Their children—four each—are U.S. born and attended primary grades in U.S. public schools. The primary language in these women's homes is Spanish; at the start of their involvement in the project, their fluency in English was minimal. Both were active and respected members of the community and highly visible in activities at St. Leo's Mission. Both joined the project as volunteers; initially, each worked closely with her own children and helped the research staff to make connections with institutional agents. They learned to use computers and telecommunication technology (e.g., designing the many materials that accompany the computer games), and also applied their new knowledge to personal and job-related areas. When the project expanded into the northern and southern regions of San Diego County, both women advanced to the ranks of "metacoordinators"—regional supervisors of other coordinators. The following brief biographical sketches of each woman highlight some of their contributions to the project and the impact of their participation on their personal development, future employment opportunities, and advocacy skills.

Lourdes Durán

If any single individual can be credited for the success of *La Clase Mágica,* it is forty-year-old Lourdes Durán. In 1989, when she and I first met at St. Leo's, the youngest of her four children was six months old and the oldest was five years old. At the time, Lourdes was the head of a catechism program, overseeing thirty teachers and more than 220 children. When I spoke about a fantasy world, an electronic entity, and a program that would provide her children and those of the community with an activity to share after school, Lourdes heard "computers," "education," and "a safe place for her children." Almost immediately, she grasped the potential value of *las computadoras* for the betterment of the community. Without hesitation, she began to show the same kind of commitment to the design and implementation of the project that she demonstrated with regard to her family and the community. She assumed an active role in the early project-sponsored community sessions, offering suggestions regarding language and cultural artifacts that helped make possible the adaptation of the 5D materials to the needs and interests of the community. She also negotiated with mission administration for a space to open the site. In her capacity as a volunteer, Lourdes attended specially designed training sessions held at UCSD's Laboratory of Comparative Human Cognition. There, she learned about the organizational and technical aspects of the project. When the site opened six months later, Lourdes and Maria Nieves (who was the mission's receptionist at the time) became the first community representatives to serve on the research implementation team.

Currently, Lourdes is acting metacoordinator of the sites in the northern region of San Diego County—covering the original site at St. Leo's Mission (and including its four age-specific activities) and three new sites. One of the new sites is located at a local housing project for Latinos in the city where Lourdes now lives; the other two sites are on American Indian reservations. She assists her seventeen-year-old daughter, a former long-term project participant, in operating the Latino site and helps a university staff member plan and develop materials for the sites on the reservations. She has trained all but one of the coordinators who head seven of the nine activities that, as of 2002, constitute *La Clase Mágica.* More significantly, she has been integral to the maintenance of an ongoing adaptation of the curricular materials, ensuring that they are both culturally and developmentally relevant to the learners at each site (excluding *La Gran Dimensión,* the adult component of *La Clase Mágica,* where a university staff member leads both the session and the adaptation of the materials). For over seven years, Lourdes has single-handedly developed and adapted the curriculum materials and has trained others in the use of the multiple computer applications that support the curriculum.

In addition to helping the emergent project gain the necessary momentum and relevance to the needs of the local community, Lourdes also has developed her own academic and advocacy skills. Her fluency in English has improved dramatically, as has her sophistication in supporting and advancing her own children's educational attainment. On numerous occasions she has intervened in their schooling, requesting and achieving positions for them in advanced placement classes despite what some school staff perceive as low academic achievement on the part of her children. In parent meetings for the project, she continuously shares the lessons she has learned in the process of ensuring that her children receive a high-quality education. Lourdes clearly knows a great deal about her children's abilities, both from observing them as they interact with the undergraduate students in the after-school project and from engaging the undergraduates in extended conversations about her children's learning.

Like her children, Lourdes also gained new skills as a result of her involvement in *La Clase Mágica* and its satellite centers. The field note excerpts presented here illustrate not only her expanding grasp of the overall nature of the project but also the multiple skills—what Gallego and Hollingsworth (2000) label personal, community, computer, and school literacies—that she developed along the way. The first (see Figure 2.1) was written in pencil in 1989, before she learned to use the computer and before she had learned much about the goals

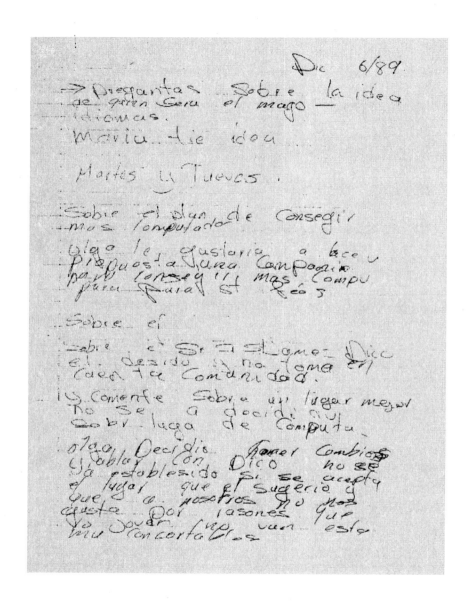

FIGURE 2.1. Lourdes Durán's First Field Note

and objectives of the project. The second excerpt (following this paragraph) was written in spring 2000, after she had learned to write ethnographic field notes and after she had internalized the project's core principles (Vásquez, 2003).[1] In the latter, she follows the coordinators' format for writing field notes, a style she adapted from the format used by undergraduate students. By the time Lourdes wrote this second field note, she was much more comfortable in the use of computers, and she was also working closely with Rick, the technical assistant, to remedy the many technical glitches that inevitably surface when using outdated technology.

Mi Clase Mágica. South Bay
Marzo 14. 2000
Lourdes Durán.
Primera sección 9:45-10:45 am

Asistencia de niños (5)
padres de familia (1)
estudiantes (3)
Coordinación (3) Vicky, Lupe, y yo
visitante: Rick

Como Empezo:
    Cuando llego lo primero que hize fue tratar de connectar el Zip, para tratar de poner los juegos que usaremos para LCM, al parecer las computadoras necesitan alguna aplicación mas para acepatar o prollectara en el en la pantalla el zip, cuando ilego Rick le hize el comentano y dice que probablemente necesite una aplicacion.
    Primeramente como a los 5 minutos que liege yo, llego Lupe, despues liego Marisa una niñas que siempre llega temprano y liro [little] Vicky y asi fueron liegando ya estaba todo listo cuando llegaron dos estudiantes nuebos mientrsa que yo trataba de darle instrucciones al uno de ellos le dije a Lupe que ella le diera instrucciones a la otra estudiante, mientras que una de las mamas me alludaba con otro niño. Rick que tambien estaba ahi le pedi que me alludara con Serjio y Christobal rato mas tarde liego otra estudianate y Vicky se encargo de darle información.

Algo importante que paso en este día:
    Algo muy interesante fue sobre Elías y su mama, ella me pregunto quieres que trabaje con Elías con el, apuntando al nibo que regularmente esta con ella y su niño en las actividades en la computadora ya que los dos estan en el mismo salon y tienen las clases en español, le

conteste que seria bueno que ella trabajara con el otro niño ya que ella sabe esactamente lo que el nibo necesita. El estudiante nuebo lo puse con Elías y le dije que el estaba en las clases de espabo y que nos ivamos a enfocar en puro espaoo, le di una introduccion sobre el record de actividades y le dije que el ya sabía bien los sonidos y conocía las a.b.c. le esplique que nos concentrariamos en alludarlo a escribir oraciones muy cortitas, le puse el juego de Kid Pix en Goodies.

Le escribi en un papel al estudiante:

    La mama de pepe
    El bebe de Niña
    El papa de Juan

y le dije alludale con estas oraciones, me hacerque al ni niño y le dije escribeme llllllllll y el la escribia aaaaaaaaaaa (la) y el la escribja y le di Un sacudida en el ombro y le dije riendome ves ya sabes escribir, al niño le dio nsa, le dije al estudiante asi es como debes repetirle el sonido de la letra para que el balla escribiendo, asi se lo fue lievando hasta que el nioo escribjo las tres oraciones al terminar el estudiante me dice ya las termino de escribir, le dije ok ahora ayudalo a que el solo balla leyendp lo que escribio y asi lo hizo el nibo fue leyendo por silabas las oraciones y las iva repitiendo hasta que decia la palabra completa, le dije ahora enzeñale a tu mama que tu sabes leer, y la mama que escuchaba al niño ir leyendo sus primeras oraciones nomas le daba nsa, y me hizo el comentano, estoy tan sorprendida de como este programa a ayudado al nioo el ya esta empezando a leer me decia que la maestra le comentaba que ella esta mirando que al nioo se le nota que esta avanzando. Le dije es bien importante que esto que tu miras en el programa 10 lieves a las maestras y al director, me contesto, Si 10 voy a hacer porque deberas que este programa les esta ayudando a los nioos.

Reflexión:
    Esta esperiencia con Elías, me recuerda que esta manera de enzeñar la aprendi recordando mi necesidad a raiz de mi esperiencia a los 6 años la confucion que me ~auso la manera en que la maestra me enzeño. y partiendo de esto entiendo por mi propia esperiancia confucion la mejor manera de enzeñar al niño sin causar tanta confucion, tal ves no es lo mejor pero lo he practicado con mis hijos y es tan facil enzeñar a un niño a leer español. Se necesita paciencia tiempo una y mucho amor a los chiquillos cabezones.

It is impossible to know exactly how much influence Lourdes's participation in *La Clase Mágica* had on the multiple levels of development apparent across these two notes, but it is clear that the project provided her ample opportunity to maximize her skills almost daily. As the second note makes evident, eleven years later, it is she who is in control and not the computer. Gone are all traces of the reticent young woman who became easily overwhelmed with the almost magical qualities of the technology. She no longer giggles and asks someone else to solve her problem, as she did during the first several years of the project. Now, she confidently figures out that she needs a particular application in order to access the Zip drive that contains the games for the site. Just as important, she has developed a facility to manage social relations, pedagogical goals, and theoretical underpinnings of the activities with the ease of one who has been trained in language acquisition, literacy, and sociohistorical theory. On several occasions, Lourdes has used the PowerPoint presentation I developed for academic talks to address parents from the various communities she works with in advancing the goals of the program.

Angelina Torres

As did many of the coordinators, Angelina spent considerable time at *La Clase Mágica* observing her children's interactions with the undergraduate students before she joined the staff in spring 1999. She was thirty-two years old at the time; her four children ranged in age from five to twelve. Living in the rectory with her family, she was directly involved in both the pastoral and administrative functions of St. Leo's Mission. She had received a nursing degree in Mexico but she had little or no experience with computers, other than the word processing she performed as the mission's part-time receptionist. Recalling a question I asked her years earlier about her knowledge of computers, Angelina remarked, "Yo no sabía lo que era el Internet" ("I did not know what the Internet was"). When her home situation required that she earn a second income, the project was recruiting a new coordinator. Angelina was approached as a likely candidate. Initially, she was nervous about assuming a responsibility that demanded knowledge of English, computers, and management of the site. However, encouraged by Lourdes's willingness to provide support by phone at all hours of the day and night, and to work at the site two days a week, Angelina began coordinating the operations of the activity designed for elementary-school-aged children. Although she had lingering worries, she resolved to do the best she could. Almost immediately, the appearance of the site, organization of the materials, and coordination of the activities and participants significantly improved. Angelina's site reforms were transformative: *La Clase Mágica* was, at that point, located in the kitchen of the mission, where large stacks of day-old bread gave off a suffocating stench on hot days. The freshly organized and brightened space made it easier for the demoralized staff (who also conducted other activities in the kitchen) to suffer through the displacement until the project was permitted to reoccupy its original quarters.

Today, Angelina is the metacoordinator of two of the sites in the South Bay: one at Bayside Elementary School, where there are two sessions for kindergartners and one for children in the upper grades, and the other at a community center on the U.S.-Mexico border, where there are two sessions for children age five through twelve and their parents. Like Lourdes, she oversees the staff and the evaluation, the orientation, and guidance of the undergraduates (in the South Bay these students come mainly from Southwestern Community College, which offers a course in partnership with the project). Angelina updates all the materials and writes biannual reports (see the report following) that are sent to the professor and the class at Southwestern. Her management style reflects the depth of understanding she has acquired over the past two years of intensive involvement and the previous five years she spent as a peripheral participant. For example, she deliberately allows child participants known as Wizard Assistants to share their knowledge with the incoming undergraduate students in the best way they can while she provides supportive materials to amplify their presentation. In this way, she remains on the sidelines as she scaffolds the development of these "experts," exemplifying the core principle of enhancing learners' optimal development. In the summer of 1999 she and Lourdes designed and implemented a seven-week summer program without any assistance from UCSD. Two years later, serving as the main workshop leaders, Angelina and Lourdes used the program to train incoming staff. They translated my theoretically informed talks into lay terminology and developed training packets on computer use, data management, the writing of field notes, and evaluation.

Angelina began her involvement in the project with more extensive skills and training than many of the other community staff. However, her developmental trajectory in the theories, practice, and technical aspects of the project was just as steep as that of the adults who had less formal education. Her previous training allowed her to start at a higher skill level and to experiment with the form and content of the field notes that coordinators are expected to submit. Yet at the beginning she did not know how to use computers or related telecommunications technology. Maximizing her prior knowledge, she learned to use the commercially designed application Microsoft Publisher on her own. She then adapted the three-part essay format of the field notes to a newsletter template. Figure 2.2 is an example of one of the first field notes she submitted in this form. The second excerpt (translated from the original Spanish in Appendix B) is a statement of appreciation, but, as part of a regular, midterm evaluation Angelina provides the professor in charge of the course at Southwestern College, it also delineates the specific responsibilities and contributions of the undergraduate students.[2]

South Western College
Prof Barbara Canaday
03/21/02

To whom it may concern:
    La Clase Magica, (LCM) Bayside y Casa Familiar agradece a South Wester College (SWC), y a la profesora Barbara Canaday, tutora de la materia Practicum 201, y a Profesora Celia Gonzalez, tutora de la materia HDP 135 de UCDS, por su participacion y coolaboracion en este periodo de Invierno 2002. Gracias a la participacion de los Ug's llie posible llevar a cabo el programa de LCM en el area Sur del Condado de San Diego en los siguientes sitios, la Escuela primaria Bayside, en Imperial Beach y el Centro Comunitano Casa Familiar, en San Ysidro. Estos dos Sitios seran nararrados acontinuacion deacuerdo a las actividades propias de cada lugar.
    En primer lugar destacaremos las actividades diarias de Bayside. Los ~gi5 llegan a la escuala y firman de asistencia en la oficina de la escuela, se colocan un gafete con la leyenda "La Clase Magica" y se dirigen al salon 27 que es donde se desempenan las actividades propias de LCM, una vez en el salon firman nuevamente de asistencia y se disponen a trabajar con los ninos que les sean asignados por el personal de LCM.
    Bayside cuenta con 25 salones de alunmos de Kinder a Sexto grado y Un total de *550* alumnos de los cuales solo participan en el programa unos cuantos ninos de Kinder, Primero, Segundo y Tercer grado. Contamos con tres sesiones de trabajo, dos de Mi Clase Magica (MCM) y

LA CLASE MAGICA
Volume 1, Issue 4

REPORTE DE ACTIVIDADES

JUEVES, MARZO 23 DE 2000

ANGELINA LEAL

LCM

HORARIO 4:00 A 6:00 PM

Niños que asistieron: 10

Alvarado, Martín
Carter, Linda
Carter, Victoria
Carter, Krina
Escobedo, Christian
Guerrero, Melany
Leal, Jorge
Leal, Karla
Rodríguez, Yoany
Toth, Melinda

W.A. que asistieron: 5

Carter, Alex
Carter, Michael
Leal, Claudia
Leal, Ruth
Núñez, Rosalía

Padres de Familia: 3

Carter, Anita
Escobedo, Ana Silvia
Toth, María Elena

Lenguaje que se usa:

Inglés y Español

LCM   EXTRA CLASES
DEL 20 AL 30 DE ABRIL

DESARROLLO DE LA CLASE:

Llegué al salón de clase y destapé las computadoras, las prendí y una de las 3 impresoras no estaba trabajando, la misma de ayer.

Preparé mi material de trabajo, la forma de sing in, saqué punta a los lápices, hice un volante con las fechas de venta para el viaje a Florida e imprimí suficientes para entregar a los WA.

Esta tarde se trabajó muy parejo en cuanto a la atención a los niños porque hubo suficientes WA para el número de niños que asistieron este día, 3 de los cuales llegaron haciendo tarea y posteriormente entraron al Maze.

Hablé con la Sra. Anita Carter sobre el propósito de la venta de los Domingos, le aclaré sobre lo que ella tenía dudas y quedó contenta y animada a participar.

A las 5:30 despedí a los niños y los WA se pusieron a redactar sus notas que Susy les pidió porque necesita enviarlas.

Se barrió el salón, se recogieron los materiales y se dejó listo para la siguiente clase.

REUNION CON LOS WA

Se repartieron los volantes que les indicaba el Domingo que trabajarán en la venta pro-viaje a Florida.

Hablé con Susy sobre hacerles algo a los WA por su trabajo cubriendo este periodo de vacaciones que estamos justo a la mitad, yo propuse rentar una película, preparar agua fresca y palomitas y verla en mi casa. Le pareció buena idea pero ahora el problema es elegir la película que sea adecuada y educativa para ellos.

COMENTARIOS:

Esta tarde tomé varias fotos de la clase, me sentí motivada a hacerlo porque el ambiente se sentía muy agradable.

Yo me llevé a mi casa el SITE BK-UP, para tenerlo en un lugar más protegido mientras se consigue el file para tenerlo bajo llave.

LOQUE APRENDI HOY:

La comunicación constante con los padres de familia facilita realizar las metas que tenemos en común.

FIGURE 2.2. Angelina Torres's Field Note Adapted to a Newsletter Template

una sesión de La Clase Mágica (LCM) Cada sesión tiene actividades propias como lo indica el Maze que se sigue en cada actividad. MCM am es la primera sisión que se lleva a cabo los Mates y Jueves de las 9:45 a 10:45am contamos con 6 niños de Kinder y 3 Ug's de SWC a la semana. MCMpm segunda sesión de 11:30 a 12:3Opm, en esta clase tenemos 12 niños de Kinder con un Ug de SWC y dos Ug's de UC SD, cada Martes y Jueves.

LCM tercera sesion, de 2:00 a 4:00pm contamos con 18 ninos de Primero, Segundo y Tercer grado y dos Ug's de SWC una vez a la quincena, los Jueves.

Casa Familiar es un Centro comunitarlo donde atiende gente Hispana de todas las edades y participan en diferentes actividades que tal centro ofrece, principalmente clases de computacion y arte. En Casa Familiar tenemos dos sesiones los Miercoles, la primera es de 3:00 a 4:30pm, y contamos con la participacion de 15 ninos y la ayuda de tres Ug's de SWC y cuatro Ug'5 deUCSD En la segunda sesion de Casa Familiar tenemos 15 ninos y la participacion de dos Ug's de SWC y cuatro Ug's de UCSD.

En este sitio los Ug's firman de asistencia al liegar y se preparan para atender a los ninos que les sean asignados. Toman el folder del nino y se dirigen a la computadora que tiene el juego que se necesita para trabajar. Tanto en Bayside como en Casa Familiar se llenan formas antes de que el nino comienze Un juego nuevo, esto es para darles Credito a los ninos por cada juego terminado en el nivel Good 0 Expert.

Los Ug's son los encargados de llevar al nino al maximo aprovechamiento del juego y evaluar el nivel jugado. Una vez observado el desempeno del nino, el Ug hace anotaciones en el folder del nino vaciando en el, la signiente informacion:

Date (fecha del dia)
Amigo (nombre del Ug)
Room (numero del cuarto se eligio parajugar)
Game (nombre del juego)
1St. Stepp Pass (forma que se llena antes de jugar el juego y lo que el nino cree que aprendera)
Begginer, Good, Expert (evaluacion del nivel jugado)
Credit (si el nino termino el juego en Good 0 Expert, se llena esta forma dando credito al nino)
Progress to game (anotaciones informando la opcion del juego en la que se trabajo y las actividades que se hicieron para reforzar el tema)
Learning Observed Cog/Linguistic (anotaciones sobre lo aprendido y aspectos que resaltar)

Despues de cada una de las sesiones, nos reunimos para enriquecer el dia de trabajo expresando los comentarios sobre la experiencia perosonal. Cada uno de los Ug's tiene la oportunidad de decir abiertamente su punto de vista, ellos dicen como trabajaron con el nino, que juego jugaron, que nivel ilegaron, que piensa del juego para la edad del nino, 51 file muy facil 0 dificil, Si el nino sigue indicaciones, comentamos sobre el idioma que se uso, en fin todo lo que el Ug's quiera comentar se toma en cuenta y hay intercambio de ideas entre el personal de LCM y los demas companeros de SWC y UCSD.

Cabe mencionar que las dos escuelas, SWC y UCSD, se integraron en un ambiente favorable para ellos mismos y sobre todo para los ninos que participan en el programa, nunca se hicieron grupos diferentes, sino que trabajaron conjuntamente. La dedicacion y los conocimientos de los estudiantes, asi como la convivencia con los ninos, permitieron el mayor aprovechamento y logro de los fines por los cuales trabaja La Clase Magica, que es: fortalercer el aspecto social y academico de los ninos.

Gracias a SWC y UCSD por tener en cuenta a Bayside y Casa Familiar como sitio de practica para los creditos de sus estudiantes. Esperamos seguir contando con su participacion y apoyo ya que de eso depende que podamos continuar nuestra labor academica y social.

Sincerely,
Angelina

These two documents illustrate the facility with which Angelina carried out her responsibilities as a project leader. They also show how *La Clase Mágica* makes it possible for her to actualize her skills and talents. "Me sentía libre de hacer lo que podía" ("I felt free to do what I could"), she related to parents at a monthly meeting. Although still uncomfortable with her knowledge of English, she too has conquered what seemed an insurmountable challenge at the initial stages of her involvement: the computer. Afraid even to touch the laptop at the beginning, she learned to incorporate the computer into both her personal and professional activities. She eventually bought a computer to work with at home. Today, she manages the database for the project, uses e-mail to communicate with staff and students, and uses the computer to develop new curricular materials. Her public speaking abilities also progressed dramatically. Initially, she experienced great panic in facing the undergraduate students as a critical audience, but in her later interactions with them she drew their visible admiration. As one Spanish-speaking student wrote in a letter to Angelina at the end of the spring quarter (2002), "Te admiro por todas tus cualidades, y se que *La Clase Mágica* esta en buenas manos porque tu estas al frente como coordinadora" (I admire you for all your qualities, and I know that *La Clase Mágica* is in good hands because you are the coordinator").

A NEW DEFINITION OF PARENT INVOLVEMENT

While each of the parent-participants described here is unique in her own right, together they provide a preliminary vision of a type of participatory involvement that draws heavily on the symbolic and material resources of low-income, Spanish-dominant participants. The level of involvement of these two coordinators makes evident the high level of involvement among minority parents who willingly assume and competently execute, provided proper training and financial remuneration consistent with their position.[3] Under the right conditions, these parents can and do effectively facilitate their children's access to educational resources and institutional support. They also contribute to their own development and to the projects in which they become involved. As one recent newcomer to the staff said, "I can't wait for my children to become Wizard Assistants like Angelina's children, so I can talk about their accomplishments with such pride." This same parent announced at the annual CREATE conference, "Linking Communities of Learners," that she wanted to take *La Clase Mágica* beyond the school and the PTA. Parent-participants learn very quickly the potential impact of the project and commit themselves readily to its success, knowing the benefits to the community, their children, and themselves.

Although the type and degree of parent involvement with in-school and after-school activities is governed by different institutional structures, goals, and clientele, there are a range of valuable lessons that have resulted from forging such connections. First, parents are expected to participate in their children's schooling and often do not possess the social and cultural knowledge to do so in a meaningful fashion. Second, school personnel is often ineffective in establishing strong connections with parents from low-income minority communities. Involvement in after-school projects such as *La Clase Mágica* can introduce nonmainstream parents to school culture within a warm and supportive environment. Although Lourdes Durán and Angelina Torres chose to participate in their children's intellectual and social development in a setting apart from the educational system, their lives and work teach us volumes about participatory parent involvement. Their example demonstrates that minority parents do have a commitment to participate effectively at high levels of involvement, that these parents have valuable capital to contribute to

the education system, and that the educational experience of historically underserved populations can be enhanced by systematic efforts
to incorporate the symbolic as well as the human resources of minority parents.

Thirteen years of reforming and redefining this model of participation has led to the development of the following principles optimal
for meaningful involvement:

1. Situate involvement within the context of a community of learners.
2. Ground all action in cultural relevance.
3. Accentuate the relative strengths of participants, and amend
   their weaknesses through apprenticeship.
4. Exercise bidirectional relations of exchange at all levels.
5. Promote a continuity of experience across language and culture.
6. Enable the transformation of the learning context as well as the
   learner.
7. Institute strategies to recycle knowledge to newcomers.

This participatory model of parent involvement has important implications for schools and communities. It emphasizes the central
role educational institutions assign to parents and calls for funding
that provides parents with the same remuneration others receive for
their time and effort in settings that promote children's academic and
social development. Communities as well as schools must work together to provide transitional experiences such as those provided by
La Clase Mágica to help nonmainstream parents acquire the social
and cultural capital required to negotiate public institutions in demanding equity in programming. It also indicates the demand for
teachers who know how to draw on community sources to adequately
teach students from diverse backgrounds. This means that teacher
training programs need to provide training for preservice teachers on
issues and benefits related to bilingualism and biculturalism.

Importantly, this model offers those committed to a multidimensional model of global citizenship education the ability to benefit society (Cogan and Derricott, 1995). By devoting themselves to the ideals and philosophy of *La Clase Mágica,* individuals such as Lourdes
and Angelina practice ethical civic involvement that has long-lasting
impact on their lives and those with whom they serve. The pride and

confidence in their bilingual, bicultural skills and experiences enriches the lives and work of both minority and mainstream children, parents, and school personnel.

APPENDIX A

My Magic Class. South Bay.
March 14, 2000
Lourdes Durán
First Session, 9:45-10:45 a.m.

Children's Assistants (5)
Parents (1)
Students (3)
Coordinators (3) Vicky, Lupe, and myself
Visitor: Rick

How it started:
When I arrived, the first thing I did was to try to connect the ZIP to try to install the games we would use for LCM. It seems that the computers need some type of program to open the ZIP on the screen. When Rick arrived I mentioned this to him and he said that it probably needs a program.

First, about five minutes after I arrived, Lupe arrived, then Marisa, a child who always arrives early and little Vicky, and then they all began to arrive—everything was set up when two new students arrived. While I gave instructions to one of them, I told Lupe to give instructions to the other. Meanwhile one of the mothers helped me with another child. Rick, who was also there, I asked him to help with Sergio and Christobal. Later another student arrived and Vicky took responsibility to give her information.

Something important that happened today:
Something very interesting was about Elias and his mother. She asked me, do you want me to work with Elias and pointing to the child who is normally with her and her child on the computer activities, since both are in the same class and have classes in Spanish. I responded and said that it would be good for her to work with the other child since she knows exactly what the child needs. I placed the new student with Elias and told him he was in the Spanish classes and that we would focus only in Spanish. I gave him an introduction to the activities file and told him he knew well the sounds and knew the abc's. I explained that we would concentrate in helping him write short sentences and I played the Kid Pix in Goodies game for him. I wrote on a paper for the student:

Pepe's mother.
Nina's baby.
Juan's father.

and I told her [?] to help him with these sentences, I got close to the child
and told him to write 111111 for me and he would write a a a a a (la)—I gave
him a push on the shoulder and smiling told him, see, you know how to
write. The child smiled. I told the student this is how you should repeat the
sound of the letter so that he can write it down, this is how he moved him
along until the child wrote all three sentences. When they finished, the student told me he finished writing them. I told him OK, now help him so that
he can read what he wrote, and he did: the child read the sentences by sylla-
bles and repeated them until he read the complete word. I told him now
show your mother that you know how to read and the mother listened and
while he read his first sentences, she smiled and laughed and commented
that she is so amazed at how this program has helped her child, he is now beginning to read. She told me that the teacher comments to her that she no-
tices that the child is advancing. I told her, it is very important that this is
what you observe in the program, that you take it to the teachers and the director. She responded with, yes, I will do that because this program is truly
helping the children.

Reflection:
    This experience with Elias reminds me that this manner of teaching—
I learned it remembering my need at the root of my experience at the age of
6, the confusion it caused me, the manner in which the teacher taught me.
And now after this, I understand from my own experience of confusion, the
best way to teach the child without causing so much confusion. Perhaps it is
not the best, but I have practiced with my own children and it is so easy to
teach a child to read Spanish. You need to have patience, time, and lots of
love of the "big headed" kids.

APPENDIX B

To Whom It May Concern:
    La Clase Mágica (LCM) Bayside and Casa Familiar would like to ac-
knowledge South Western College (SWC); Professor Barbara Canaday, tutor for the material in Practicum 201; and Professor Celia Gonzalez, tutor
for material in HDP 135 of UCSD, for their participation and collaboration
during the Winter of 2002. Thanks also to the undergraduates who made it
possible to implement the LCM in South San Diego County at the following
sites: Bayside Elementary, Imperial Beach, and the Casa Familiar Commu-

nity Center in San Ysidro. These two sites will be continuously narrated in accordance to the activities at each site.

First, we will outline the daily activities at Bayside. The GI 5 arrive at the school and sign off on attendance at the school's office. They wear a badge with the title "La Clase Mágica" and they go to room 27, which is where the LCM activities take place. Once in the classroom, they sign again the attendance and they begin to work with the children to whom they have been assigned by the LCM staff.

Bayside consists of 25 classrooms from K to 6th grade, with a total of 550 students, of which only a few from K, 1st, 2nd, and 3rd grade participate in the program. We provide three work sessions: two of My Magic Class (MCM), and one of the Magic Class (LCM). Each session has its own activities as indicated by the MAZE that is part of each activity. MCM a.m. is the first session that takes place on Tuesdays and Thursdays from 9:45 to 10:45 a.m. We have six children from K and three undergraduates from SWC each week.

MCM p.m., the second session, from 11:30 to 12:30 p.m. In this class we have 12 children from K with one undergraduate from SWC and two undergraduates from UCSD every Tuesday and Thursday.

LCM third session, from 2 to 4 p.m. with 18 children from 1st, 2nd, and 3rd grades and two undergraduates from SWC, once every two weeks on Thursdays.

Casa Familiar (CF) is a community center attended by Hispanics of all ages and they participate in different activities that the center offers, primarily computer and art classes. At Casa Familiar we have two sessions on Wednesdays, the first is from 3 to 4:30 p.m., with 15 children participating with the help of three undergraduates from SWC and four from UCSD. In the second session at Casa Familiar we have 15 children, with two undergraduates from SWC and four from UCSD participating.

At this location, the undergraduates sign in as they arrive and they prepare to attend to the children assigned to them. The take the child's folder and go to the computer that has the game needed to work on. Both at Bayside and at CF, forms are filled out before the child starts a new game, this is to give them credit for each game completed at good or expert level.

The undergraduates are responsible for taking the child to maximum use of the game and evaluating the level of performance. Once observing the child's attempts, the undergraduate takes notes in the child's folder and provides the following information:

Date
Friend (name of undergraduate)
Room (room number chosen to play)
Game (name of game)

1st Stepp Pass (form that is filled out before playing the game
and what the child thinks he will learn)
Beginner, Good, Expert (evaluation of level of performance)
Credit (if child finishes the game with good or expert, the form is
filled out giving credit to the child)
Progress to game (notes informing the object of the game that
was worked on and the activities that were done to reinforce the
theme)
Learning observed cog/linguistic (notes on what was learned
and aspects that stand out)

After each of the sessions, we gather to enrich the working day by ex-
pressing comments of the personal experience. Each of the undergraduates
has the opportunity to speak freely their point of view. They state how they
worked with the child, what game they played, what level they reached,
what they think of the game according to the age of the child, if they feel that
it's too easy or difficult, and if the child followed instructions. We comment
on the language spoken, and in the end everything that the undergraduates
want to say is taken into consideration and there is an interchange of ideas
between the LCM staff and other members from SWC and UCSD.

I just finished mentioning that the two schools, SWC and UCSD, joined a
good environment for themselves and above all for the children who participate in the program. Different groups were never made; they worked together. The dedication and the knowledge of the students and the interactions with the children allowed for the major utilization and achievement for
the purpose of which the La Clase Mágica works for, which is to strengthen
the social and academic aspects of the children.

Thanks to SWC and UCSD for considering Bayside and Casa Familiar as
a site of practice for their students' credits. We hope to continue relying on
your participation and support, since that depends on our ability to continue
our academic and social labor.

Sincerely,
Angelina

NOTES

1. Spelling and grammar have been preserved in this note, with the exception of
incorrect diacritical marks, which have been corrected. See Appendix A for translation.
2. Submitting midterm evaluations such as these is a strategy that has been followed since the early stages of the project, when Lourdes co-authored the end-of-

the-year reports to the Andrew Mellon Foundation (the Fifth Dimension's major funding agency). See Appendix B for English translation.

3. Teachers are typically paid for their involvement while parents are expected to participate without remuneration. At the site located on school grounds, teachers were paid $25.00 per hour to attend project-related meetings.

REFERENCES

Alvarez, C. and Vasquez, O. A. (1994). Language socialization in ethnic minority communities. In F. Genesee (Ed.), *Educating second language children: The whole child, the whole curriculum, the whole community* (pp. 52-102). New York: Cambridge University Press.

Buriel, R. (1993). Acculturation, respect for cultural differences, and biculturalism among three generations of Mexican American and Euro American school children. *Journal of Genetic Psychology* 154(4): 531-544.

Buriel, R. and Cardoza, D. (1988). Sociocultural correlates of achievement among three generations of Mexican American high school seniors. *American Educational Research Journal* 25: 177-192.

Cogan, J. J. and Derricott, R. (1995). *Citizenship for the 21st century: An international perspective on education.* London, UK: Kogan Page.

Cole, M. (1996). *Cultural psychology: Once and future discipline.* Cambridge, MA: Harvard University Press.

Cole, M. and Nicolopoulou, A. (1991). *Creating sustainable new forms of educational activity in after-school settings.* Final report to the Spencer Foundation. Laboratory of Comparative Human Cognition, University of California, San Diego.

Delgado-Gaitan, C. (1990). *Literacy for empowerment: The role of parents in children's education.* New York: Falmer Press.

Delgado-Gaitan, C. (1996). *Protean literacy: Extending discourse on empowerment.* Washington, DC: Falmer Press.

Dewey, J. (1938). *Experience and education.* New York: Collier Books.

Durán, R., Durán, J., Perry-Romero, D., Sanchez, E. (2000). "Latino immigrant parents and children learning and publishing together in an after school setting." Paper presented at the annual meeting of the American Educational Research Association, New Orleans, LA.

Edwards, P. A. (1987). *Educating black children: America's challenge.* Washington, DC: Howard University, Bureau of Educational Research, School of Education.

Gallego, M. and Cole, M. (2000). Classroom culture and culture in the classroom. In V. Richardson (Ed.), *The handbook of research on teaching* (Fourth edition) (pp. 961-997). Washington, DC: American Education Research Association.

Gallego, M. and Hollingsworth, S. (Eds.) (2000). *What counts as literacy: Challenging a single standard: Multiple perspectives on literacy.* New York: Teachers College Press.

Gibson, M. A. and Ogbu, J. U. (1991). *Minority status and schooling: A comparative study of immigrant and involuntary minorities.* New York: Basic Books.

Griffith, J., Wade, J., and Loeb, C. (1997). *An evaluation of family-school partnership initiatives in sixteen elementary schools.* Montgomery County, MD: Department of Educational Accountability, Montgomery County Public Schools.

Heath, S. B. (1983). *Ways with words: Language, life and work in communities and classrooms.* Cambridge: Cambridge University Press

Lareau, A. (1986). "Perspectives on parents: A view from the classroom." Paper presented at the annual meeting of the American Research Association, San Francisco, CA.

Lareau, A. (1989). *Home advantage: Social class and parental intervention in elementary education.* New York: Falmer Press.

Moll, L. C. and González, N. (1994). Lessons from research with language minority students. *Journal of Reading Behavior* 26(4): 439-456.

Moll, L. C., Velez-Ibañez, C. G., Greenberg, J., Whitmore, K., Dworin, J., Saavedra, E., and Andrade, M. (1990). *Community knowledge and classroom practice: Combining resources for literacy instruction.* Tucson: College of Education and Bureau of Applied Research in Anthropology, University of Arizona.

National Education Goals Panel (1995). *The national education goals report: Building a nation of learners.* Washington, DC: U.S. Government Printing Office, Superintendent of Documents.

Nieto, S. (1996). *Affirming diversity: The sociopolitical context of multicultural education* (Second edition). White Plains, NY: Longman.

Rogoff, B. (1994). Developing understanding of the idea of communities of learners. *Mind Culture and Activity: An International Journal* 1(4): 209-229.

Sosa, A. S. (1996). Involving Hispanic parents in improving educational opportunities for their children. In J. L. Flores (Ed.), *Children of La Frontera: Binational efforts to serve Mexican migrant and immigrant students.* Charleston, WV: ERIC, Clearinghouse on Rural Education and Small Schools.

Stanton-Salazar, R. (2001). *Manufacturing hope and despair: The school and kin support networks of U.S.-Mexican youth.* New York: Teachers College Press.

Suarez-Orozco, C. and Suarez-Orozco, M. (1995). *Transformations: Immigration, family life, and achievement motivation among Latino adolescents.* Stanford, CA: Stanford University Press.

University of California Black Eligibility Task Force (1992). *Making the future different: Report of the task force on black student eligibility.* Berkeley, CA: Author.

University of California Latino Eligibility Task Force (1997). *Latino student eligibility and participation in the University of California: YA BASTA.* Berkeley, CA: Author.

Utterback, P. H. and Kalin, M. (1989). A community-based model of curriculum evaluation. *Educational Leadership* (October): 49-50.

Valdes, G. (1996). *Con respeto. Bridging the distance between culturally diverse families and schools: An ethnographic portrait.* New York: Teachers College Press.

Vásquez, O. A. (2003). *La Clase Mágica: Imagining optimal possibilities in a bilingual community of learners.* Mahwah, NJ: Laurence Erlbaum.

Vásquez, O. A., Pease-Alvarez, L., and Shannon, S. M. (1994). *Pushing boundaries: Language and culture in a Mexicano community.* Cambridge: Cambridge University Press.

Wiggington, E. (1985). *Sometimes a shining moment: The Foxfire experience.* Garden City, NY: Anchor Books.

Wong-Fillmore, L. (1991). When learning a second language means losing the first. *Early Childhood Quarterly* 6(3): 323-346.

Zentella, A. C. (1997). *Growing up bilingual: Puerto Rican children in New York.* Malden, MA: Blackwell.

Chapter 3

Building Community, Research, and Policy: A Case of Community Health and Central Americans in Los Angeles

Claudia Dorrington
Beatriz Solís

INTRODUCTION

This chapter explores the concepts of empowerment evaluation and participatory action research methods within the context of a community health education initiative developed and implemented by a grassroots organization established to respond to the needs of low-income Central American and Mexican immigrants in the Pico Union and Westlake areas of Los Angeles. Empowerment evaluation relies on evaluation concepts, methods, and findings to promote program improvements and foster self-determination among program participants (Fetterman, 2001). The emphasis is on capacity-building and democratic processes that aim to "legitimize community members' experiential knowledge, acknowledge the role of values in research, empower community members, democratize research inquiry, and enhance the relevance of evaluation data for communities" (Fawcett et al., 1996, p. 162). Participatory action research (PAR) has similar capacity-building and empowerment goals. In the PAR model, members of the community and/or organization working with a community select the topic to be explored, design the methods to be used to collect the data, gather the information, and analyze the results, either alone or within collaborative research partnerships with academics (Stoecker, 1998; Nyden et al., 1997).

This chapter (1) describes the community and organizational context, (2) outlines the community partnership and methods utilized to develop and evaluate community health education programs, illustrated through a case study, and (3) discusses the benefits and challenges of empowerment evaluation in this context. The processes of involving community members in conducting a community needs assessment, designing interventions, and developing and implementing an evaluation to monitor program processes and outcomes are central to this approach. A needs assessment, conducted in early 1997, was developed to assess the extent to which and in what way residents of the Pico Union/Westlake area in central Los Angeles perceived HIV/AIDS to be an issue of concern in their community and to obtain residents' general perceptions of other critical issues affecting their lives. Interventions in response to the results of the needs assessment were developed and implemented in the same year and evaluated over the next three years. The evaluation approaches and activities were used to enhance the planning and preventive intervention strategies of Clinica Para Las Americas, a small community clinic providing primary health care and health education services to a predominantly uninsured Latina/o immigrant population.

ORGANIZATIONAL AND COMMUNITY CONTEXT

The Agency Setting

Clinica Para Las Americas (CPLA) was founded in 1989 by a group of health care providers and health care advocates who had worked with the Central American refugee movement during the 1980s. The agency emerged in response to the perceived changing needs of what had become, by the early 1990s, a settled refugee population (Hamilton and Chinchilla-Stoltz, 2001). The central goal was the provision of accessible, quality primary health care services and health education to uninsured immigrants and refugee children and adults who had begun to establish their lives in the Pico Union/Westlake area. HIV counseling and testing services and a prevention program were added in 1993. By the mid-1990s, CPLA's primary care patients closely reflected the demographics of the area: 55 percent were Central American and 45 percent Mexican in 1995. The majority of the agency's full- and part-time staff are hired from within the local community, also reflecting the area's sociodemographic characteristics—predominantly monolingual, Spanish-speaking, Mexican and Central American immigrants. During the 1990s, most of the clinic's health educators, outreach workers, and HIV-testing counselors, among others, were provided with training through the agency. Several were recruited after their participation in one of the clinic's health education programs.

Similar to other small community-based agencies, CPLA is characterized by a lack of discretionary resources including funds, time, space, and people, as well as limited technical and structural support. Activities are frequently shaped by the requirements of funders, fee-for-service contracts, and licensing agencies. In the public health arena, as in other social service arenas, these requirements have become increasingly complex, with funders placing a greater emphasis on quality assurance and demonstration of program effectiveness and utilizing more traditional methods of program evaluation, often taxing the resources of small agencies (Gómez and Goldstein, 1996). Despite the challenges of responding to limited resources and growing demands, CPLA is nonetheless strongly committed to remaining responsive to its community by fostering patient and community empowerment, participation in agency activities and program development, and decreasing the barriers that hinder residents from receiving timely and needed health care. Furthermore, and in part because of the limited resources and the high cost of making mistakes, ongoing review, analysis, and evaluation are viewed as important tools to ensure the agency remains in step with its community.

During 1996, under new leadership, the agency reaffirmed its mission "to provide and advocate for accessible, quality primary health care and prevention services in settings that are responsive to the specific needs of the community, and to strengthen community involvement in health promotion and disease prevention" (Clinica Para Las Americas, 1997) and embarked on a strategic plan to expand its health education and prevention work with the community. The plan, as well as the possibility of funding opportunities available for HIV prevention in the immediate future, led to the creation of a work group consisting of an agency task group and a support team. The fifteen-member task group included CPLA's peer health educators, outreach workers, HIV-testing counselors, members of its community advisory committee, and volunteer participants from an existing HIV-prevention program. The support group included the authors. Dr. Octavio Vejello, a consultant researcher in HIV/AIDS from the University of California, School of Public Health, joined the work group during the planning stage of the initiative and during the first phase of program implementation.

The Community Setting

In the mid-1990s, a growing number of Latino men and women were becoming infected with HIV in Los Angeles County. The rate of AIDS among Latino men, for example, had increased from sixty-four per 100,000 in 1989 to seventy-one in 1995; among women the number had increased from two per 100,000 to ten in the same time period (Los Angeles County Department of Health Services, HIV Epidemiology Program, 1996). In 1994, AIDS was the seventh leading cause of death in the county, but in the Pico Union/Westlake area it was the fourth leading cause (United Way of Greater Los Angeles, 1996).

The Pico Union/Westlake area, just west of downtown Los Angeles, is the most densely populated area in the city, with 18,884 residents per square mile compared to 2,281 in Los Angeles County in 1995 (United Way of Greater Los Angeles, 1996). While historically a "first stop" location for newly arriving immigrants from Latin America, during the 1980s the area became known, at least informally, as "Little Central America" or "Little San Salvador," reflecting the growing number of Central American refugees and immigrants, particularly Salvadorans and Guatemalans, that arrived during that decade (Chinchilla and Hamilton, 1988, 2001; Dorrington, 1992). In 1995, 67 percent of the population in the larger Pico Union/Westlake area served by CPLA was Latino and 75 percent were foreign-born in 1990. However, within three zip codes (90006, 90017, 90057), a 3.4-square-mile area where over half of CPLA's primary care patients resided in 1996, 79 percent of the population were Latino in 1995, among whom almost half were of Mexican origin (45.4 percent) and half of Central American origin (49 percent). Population density in this area was 36,255 per square mile. In 1990, 83 percent of this smaller area's population were foreign-born and 83 percent exclusively spoke Spanish at home (United Way of Greater Los Angeles, 1996; U.S. Bureau of the Census, 1990). The poverty rate was 58 percent in 1995 and the estimated unemployment rate was 12.6 percent in 1996, as compared to 24.4 percent and 8.3 percent, respectively, in Los Angeles County for the same years. Among this relatively young population, 42.4 percent under the age of twenty-five and 67 percent age sixteen and older participated in the labor force in 1996, compared to 64 percent countywide, though an estimated 43 to 53 percent of adults ages eighteen to sixty-five had no health insurance coverage in 1997. With respect to formal education, in 1990 almost two-thirds (61.2 percent) of the adult population in this area, age twenty-five and over, had not graduated from high school and 42 percent had less than a ninth grade education (United Way of Greater Los Angeles, 1996).

The sociodemographic profile of this community, developed by the CPLA task group during its needs assessment, revealed multiple indicators of risk. However, these indicators in themselves mask the strengths and dynamic nature of this area, a community that despite multiple obstacles has a history of locally based political and social advocacy. Leaders and residents who participated in the needs assessment all emphasized the resiliency and self-determination of the community. Common themes reported were

1. strong commitments to family and community;
2. willingness and ability to work collaboratively;
3. resiliency under frequently very adverse economic and environmental conditions;
4. a strong motivation to work toward improving the lives of their children, their families, and themselves through self-development, education, and hard work;
5. a strong emphasis placed on education for their children; and
6. a high level of resourcefulness in seeking out resources that aid in improving their lives and those of their children, including opportunities for engaging in activities that aim to address problems in their community.

Many of the Central American immigrants and refugees in the United States who arrived during the 1980s had a history of community organizing, particularly Salvadorans and indigenous Guatemalans who had been members of community-based organizations or community leaders establishing organization in their home countries. In that decade, as an estimated 310,000 to 430,000 Salvadorans and Guatemalans arrived into the Los Angeles area (Ruggles and Fix, 1985; Aguayo and Weiss Fagen, 1988), they began organizing and were instrumental in establishing political advocacy and service delivery organizations in Pico Union/Westlake, on their own or in conjunction with local activists (Cordoba, 1986, 1992; Dorrington, 1992). The organizations that survived into the next decade adapted to respond to the needs of a more settled Central American refugee community and to the needs of new immigrants arriving to join family members and/or spurred by continuing economic difficulties in El Salvador and Guatemala, as well as the needs of other Latino immigrants in the area. By the time peace accords had been signed in El Salvador in January 1992, twelve years after civil war had begun, and in Guatemala in 1996, sixteen years after escalation of conflict in a protracted thirty-year civil war, many Central Americans who had initially intended to return to their homelands had permanently established their lives in the United States.

However, the 1990s did not necessarily translate into increased security or stability for the Central Americans in Pico Union/Westlake. The majority of Salvadorans and Guatemalans arriving in the previous decade were "undocumented" and many were not eligible for the amnesty provision of the 1986 Immigration Reform and Control Act (IRCA) that required continuous residence in the United States since or before January 1982 (U.S. Committee for Refugees, 1990, 1991). Interim policies that provided Salvadorans with temporary protected status (TPS) and, later, deferral of enforced departure (DED) expired in June 1992 and December 1994, respectively (U.S. Bureau of Citizenship and Immigration Services [BCIS], 2002). Thus, while a proportion of the Pico Union/Westlake Central American community have secured legal status, many remain in "a form of legal limbo" (Chinchilla and Hamilton, 2001, p. 191). Clients and patients served by Clinica Para Las Americas frequently live in families or households characterized by differential legal status, ranging from citizen children to "undocumented" parents.

The 1990s were also characterized by increased economic decline and renewed hostility toward immigrants, adversely affecting the lives of the Pico Union/Westlake Latino community. The employer sanctions provision of IRCA, as well as an economic recession that began in 1990, resulted in an increasingly competitive labor market compounded by the 1992 civil disturbance in Los Angeles—Pico Union/Westlake shouldering much of the social and economic costs of this disturbance (U.S. Committee for Refugees, 1988; Chinchilla and Hamilton, 2001). By the end of 1996, hostility toward immigrants, spurred in part by the prevailing economic conditions, was clearly reflected in both state and federal legislation, including the passage of Proposition 187 in California, the Illegal Immigration Reform and Immigrant Responsibility Act of 1996, and the 1996 welfare reform act (the Personal Responsibility and Work Opportunity Reconciliation Act of 1996), legislation that severely restricted immigrant access to public benefits, in particular health care and social welfare services. Though subsequent amendments eased some of these restrictions, by early 1998 fear and misinformation had led to a decline in applications for public benefits, such as MediCal, welfare (CalWorks), and food stamps, among eligible immigrants countywide (Zimmerman and Fix, 1998). When Clinica Para Las Americas began its needs assessment project in late 1996, its activities were already being shaped by this social, political, and economic context and the resulting atmosphere of fear and mistrust. The agency's *promatoras* (health education workers), for example, had to substantially increase their outreach efforts to assure community members that the clinic's free services were in actuality *free,* independent of immigration status. The work presented in this case study could have been accomplished only through a partnership with the *promatoras* and other agency staff from the local community.

COMMUNITY PARTNERSHIP METHODOLOGY

Empowerment evaluation, in this perspective, is essentially a capacity-building process conducted in the context of balancing community self-determination with contributing to a particular field of knowledge and, in service delivery settings such as CPLA, meeting the requirements of funders as well (Fawcett et al., 1996). Health-related funding agencies such as the Centers for Disease Control and Prevention (CDC) and Center for Substance Abuse Prevention (CSAP) are increasingly recognizing the value of participatory and empowerment approaches. The W. K. Kellogg Foundation, also, has long promoted and advocated for such methods. The Kellogg Foundation's Community Health Scholars Program refers to their model of community-based participatory research (CBPR) as a collaborative approach to research that equitably involves all partners in the research process and recognizes the unique strengths that each brings. CBPR begins with a research topic of importance to the community, has the aim of combining knowledge with action and achieving social change to improve health outcomes and eliminate health disparities. (Community Health Scholars Program, 2001)

The concepts and underlying philosophy of empowerment evaluation have been important contributions to the literature related to the practice of community organizing, community psychology, popular education, and public health (Zimmerman, 2000; Fetterman, 2001; Rubin and Rubin, 2001). Within the field of community psychology, Rappaport (1981, 1987) outlines the underlying philosophy of an empowerment approach. The approach assumes that communities have existing strengths and are capable of increasing these capacities. If competence is not demonstrated, then the fault lies in the failure of social systems to provide or create appropriate opportunities for the demonstration or acquisition of skills, rather than in the realm of individual deficits. In addition, when existing capacities need to be enhanced or new skills learned, it is through direct experiences in influencing significant life events that these skills are best acquired, integrated, and "owned." The "expert" (researcher or program evaluator) is as much the "learner" as the "teacher."

Within the field of popular education, Paulo Freire's pedagogy, or the "Freirian Praxis," proposes a dialogic, problem-posing process, with equality and mutual respect between learner-teacher and teacher-learner. Problem posing contains a cycle of "listening-dialogue-action" that enables all participants to engage in continual reflection and action. Through structured dialogue, participants (learners and teachers) listen for the issues contained in their own experiences, discuss common problems, search for root causes and the interconnections between the "problems behind the problems-as-symptom," engage in action research, devise strategies to help transform their reality, and reflect on and evaluate the processes and outcomes of their action. "Conscientization," a desired outcome, is the consciousness that comes through the social analysis of conditions and people's roles in changing those conditions. In the context of practice, community empowerment starts when people listen to one another, engage in "participatory/liberatory" dialogue, identify their commonalities, and construct their own strategies for change (Freire, 1973, 1986).

Empowerment evaluation has also been strongly influenced by the field of action research. Action research, as defined by Greenwood and Levin (1998), is "social research carried out by a team encompassing a professional action researcher and members of an organization or community seeking to improve their situation" (p. 4). Action research aims to promote "broad participation in the research process and supports action leading to a more just or satisfying situation for the stakeholders" (p. 4). The process begins with a collective definition of the problem based on a collective sharing of knowledge and incorporates a social change agenda, specifically change that enhances the capacities of the community and organizational participants involved to have greater control over their own lives and the future social reconstruction of their community. Action research embraces diverse research methods, both qualitative and quantitative, but always with the agreement of the collaborators. According to Fetterman (2001), both action research and empowerment evaluation "are characterized by concrete, timely, targeted, pragmatic orientations toward program improvement" (p. 11), requiring cycles of reflection and action and focusing on "the simplest data collection methods adequate to the task at hand" (p. 11) and relevant to the aims of the collaboration.

Case Study

The conceptual framework for empowerment evaluation utilized in this case study was adapted from the framework for community health initiatives outlined by Fawcett and colleagues (1996). The authors' model incorporates four components, each involving extensive community and organizational participation facilitated by a *support team.* The first component, *agenda setting,* is the process through which community concerns and resources are researched and assessed, creating the context for the second step, *planning.* The planning phase involves establishing or modifying missions (or goals), objectives, and strategies, as well as developing an action plan outlining specific changes sought in relevant community programs, policies, and/or practices. The third component of the model, *implementation,* involves monitoring processes and outcomes, providing ongoing feedback, and disseminating information about the initiatives under-taken to relevant stakeholders, including participants and funders. The final component of the model is *outcome,* involving the documentation of community capacity building and outcomes, and assessing and promoting "adaptation, renewal, and institutionalization" of effective initiatives (Fawcett et al., 1996, p. 165).

The empowerment evaluation framework used by CPLA's task group and support team included the following five components adapted from the model proposed by Fawcett and colleagues (1996):

1. Assessing community concerns and resources (needs assessment), with a primary focus on HIV/AIDS, in the Pico Union/ Westlake area of Los Angeles County
2. Planning an initiative in response to the results of the assessment (setting goals and objectives and developing strategies and action plans)
3. Monitoring the process and outcomes of the intervention
4. Disseminating information to stakeholders

This next section addresses the processes involved in implementing this research strategy.

Needs Assessment

The focus of the needs assessment emerged from the observations of CPLA's HIV-testing counselors and internal data indicating a growing number of HIV-positive test results among the agency's anonymous HIV test-site patients during 1995 and 1996. In addition, the clinic's peer health educators and outreach workers were reporting an array of misinformation concerning HIV among members of the community. As noted earlier, an agency task group and support team were established to assess the extent to which, and in what way, residents of the Pico Union/Westlake area perceived HIV/AIDS to be an issue of concern in their community and to obtain residents' general perceptions of critical issues affecting their lives. Table 3.1 outlines the methods used to gather information for the needs assessment and the participatory role of members of the agency task group and support team. The overall needs assessment plan, data collection methods, brief survey instruments, and the focus group and in-person interview guides were collaboratively developed by members of the

TABLE 3.1. Needs Assessment Activities (December 1996 to March 1997)

Data Collection Methods	Work Group Involvement
Fifteen focus groups with 214 Latino adult men, women, and youth	Agency Task Group: Peer health educators and HIV-testing counselors
A brief survey among 88 men and 112 women (34 percent Mexican, 42 percent Salvadoran, and 20 percent Guatemalan)	Agency Task Group: Outreach workers and peer health educators
In-person interviews with twenty-eight HIV-positive Latino men and women and fifteen gay Latinos	Agency Task Group: Peer health educators and HIV-testing counselors
Guided interviews with twenty-five key informants (five Latino community leaders, twelve Latino service providers, and eight experts conducting research in HIV/AIDS among the Latino population)	Agency Task Group: Lead health educator, program coordinators
Telephone survey to identify and manually map available HIV/AIDS and related support services in the Pico Union/Westlake area and close surroundings	Agency Task Group: Outreach workers, peer health educators, volunteers
Telephone survey among fifty identified health care providers (for-profit individual private physician practices, partnership physician practices, and small health clinics) to assess HIV-related health care provision	Agency Task Group: Outreach workers, peer health educators, HIV-testing counselors, volunteers
Sociodemographic profile of the Pico Union/Westlake area from available census data	Support Team
Compile and review available epidemiologic data on HIV/AIDS, STDs, and TB	Support Team and Agency Task Group
A review of the literature relevant to HIV/AIDS and Latinos, including review of preliminary results of research studies conducted among CPLA patients or members of the community accessed through CPLA's outreach workers*	Support Team with search assistance from members of Agency Task Group

*For example, Dr. Annette Maxwell (UCLA, School of Medicine) was researching "HIV and risk behaviors" among young Latino adults (fifty-six men and thirty-four women) at this time.

work group. The support team provided technical support, training in conducting focus groups, individual interviews and survey adminis-tration, assisted in gathering information, and synthesized the results for purposes of dissemination. The agency task group members were instrumental in assessing community resources and compiling recent and sometimes unpublished epidemiologic data through their net-work of contacts. In addition, they were instrumental in expanding community participation in the assessment process through conduct-ing the focus groups, surveys, and interviews among community resi-dents at housing developments, continuing education and ESL classes, other known gathering centers (for example, churches, recreational centers, and social service agencies), and among CPLA's primary care patients. The work was conducted over four months, between December 1996 and March 1997.

The appendix to this chapter includes selected findings from the needs assessment, relevant to HIV prevention, that illustrate exam-ples of common themes found within the data gathered from commu-nity participants through focus groups, individual interviews, and the community survey, supported by information from key informants and in part by the research literature on Latinos and HIV/AIDS avail-able in 1996 (e.g., Shelby, 1995; Diaz et al., 1993; Flaskerud and Uman, 1993; Gomez and Marin, 1993; Forrest et al., 1993). Commu-nity participants and key informants also provided other important in-formation applicable to developing HIV-prevention strategies. Women, for example, expressed the view that they would feel more comfort-able learning about HIV with other women alone, they wanted to learn from the stories and experiences of women like ourselves. However, they also felt that their partners should be involved sometimes. They primarily wanted to learn how best to talk with their partners, chil-dren, or other family members about HIV and related issues. Other common themes that emerged included the need for

1. more knowledge on human sexuality, including homosexuality;
2. ongoing reinforcement and follow-up HIV/AIDS education, as well as basic HIV education;
3. protection of individual privacy;
4. family involvement and family education;
5. negotiation/communication skills training; and

6. the need to promote self-esteem and a positive self-concept, as well as address barriers such as homophobia and stigma associated with HIV/AIDS, which were more prevalent at that time.

The importance of peer educators, the use of personal testimonies, and particularly the creation of a supportive environment within a culturally relevant context were also emphasized. Among Latinos, community-based, family-oriented HIV-prevention services were seen as likely to be most successful, as illustrated by Singer and colleagues (1990):

> a community based program, whose staff matches the linguistic, cultural, historic, experiential, and social background of its clientele, can . . . create a familiar and comfortable intervention setting in an otherwise threatening social environment, raise socially difficult issues, develop authentic bonds of relationship [and reach] so-called hard-to-reach individuals. (p. 206)

The Planning Process

As noted by Fawcett and colleagues (1996), funding agencies frequently predefine the overall mission or goals, objectives, and sometimes the strategies of community-based organizational initiatives. In this case study, while funders essentially determined the overall goal and approved or redefined specific objectives, there was substantial latitude to develop strategies and corresponding action plans that reflected the assessed needs of the Pico Union/Westlake community in respect to HIV/AIDS prevention. Through a series of meetings, the work group created a multilevel strategy designed to counter barriers to HIV prevention and incorporate HIV-related issues identified in the needs assessment. With some guidance from the support group, the agency task group developed action plans for each program component outlining the specific objectives, potential changes in service delivery, the steps required to implement the components, and the estimated time frame. In addition, the agency task group developed a corresponding management plan identifying the resources that would be required, including funds, materials, staffing, skills, training, and partnerships with others in the community, as well as the division of tasks and responsibilities. The strategy and action plans were subsequently reviewed by other CPLA staff, members of the agency's board, and volunteer participants from among CPLA's clients to further assess feasibility and acceptance.

The intervention strategy implemented between June 1997 and July 2000 and funded by the CDC and Los Angeles County Office of AIDS Programs and Policies (OAPP) was designed to

1. address HIV prevention from a systemic perspective, through three closely interacting systems—community, family, and individual;
2. incorporate the main tenets of behavior change models aimed at HIV-risk behavior—information, motivation, and skill development (Fisher and Fisher, 1992);
3. counter barriers in the community that inhibit HIV risk reduction, as identified in the needs assessment; and
4. interconnect the intervention with existing agency services and activities and provide options for entry into the different program components through multiple paths, as illustrated in Figure 3.1.

The intervention design was also based on the premises that behavior change can better occur when individuals feel a strong sense of sup-

FIGURE 3.1. HIV-Prevention Initiative

port and belonging, when program providers reflect the values and culture of the participants, and when providers and program content are responsive to the cultural, political, social, and economic factors that render Latinos as vulnerable to HIV. Together with increased knowledge about HIV/AIDS and safe-sex practices, the intervention aimed to address issues identified as barriers to HIV prevention in the needs assessment. Thus, it also sought to reduce homophobia, social barriers limiting discussions about sex with partners, and misinformation about human sexuality and increase awareness of the stresses associated with adapting to a new environment. Specifically in respect to addressing difficulties associated with reaching Latino men at higher risk for HIV, the intervention allowed for multiple points of entry—reaching men in their community, with their families, in groups with the support of other men, and individually. In addition, the goal was to provide HIV prevention for men in settings that were not specifically "gay-identified" but supportive of all men, in the context of male sexuality in general, and within the broader cultural, political, and socioeconomic context of the lives of participants.

The intervention consisted of three community outreach components, three group-level components, and individual support services. Community outreach was conducted through expanded street outreach and two-hour human sexuality workshops held at multiple locations, including adult education schools, housing developments, churches, and other agencies. In addition, a media campaign—"No Ignores Al Sida" ("Don't Ignore AIDS") was launched during the first quarter of 1999, in collaboration with Advocates for Youth; Casanova and Prendrill Publicidad and Associates, an advertising agency that developed the creative materials on a pro bono basis; XXL Pictures, a production company; Laura Keller, an advertising consultant; and Primary Colors, a print company. Both TV and radio public service announcements and print media (billboards; posters for bus shelters, bus benches, and catering trucks; and educational pamphlets and flyers distributed throughout Pico Union/Westlake), were developed to promote HIV/AIDS awareness and HIV testing. The media theme was selected after extensive focus-testing among Latino members of the community.

The group-level components included three multisession programs. The first, *Entre Familias* (Between Families), a three-session program, was designed to address barriers against safe-sex practice

within a family-focused context and aimed at providing an environment that allowed discussion and learning about potentially sensitive
topics, such as homosexuality and "talking about sex" with partners
and children. Second, *Entre Mujeres (y sus Parejas)* (Between Women
[and Their Partners]), a twelve-session program with ongoing monthly
follow-up meetings, addressed HIV prevention within a broader
framework of issues identified as relevant to women's lives and promoted knowledge, skill development, and leadership. The third group-
level intervention, *Hablando Entre Hombres* (Men Talking), was a
five-session program with ongoing monthly follow-up meetings. The
content aimed to address male identity issues and self-concept/accep-
tance within a Latino cultural context and within the context of a population in cultural transition. It focused on communication/negotia-
tion skill development as a tool in safe-sex practice and included
techniques to promote critical self-evaluation and reflection to develop insight into sexual behavior and raise awareness of the multiple
factors that influence one's life choices and behaviors. Individual
support services included individual counseling on request, referral
services, and assistance with transportation and child care to increase
program accessibility.

Monitoring the Process and Outcomes of the Intervention

An integral part of the planning process in this case study was the
identification of the types of evidence needed to document progress
toward achieving the objectives of the HIV-prevention strategy and
appropriate methods to monitor both the implementation process and
intermediate program outcomes. The CDC defines process evaluation as the "[a]ssessment of a program's conformity to its design, program implementation, or the extent to which it reaches its intended
audience" (1999, p. IV-1). In addition, they make a distinction between two types of outcome assessment—*outcome monitoring* and
outcome evaluation. Outcome monitoring is a method used to assess
whether expected program outcomes occurred and is limited in so far
as any changes that might occur cannot be attributed with any cer-
tainty to the intervention alone. This method requires the utilization
of a pre- and postintervention measure to access possible changes in
factors such as behaviors, knowledge, attitudes and beliefs, and skills
among participants and, when possible, a follow-up measure to deter-

mine whether changes have been sustained over time. In contrast, outcome evaluation seeks to determine whether an intervention caused the expected outcomes utilizing a quasi experimental or experimental research design, requiring random assignment of participants to an intervention group and to a nonintervention control group or use of a comparison group (CDC, 1999, 2002).

In this case study, the agency task group and support team collaboratively developed and implemented an evaluation plan that included both process evaluation and outcome monitoring. The types of process and outcome monitoring evaluation questions asked corresponded to the objectives of the intervention components. Examples of the questions and the client- and program-level data sources are shown in Table 3.2. While recognizing its limitation, outcome monitoring was selected as the method that would best fit within the context of the agency's resource constraints, the intervention strategy, and the needs of the participants. The evaluation plan was pilot tested during the first three months of the intervention, August to October 1997, and modified based on the results of the pilot test. Members of the agency task group had skills and prior experience in conducting process evaluation, including developing program policies and procedures and manual logs to track program implementation activities, program modifications, the type and extent of services provided, sociodemographic information on participants, and participant satisfaction or feedback information. In this case, the group also became actively involved with the support team in developing pre-, post-, and follow-up survey questionnaires to monitor whether the expected outcomes in the group intervention components of the HIV-prevention strategy had occurred and were instrumental in devising appropriate methods to administer the questionnaires. In addition, the group collected all program evaluation data. The support team coded, analyzed, summarized the data, and reported the results back to the agency and program staff on a regular basis.

It was important that the outcome-monitoring measures be acceptable to both the intervention participants and the agency task group who both facilitated the intervention and are members of the Pico Union/Westlake Latino community themselves. Examples of the task group's work included assessing the relevance of the surveys in respect to the content and objectives of the interventions and helping assure that the language and meaning of survey items were under-

Table 3.2. Examples of Program Evaluation Questions and Data Sources (1997-2000)

Process Evaluation Questions	Client- and Program-Level Data Sources
Did we serve the number of people anticipated?	Number of people served in each program component Program promotion activities
Did we serve the anticipated target population?	Sociodemographic and HIV/AIDS risk profile of participants
Did participants receive the level of intervention anticipated (e.g., number of sessions in the group-level interventions)?	Group session attendance records Number of participants attending follow-up meetings
Did we implement the intervention as intended?	Description of the content and structure of the interventions, including where, when, and who facilitated; materials used; facilitators' self-evaluation; and staff trainings and supervision
Did we meet participants' expectations?	Participant feedback through post-intervention discussion groups, written responses, and unsolicited letters to program staff

Outcome Monitoring Questions	Client-Level Data Sources
Did participants' knowledge of HIV/AIDS transmission, safe-sex practices, and human sexuality increase?	Pre-, post-, and follow-up knowledge survey
Did participants' use of condoms increase?	Participants' self-reports on frequency of condom use before and after intervention
Did participants' intention to use safe-sex practices increase?	Participants' self-reported intentions in respect to safe-sex-related behaviors at end of the intervention
Did participants' attitudes/beliefs change (e.g., in respect to homosexuality and AIDS)?	Pre-, post-, and follow-up survey
Did participants increase their skills in "negotiating" safe-sex practice with partners?	Participants' self-reports on (1) comfort level in talking about sex to partners; (2) condom use in sexual encounters; (3) success in persuading partners to use condom; (4) intent to use safe-sex practices, before and after the intervention

Did the demand for the agency's HIV-counseling and -testing services increase among "higher-risk" members of the community after the media campaign?	Record of how HIV-testing clients learned of agency test site (i.e., via media campaign or other means) Number and risk profile of clients in three months after campaign compared to same three months in prior year

stood. As a result of the pilot test and feedback from participants and facilitators, the surveys were reduced, simplified, and reformatted. Several issues emerged in respect to data collection, including a certain reluctance on the part of program participants to complete forms and questionnaires, at least in part due to mistrust and/or fear about how the information would be used, irrespective of assurances of confidentiality, as well as an association of "official-looking" forms with institutions of "authority," both the Immigration and Naturalization Services (INS) (now the BCIS) and the police were mentioned as examples. Reducing the survey and changing the format helped address this issue. Another issue creating difficulty for participants was the use of five-point Likert scales as response options for some of the items on the initial surveys. This type of scale was unfamiliar to many participants and was subsequently modified. The overall evaluation plan was also modified. The initial intention to gather three-month and six-month follow-up information from participants in the group-level intervention components proved to be unrealistic. The alternative, a one-month follow-up, yielded only limited information, and was primarily from female program participants. Agency records indicate that over one-half of the primary care patients of Clinica Para Las Americas cannot be contacted, either by phone or home visit, within four to six months after their first appointment, suggesting a considerable level of mobility within the community.

Disseminating Information to Stakeholders

One of the difficulties associated with conducting any form of program evaluation is the issue of *ownership* or "buy-in" among community agencies: Will the information gathered be both used and useful? (Gómez and Goldstein, 1996; CDC, 1999). Empowerment evaluation requires the regular sharing and discussion of the accomplishments and challenges of an initiative, which in turn helps to maintain the support of stakeholders, including agency staff, program participants, and funders, among others (Fawcett et al., 1996). In addition, seeking avenues through which program staff can present their own work promotes ownership. In this case study, members of the agency task group were trained by the support team to present information on the initiative to various groups. Subsequently information was shared with program participants, the agency staff as a whole, and its board of directors, as well as other members of the community through local planning and network meetings. Members of the task group also helped prepare and then present a Spanish-language workshop and a poster at the 1999 U.S. National Conference on AIDS (Dorrington, Campos, et al., 1999; Dorrington, Debose, et al., 1999).

LEARNING FROM THE INITIATIVE: CHALLENGES AND BENEFITS

Empowerment evaluation is an interactive process that aims to "create a dynamic community of transformative learning" (Fetterman, 2001, p. 7), one that is flexible and incorporates self-evaluation and adaptation or adjustment of intervention activities in accordance with this learning. At the same time, researchers and evaluators involved in empowerment evaluation and action research methods seek to ensure that their work maintains scientific integrity, *rigor,* and usefulness (Gómez and Goldstein, 1996). Critics of the methodologies question whether they can in fact meet the standards of traditional evaluation and systematic inquiry (Stufflebeam, 1994). Fetterman (2001), however, describes the range of mechanisms used to promote rigor in empowerment evaluation efforts, including

> workshops and training; democratic participation in the evaluation to ensure that majority and minority views are represented; quantifiable rating matrices to create a baseline measure of progress; discussion and definition of terms and ratings (i.e., norming); scrutinizing documentation; and questioning findings and recommendations. (p. 102)

(See also Fetterman's discussion on *objectivity* and *bias,* pp. 103-105.) Ultimately though, while "rigor can be maintained, . . . usefulness supercedes academic precision" (p. 107). In this case study, agency participants reported benefiting most from the learning process itself, from sharing what they had learned with others, and from using the knowledge and information gathered to improve or create new services in their community. Toward the end of the three-year intervention, the group developed a new initiative and adapted components of the existing one, incorporating Paulo Freire's pedagogy and participatory educational methods into their practice, as well as evaluation strategies. Changes were designed to build on the previous work and were based on the lessons learned, feedback from program participants, as well as an assessment of changes in the problem of HIV/AIDS itself within the community.

Zimmerman (2000) describes the relationship and roles of "the professional" in empowerment approaches to intervention planning, implementation, and evaluation as collaborator, facilitator, and a potential community resource, emphasizing also the benefits to the professional who learns through the life experiences and cultural lens of community participants. Wallerstein and Bernstein (1994) state that a crucial role is to "engage in the empowerment process as partners, plunging ourselves equally into the learning process" (p. 144). From this perspective, social problem definitions and the range of possible solutions can become more responsive and more closely aligned with the actual needs and culture of a community and expand our ways of knowing. Empowerment approaches can serve to build capacity and demystify academic knowledge, broadening participation in the development of new knowledge (Fetterman, 2001). Fawcett and colleagues suggest that empowerment evaluation also leads to "reinvention of [or new] evaluation methods and instruments" (1996, p. 181). In the authors' case studies, similar to the one presented here, agency participants adapted and created evaluation tools and methods to administer them within the sociocultural context of their communities and in consideration of what would be both useful and feasible. Such involvement promotes self-determination and can aid in the institutionalization of evaluation and action research activities within community organizations and initiatives.

Institutionalization of such activities and maintaining the momentum and capacity in service agency settings can be challenging, as they were in this case—"[a]lthough the value of learning evaluation skills and conducting an evaluation of one's own services is great, so is the burden" (Gómez and Goldstein, 1996, p. 119). Agency financial constraints, limited time, outdated and inadequate technology (computer hardware and software), a certain degree of staff turnover, and day-to-day service delivery demands contributed to these difficulties, none of which are necessarily uncommon in resource-strapped, community-based organizations. Conversely, agency commitment to the process and the involvement of a relatively large number of agency staff, ranging from the director to the outreach workers, as well as the support and flexibility of the CDC as one of the funders, were important in countering these difficulties. For the support team, staff turnover was perhaps one of the most challenging aspects, not only in the additional time required to provide training and orientation but also in seeking to maintain the established intervention and evaluation plans, while fostering the engagement and commitment of new participants who had not been part of creating the original project. New participants bring new perspectives and different life experiences. This strategy served the agency and enhanced the project since these perspectives were integrated and reflected the methodology which, at least to some extent, promoted ownership and maintained commitment. Challenges to institutionalizing evaluation and action research activities, and maintaining community participation and momentum are also related to difficulties in sustaining resources. In this case, at the time that the agency sought refunding, toward the end of the three-year initiative, very enthusiastic about changes it had made in its practice, the Los Angeles County OAPP also changed its prevention strategies, adopting a more uniform and structured approach in its grant-making process and program expectations (Los Angeles County HIV Prevention Planning Committee, 2000). The agency found that parts of its redesigned initiative and methodological approaches were no longer applicable. In addition, large reductions in funding for programs targeting women countywide, including CPLA's intervention component for Latinas, resulted in agency cutbacks, a loss of several key agency task group members and demoralization among remaining members.

Despite these challenges and later setbacks, the empowerment evaluation framework and partnership illustrated in this case study with Latino/a immigrants was successful in building both community capacity and contributing to a field of knowledge (Fawcett et al., 1996). Approaches to intervention planning, implementation, and evaluation that are inclusive, and "designed to empower rather than judge, to share skills and knowledge rather than to find fault, to improve services rather than shut them down, [provide] for the kind of learning necessary in [this third] decade of the AIDS epidemic" (Gómez and Goldstein, 1996, p. 121). Such approaches also, irrespective of unanswered questions about how best to incorporate methodological rigor, enrich our ways of knowing, teach us what is possible and important in the context of diverse social, cultural, political, and economic realities, and value the knowledge from different ways of learning.

APPENDIX: SELECTED FINDINGS FROM THE NEEDS ASSESSMENT

Participant Profile

The majority of community participants were immigrants who had arrived in this country during the past ten to twenty years, primarily from Mexico, El Salvador, and Guatemala. Twenty-four percent had been here less than five years. All participants had incomes below the poverty level, no health insurance, and the majority of the adults had not graduated from high school. Thirty-four percent had zero to six years of formal education, 27 percent had seven to nine years, and 32 percent had ten to twelve years. However, despite different ethnic origins, participants reported common needs and concerns that related to the quality of their lives and those of their families.

Basic Needs

The primary needs reported by community participants centered on economic and environmental conditions: low incomes; unemployment or under employment and few or no benefits; lack of adequate housing and poor quality housing; perceived high levels of neighborhood violence, gang, and drug and alcohol related problems; and lack of services or difficulty accessing services, including health, social, and educational services; child care; and transportation. Reported problems related to accessing services included: costs; lack of bilingual providers, child care, and transportation; immigration status; inaccessible service hours (e.g., nine-to-five operating hours); no health insurance; and lack of information about services. These basic needs were similar to those reflected in the research literature on low-income Latinos in Los Angeles County and nationwide (e.g., Zambrana, 1995; Los Angeles County HIV Prevention Planning Committee, 1995).

HIV/AIDS Risk

All participants considered AIDS to be a serious or very serious problem in their community. They saw the Latino community as not protecting itself well against HIV, although many tended to minimize their own personal risks, stating that HIV was a "disease of homosexuals" and "promiscuous women" only. However, women participants expressed the view that they were particularly vulnerable to becoming infected with HIV based on their belief that men tended to have more sexual partners, both with other women and men, and that often this information was not shared. They also perceived themselves has having less control over decisions related to sexual activity; for example, in regards to persuading partners to use condoms or get tested for HIV and learning about partners' current or past sexual activity. Younger, single women perceived themselves at being at somewhat less risk as they were more inclined to use condoms and to talk to their partners about sex. However, over 80 percent of the women participants of all ages reported never using condoms. By mid-1996, adolescent and adult Latinas with AIDS constituted 33 percent of all women in the county with AIDS, with 48 percent having become infected through heterosexual contact, compared to 39 percent of white women and 43 percent of African-American women. Latino men constituted 25 percent of all cumulative cases of AIDS among men, 81 percent had contracted the virus through male-male sexual contact (75 percent) and/or male-male sexual contact/intravenous drug use (6 percent) (Los Angeles County Department of Health Services, HIV Epidemiology Program, 1996).

Potential Barriers to HIV Prevention

The following potential barriers to HIV prevention were identified.

Misconceptions and misinformation about HIV/AIDS transmission and ways to protect oneself. For example, methods of protection, other than condom use (mentioned by only a minority of participants), included "taking care to keep clean," "knowing your partner takes care of himself," and "confidence in your partner." Among women, getting tested for HIV was seen as important primarily when a woman was pregnant or did not have confidence in her partner. Most often, they believed there was nothing they could do if their partners refused to use a condom, a belief reinforced in some by a fear of domestic violence. Participants reported not knowing how to prevent HIV or enough about HIV/AIDS to inform partners, friends, or family members. Much of their existing information came from the media (TV/radio). Research indicates that Latinos may be less knowledgeable about HIV and related risk factors than non-Latinos (e.g., Marin, 1989).

Lack of accurate knowledge about human sexuality was seen as a contributing factor to HIV in the community. Participants all expressed the need and desire for more general education in this area. Self-identified gay Latino men reported that the lack of understanding about sexual orientation contributed to the reportedly widespread homophobia in the community. Homosexuality was seen as resulting from such factors as: "being badly brought up by parents"; "being molested as a child"; "imitating others"; "just being rebellious"; or "having a hormonal imbalance." They also reported that among Latino men, sexuality is not necessarily categorized by sexual orientation (e.g., heterosexual, homosexual, bisexual). Latino men who may occasionally have sex with men identified themselves as "exclusively heterosexual." Results from the community survey found that 33 percent of the eighty-eight men who participated reported that they had had one or more same-sex encounters during their lifetime.

"Sexual silence," meaning a lack of communication between partners or within families about sex, is considered normative within Latino communities (Diaz, 1996). The Latinos/as are generally reported as "sexually conservative," though there is much variation depending on such factors as level of acculturation—including generational status and length of time in the United States, socioeconomic status, and whether a family originated from a traditional patriarchal system (Vega, 1990). Most community participants reported being raised in families where sex (in any context, e.g., "being taught about the facts of life") was never discussed and where such discussion would be considered inappropriate or outside the norm.

Cultural transition may lead to "behavior changes" during the process of immigration, adaptation, and transition from one culture to another with resulting increased risks for exposure to HIV. Examples given were the move from a more "sexually conservative" society to one that is perceived as ostensibly more "sexually open," where individuals may be "suddenly exposed to potentially more provocative material (e.g., in movies, TV, magazines) with sexual content not available in their countries of origin." The subsequent "false" sense of "freedom from risk" that this can give, as well as limited accurate knowledge about HIV/AIDS and the immigrant's increased isolation or loneliness, may result in increased sexual activity with both same-sex and opposite-sex partners.

"Machismo" was seen by many of the participants in the focus group as a barrier to reducing the spread of HIV among both men and women—the concept interpreted here not in the sense of male responsibility, but in the sense of male authority—the "right" to or "pride" in extensive sexual experience. "Machismo," according to Vega (1990), is a strong underlying force in many Latino communities and encourages men to be sexually dominant, particularly over the "feminine" (whether a woman or an "effeminate" man).

Homophobia was considered to be widespread within the community. Participants reported that it was difficult being openly gay in the Latino community; people are "rejected and mistreated," "discriminated against by society and churches, and many themselves would feel shame and reject a family member found to be gay. The gay and transsexual participants all reported having experienced isolation and rejection, some had been suicidal, many had felt depressed or anxious from "living double lives," and some had left their countries of origin in the hope of finding greater acceptance. Most who had told their families had experienced pressure to change, for example, being taken to a psychiatrist or "forced" to date women. The majority also reported that they did not participate actively in "the gay community" or with identified "gay community" activities, events, and organizations. Self-identified heterosexual Latino men who have sex with men have also been found to be very unlikely to participate in organizations associated with the gay community (Peterson and Marin, 1988).

The "stigma" of AIDS or the fear expressed by participants in regards to contracting HIV centered around the expected reactions from their families and community. For example, the expected response for a woman with HIV was "divorce," "pity," "criticism," and "gossip" about her behavior within the community (that is, promiscuity, drug use, or prostitution would be assumed) and rejection and isolation from friends and family.

REFERENCES

Aguayo, S. and Weiss Fagen, P. (1988). *Central Americans in Mexico and the United States.* Washington, DC: Georgetown University, Hemisphere Migration Project, Center for Immigration and Refugee Assistance.

Centers for Disease Control and Prevention (1999). *Evaluating CDC-funded health department HIV prevention programs,* Volume 2: *Supplemental handbook* [draft]. Available online: <http://www.cdc.gov/hiv/aboutdhap/perb/hdg.htm#vol2>.

Centers for Disease Control and Prevention (2002). *Evaluation guidance handbook: Strategies for implementing the evaluation guidance for CDC-funded HIV prevention programs,* Volume 2. Available online: <http://www.cdc.gov/hiv/aboutdhap/perb/guidance/chapter6.htm>.

Centers for Disease Control and Prevention, National Community AIDS Partnership (1995). *Evaluating HIV/AIDS prevention programs in community-based organizations.* Rockville, MD: CDC National AIDS Clearinghouse.

Chinchilla, N. S. and Hamilton, N. (1988). *Central American enterprises in Los Angeles.* A report to the International Program for Latino Research and the Social Science Research Council.

Chinchilla, N. S. and Hamilton, N. (2001). Doing business: Central American enterprises in Los Angeles. In M. López-Garza and D. R. Diaz (Eds.), *Asian and La-*

tino immigrants in a restructuring economy: The metamorphosis of Southern California (pp. 188-214). Stanford, CT: Stanford University Press.

Clinica Para Las Americas (1997). About CPLA: Information for board members. In *1996-1997 strategic plan.* Los Angeles, CA: Clinica Para Las Americas.

Community Health Scholars Program (2001). *Program goals and competencies.* Available online: <http://www.sph.umich.edu/chsp/program/index.shtml>.

Cordoba, C. (1986). "Migration and acculturation dynamics of undocumented Salvadorans in the San Francisco Bay area." Unpublished doctoral dissertation. San Francisco, University of California.

Cordoba, C. (1992). Organizing in Central American immigrant communities in the United States. In F. G. Rivera and J. L. Erlich (Eds.), *Community organizing in a diverse society* (pp. 181-200). Boston, MA: Allyn & Bacon.

Diaz, R. M. (1996). Latino gay/bisexual men: Barriers to safer sex practices. *Psychology and AIDS, 21,* 3-8.

Diaz, T., Buehler, J. W., Castro, K. G., and Ward, J. W. (1993). AIDS trends among Hispanics in the United States. *American Journal of Public Health, 83*(4), 504-509.

Dorrington, C. (1992). "Central American organizations in Los Angeles: The emergence of 'social movement agencies.' " Unpublished doctoral dissertation. Los Angeles, University of California.

Dorrington, C., Campos, R., and Aguilar, A. (1999). "Entre Mujeres [y sus parejas]": HIV Prevention Among Latinos in Pico Union, Los Angeles [workshop]. Denver, CO: The U.S. National Conference on AIDS, November 4-7.

Dorrington, C., Debose, H., Aguilar, A., and Hernandez, C. (1999). *"Hablando Entre Hombres": HIV Prevention Among Latino Men in Los Angeles* [poster]. Denver, CO: The U.S. National Conference on AIDS, November 4-7.

Fawcett, S. B., Paine-Andrews, A., and Francisco, V. T., Schults, J. A., Richter, K. P., Lewis, R. K., Harris, K. J., Williams, E. L., Barkley, J. Y., Lopez, C. M., and Fisher, J. L. (1996). Empowering community health initiatives through evaluation. In D. M. Fetterman, S. J. Kaftarian, and A. Wandersman (Eds.), *Empowerment evaluation* (pp. 161-187). Thousand Oaks, CA: Sage Publications.

Fetterman, D. M. (2001). *Foundations of empowerment evaluation.* Thousand Oaks, CA: Sage Publications.

Fisher, J. D. and Fisher, W. A. (1992). Changing AIDS-risk behavior. *Psychological Bulletin, 111*(3), 455-474.

Flaskerud, J. H. and Uman, G. (1993). Directions for AIDS education for Hispanic women based on analyses of survey findings. *Public Health Reports, 108*(3), 298-304.

Forrest, K. A., Austin, D. M., Valdes, M. I., Fuentes, E. G., and Wilson, S. R. (1993). Exploring norms and beliefs related to AIDS prevention among California Hispanic men. *Family Planning Perspectives, 25*(3), 111-117.

Freire, P. (1973). *Education for critical consciousness.* New York: Seabury.

Freire, P. (1986). *Pedagogy of the oppressed* (M. Bergman Ramos, Trans.). New York: Continuum Publishing Corporation. (Original work published in 1968.)

Gómez, C. A. and Goldstein, E. (1996). The HIV prevention evaluation initiative: A model for collaborative and empowerment evaluation. In D. M. Fetterman,

S. J. Kaftarian, and A. Wandersman (Eds.), *Empowerment evaluation* (pp. 100-122). Thousand Oaks, CA: Sage Publications.

Gómez, C. A. and Marin, B. V. (1993). Can women demand condom use? Gender and power in safe sex. *International Conference on AIDS, 9*(2), 801 (abstract No. PO-D03-3502).

Greenwood, D. J. and Levin, M. (1998). *Introduction to action research.* Thousand Oaks, CA: Sage Publications.

Hamilton, N. and Chinchilla-Stoltz, N. (2001). *Seeking community in a global city: Guatemalans and Salvadorans in Los Angeles.* Philadelphia: Temple University Press.

Los Angeles County Department of Health Services, HIV Epidemiology Program (1996). *Advanced HIV disease (AIDS) surveillance summary.* Los Angeles, CA: HIV Epidemiology Program.

Los Angeles County HIV Prevention Planning Committee (1995). *Los Angeles County HIV prevention plan for fiscal years 1996/1997 to 1997/1998.* Los Angeles, CA: LA County HIV Prevention Planning Committee.

Los Angeles County HIV Prevention Planning Committee (2000). *Los Angeles County HIV prevention plan for fiscal years 2000/2001 to 2002/2003.* Los Angeles, CA: LA County HIV Prevention Planning Committee.

Marin, G. (1989). AIDS prevention among Hispanics: needs, risk behavior, and cultural values. *Public Health Reports, 104*(5), 411-415.

Nyden, P., Figert, A., Shibley, M., and Burrows, D. (1997). *Building community: Social science in action.* Thousand Oaks, CA: Pine Forge Press.

Peterson, J. L. and Marin, G. (1988). Issues in the prevention of AIDS among Black and Hispanic men. *American Psychologist, 43*(11), 871-876.

Rappaport, J. (1981). In praise of paradox: A social policy of empowerment over prevention. *American Journal of Community Psychology, 9,* 1-25.

Rappaport, J. (1987). Terms of empowerment/examplars of prevention: Toward a theory of community psychology. *American Journal of Community Psychology, 15*(2), 121-148.

Rubin, H. J. and Rubin, I. S. (2001). *Community organizing and development,* Third edition. Boston, MA: Allyn & Bacon.

Ruggles, P. and Fix, M. (1985). *Impacts and potential impacts of Central American migrants on HHS and related programs of assistance.* Washington, DC: The Urban Institute.

Shelby, L. J. (1995). Cuidandote/Take care! The Latina Health Project. HIV-Infected Women, February 22-24, 92-102.

Singer, M., Castillo, Z., Davison, L., and Flores, C. (1990). Owning AIDS: Latino organizations and the AIDS epidemic. *Hispanic Journal of Behavioral Sciences, 12*(2), 196-209.

Stoecker, R. (1998). *Are academies irrelevant? Roles for scholars in participatory research.* Available online: <http://www.comm–org.utoledo.edu/paper398/pr. htm>.

Stufflebeam, D. L. (1994). Empowerment evaluation, objective evaluation, and evaluation standards: Where the future of evaluation should not go and where it needs to go. *Evaluation Practice, 15*(3), 321-338.

United Way of Greater Los Angeles (1996). *State of the county databook: Los Angeles County 1996-97.* Los Angeles, CA: United Way of Greater Los Angeles, Community Development Division.

U.S. Bureau of the Census. *1990 Census Data: Los Angeles City* [1990 Census Lookup] Available online: <http//www.venus.census.gov/cdrom/lookup>.

U.S. Bureau of Citizenship and Immigration Services (BCIS) (2002). *Temporary Protected Status—El Salvador.* Available online: <http://www.immigration. gov/graphics/services/tps_elsa.htm>.

U.S. Committee for Refugees (1988). Salvadorans and Guatemalans after amnesty: Squeezed out of jobs, afraid to go home. *Refugee Reports, 9*(5), 1-20.

U.S. Committee for Refugees (1990). Legalization applicants. *Refugee Reports, 11*(2), 16.

U.S. Committee for Refugees (1991). 1991 statistical issue. *Refugee Reports, 12*(12), 1-16.

Vega, E. de la (1990). Consideration for presenting HIV/AIDS information to U.S. Latino populations. *SIECUS Rep., 18*(3), 1-6.

Wallerstein, N. and Bernstein, E. (1994). Introduction to community empowerment, participatory education, and health. *Health Education Quarterly, 21*(2), 141-148.

Zambrana, R. E. (Ed.) (1995). *Understanding Latino families.* Thousand Oaks, CA: Sage Publications.

Zimmerman, M. A. (2000). Empowerment theory: Psychological, organizational and community levels of analysis. In J. Rappaport and E. Seidman (Eds.) *Handbook of community psychology* (pp. 37-79). New York: Plenum.

Zimmerman, W. and Fix, M. E. (1998). *Declining immigrant applications for Medi-Cal and welfare benefits in Los Angeles County.* Washington, DC: The Urban Institute. Available online: <http://www.urban.org/url.cfm?ID=407536>.

Chapter 4

Critical Ethnography and Substance Abuse Research Among Transnational Mexican Farmworkers

Víctor García

INTRODUCTION

Anecdotal evidence indicates that there is a major, if not growing, alcohol and substance abuse problem among transnational Mexican farmworkers. These workers travel, without their families, thousands of miles from their Mexican villages to agricultural regions across the United States, and remain anywhere from a few months to two or three years before returning to their homeland. Police and medical care providers who have compiled statistics on this issue, claim that single Mexican males disproportionately are perpetrators of alcohol-related infractions of the law or victims of alcohol-related accidents and deaths. The available literature on alcohol and farmworkers, which does not include transnational migrants, is unable to substantiate or challenge these observations. This subject clearly demands further research. However, successfully conducting substance abuse studies among transnational migrants is a difficult proposition. The migrants' transnational status, judicial immigration standing (residing and working in the United States legally or illegally), and residence practices in the United States are only a few of the obstacles.

This chapter, drawing on the author's previous ethnographic research in the United States and Mexico, suggests how researchers should examine substance abuse among transnational Mexican farmworkers. The advocated prospective is centered on the use of critical ethnography to examine this social problem and argues for the ethnographic method in gathering needed qualitative data. Critical ethnography allows for exploring the relationship between the subordinate status of the transnational migrants in the United States (as non-citizens and, at times, undocumented workers) and problem drinking. Factors in Mexico that may predispose transnational farmworkers to drinking in the United States are also considered in this research approach. Specifically, there are three objectives. The first is to introduce a migrant status paradigm, based on the critical ethnography perspective, that includes the migrants' emic view of drinking and considers problem drinking a consequence of their foreign-worker status in the United States. Causes behind this crisis in both the United States and Mexico—respectively, situational (e.g., living conditions and social isolation) and predisposing (family history of drinking and community drinking norms) factors—are considered. The second aim is to identify obstacles in studying substance abuse among migrants. The discussion addresses how transnational migrants, as a hard-to-study population, pose serious methodological challenges, and how the U.S. agricultural industry, as a suspicious and reluctant collaborator, makes this type of research difficult. The third objective is to establish research strategies that address a range of obstacles. The recommendations developed from this research include using the ethnographic method and collaborating with the agricultural industry.

Critical Ethnography As Participatory Action Research

Since the early 1980s, critical ethnography, as a paradigm and a field method, has guided ethnographic inquiry in and outside of the United States (Clifford and Marcus, 1986; Fahim, 1982; Kuper and Kuper, 1996; Ohnuki-Tierney, 1984; Young, 1991). This research approach in anthropology calls for the structural examination of the causes and consequences of social, economic, and political inequality in regions, nation states, and the global economy (LeCompte and Schensul, 1999; Meillassoux, 1981; Wolf, 2001). Capitalism and its political domination over tribal people, peasants, industrial workers, and minorities and women is often the focus of this research (Kelly et al., 2001; Meillassoux, 1981; Palerm, 1980; Wolf, 2001). Critical theorists (e.g., Fahim, 1982; Whyte, 1991) also argue that the research subjects and their communities should have a voice in the research—particularly on how it is designed and carried out—and in the dissemination of findings. Of equal importance in critical ethnography is advocacy and activism on behalf of the research population (LeCompte and Schensul, 1999). Through political action, policymaking, and program implementation, the ethnographer is to bring about change and equitable distributions of political power and other resources that empower communities (LeCompte and Schensul, 1999; Stringer, 1996).

Marxism, feminism, and postmodernism, as well as other theoretical perspectives in the social sciences, contributed to the development of critical ethnography. As a paradigm, it appealed to native researchers in ex-colonies of the third world and to Native Americans and other minority groups in the United States—the objects of study in European and North American ethnographies. These "indigenous" or "native" ethnographers in the third world (e.g., Fahim, 1982; Kanaaneh, 1997; Ohnuki-Tierney, 1984; Ryang, 1997) and the United States (e.g., Mwaria, 2001; Rodriguez, 2001; Rosaldo, 1986, 1997; Thornton, 1998; Vélez-Ibáñez, 1996, 1997) called into question early ethnographies of their people and challenged the hegemony of Western political thought. Rosaldo (1997), for example, has introduced and developed new concepts of citizenship, such as Latino cultural citizenship, that give immigrant populations an identity and a place in U.S. society. Other Latinos, such as García (1998) and García and González (2001), also advocate critical ethnography and field training to recruit Latinos and other underrepresented minority groups into universities. Critical ethnography, then, is allowing the "objects of study" to have a voice, albeit one that is not always heard, in anthropology and other social sciences.

Critical ethnography, as a data-gathering method, is similar to participatory action research. Like the latter, the research subject's view of the research problem, together with the observations of other community members, is sought in critical ethnography. The information is used to define and, as is often required, redefine the research problem. In fact, the use of the insider perspective in this fashion is standard practice in traditional ethnography (LeCompte, 1994). Closely related, collaboration in program and research development with community-based organizations—particularly those that provide services to the target population—is another similarity between critical ethnography and participatory action research (Schensul and Stern, 1985). The collaboration should not compromise the researcher's study or rapport with research subjects (LeCompte et al., 1999). Advocacy is another similarity between critical ethnography and participatory action research. However, given the in situ nature of the ethnographic method, the researcher must exercise caution and should wait until after the study is completed before proposing or advocating change, especially when conducting sensitive research similar to that discussed in this chapter (LeCompte et al., 1999). In addition, advocacy in critical ethnography is a grassroots and inclusive effort, organized and directed by the local populace around issues the community considers important and including as many social groups as possible, such as local government, community-based organizations, research populations, and employers (LeCompte and Schensul, 1999).

Despite its usefulness in data collection, critical ethnography (or, for that matter, participatory action research) is seldom taught in graduate-level field methods courses. This omission occurs even though critical ethnography is taught and advocated in other courses in the graduate curriculum. In this author's opinion, based on observations and discussions with colleagues, the schism between critical ethnography as a paradigm and critical ethnography as a field method is due to the strong influence of positivism in ethnographic research methods. Positivism is an approach established to duplicate and maintain the rules, criteria, and assumptions in the social sciences. Within this framework, the researcher is expected to be an objective, neutral technician in the field. Ethnography, according to this approach, should be free of the researcher's bias or prejudices about the research subject and population under study, and should be constrained of influences in and out of the research site that may bias findings (LeCompte and Schensul, 1999). Likewise, the ethnographer is to refrain from advocating for the research population while in the field. Failure to adhere to this principle keeps the ethnographer from being objective in his or her research and calls into question his or her findings (LeCompte and Schensul, 1999). Advocacy is appropriate only when the researcher is conducting what is known in the discipline as applied anthropology, that is, the use of anthropological research outside of the academy to study and solve major social problems (Van Willigen, 1993).

In proposing research strategies for studying substance abuse among transnational Mexican farmworkers, this author will demonstrate that critical ethnography, as a field research method, and scientific inquiry are not mutually exclusive—that is, one does not exclude the other. The scientific value of critical ethnography as a field research method is that it establishes a strong research rapport between the researcher and the research population and community that is not found in conventional research. Critical ethnography allows the researcher to gain the trust and collaboration of a population that is highly suspicious of researchers. By including the "native voice" and seeking the insider perspective in research development, members of the research population view themselves as partners with a vested interest in the success of the project. Assisting community-based service-providing organizations in their development of substance abuse prevention and intervention programs also creates goodwill within the community. The assistance, it should be stressed, must be within the guidelines of the human subjects protocol and should in no way compromise the anonymity of the key informants and the confidentiality of field data. Key informants are research subjects who provide the researcher with information about their culture or a specific research problem (Bernard, 1995). Hence, the trust and partnerships facilitated by critical ethnography establish a research environment highly conducive to gathering accurate and reliable data from different segments of the community.

TRANSNATIONAL MEXICAN FARMWORKERS AND SUBSTANCE ABUSE

Transnational Farmworkers

The vast majority of the 2.5 million seasonal farmworkers employed in the United States are transnational migrants from Mexico's Central Plateau Region.[1] Increasingly, however, migrants from southern and coastal Mexico are also embarking on the long trip to the United States. Irrespective of their regions in Mexico, they enter the United States legally (i.e., with proper resident and work visas) as well as illegally (i.e., without inspection/proper visas) to work. The migrants, mainly males, journey north without their spouses and children because of the expenses associated with the trip (González, 1992, 2001; Salgado de Snyder, 1993; Mines et al., 2001). Women also migrate to the United States on a seasonal basis but are generally employed as domestics and in service industries (González, 1995, 2001). The small percentage of transnational Mexican women who are employed in U.S. agriculture work in canneries and other food-processing plants (González, 1995). Mexican women who harvest crops and work in other field-related activities are primarily U.S.-based migrants and immigrants (García, 1992a,b; Palerm, 1991).

Farmworker research (e.g., García, 1997; Griffith and Kissam, 1995; Mines et al., 2001; R. Mines, personal communication, 2001) indicates that transnational Mexican migrants are a major farm labor force across the United States. Mexican migrants make up the vegetable and fruit harvesters in the southwest United States (Cross and Sandos, 1981; Galarza, 1977; Palerm, 1991). Outside of this region, as evidence reveals, they are complementing or replacing resident farmworkers and domestic migrants from Appalachian states, south Texas, and Florida (Heppel and Amendola, 1992; Griffith and Kissam, 1995). In the Midwest, for example, where this writer has conducted research, Mexican migrants, together with their Tejano counterparts, are harvesting and packing asparagus, strawberries, and blueberries in western Michigan (García, 2001b; Griffith and Kissam, 1995). In the northeast United States, transnational migrants have replaced Puerto Rican and other resident farm laborers in the mushroom industry of southeastern Pennsylvania and the vegetable and nursery industries of New Jersey and surrounding states (García, 1997). In the South, according to accounts of other researchers, Mexican migrants are joining black and poor white farmworkers in the tobacco fields of the Carolinas and the peach orchards of Georgia (Heppel and Amendola, 1992; Griffith and Kissam, 1995).

Substance Abuse Among Transnational Mexican Farmworkers

Despite anecdotal evidence that transnational Mexican migrants engage in problem drinking while working in the United States, there is little research on the nature, prevalence, and etiology of this substance abuse problem. In this chapter, unless otherwise noted, the discussion of transnational migrants and problem drinking is based on studies conducted by this writer and his colleague.[2] Although the studies address only alcohol use among this population, the findings are also useful in understanding other types of substance use and abuse among this farmworker population.

One of the alcohol studies was conducted in La Ordena and San Antonio Tejas (real names of the communities), respectively, in the municipalities of Moroleon and Irapuato in Guanajuato, Mexico (see García and González, forthcoming).[3] The men in these two peasant communities, at one point or another in their lives, have traveled thousands of miles seeking work in the agricultural industry of the United States. Drinking norms of the inhabitants, associated with alcohol preference, gender and drinking age, and appropriate behavior when drinking, were examined. Included were challenges to traditional drinking practices, brought about by transnational migrations and resulting in problem drinking among young males.

The other study was carried out in a major mushroom production region of the United States, southern Chester County, Pennsylvania, from August 2000 to November 2001 (see García, 2001b).[4] An ethnographic study of the industry and its workforce was conducted from 1993 to 1994 (see García, 1997; García and González, 1995). The recently completed alcohol study addressed problem drinking among transnational migrants, briefly defined as binge drinking associated with negative behaviors, such as drinking and driving, injuries, and work problems. The objective of the study was to identify and examine situational factors, such as living conditions and peer pressure, that contribute to problem drinking. Information was gathered through a community-level ethnography on problem drinking and case studies of problem drinkers. The former was used to obtain information on the community context of drinking, and the latter was used to individualize the general descriptions of problem drinking discovered in the community ethnography and examine the relationship between situational factors and problem drinking.

Limited Research on the Subject

Despite their growing numbers in U.S. agriculture, there apparently are no studies on problem drinking among transnational Mexican farmworkers; this conclusion was drawn after an extensive review of the literature (for further information of the review see García and Gondolf, in press). Transnational migrants were either missed altogether in studies on the subject or are not differentiated from other farmworkers. Mexican studies, it was found, have also failed to examine the drinking behavior and drug use of the migrants in their homeland. The urban underclass and its substance abuse problems have received attention while the rural populations in the Central Plateau Region, whose residents migrate seasonally, have been ignored. The pioneering alcohol studies of de la Parra and his colleagues (1980) in San Luis Potosi and of Medina-Mora and her colleagues (1986) in Michoacan did not attempt to identify migrants in the communities of this region.

Without a question, there is a serious dearth of data on the nature, prevalence, and etiology of substance abuse among transnational Mexican farmworkers. Additional studies are essential to increase knowledge in this topic, and new paradigms are also needed. The research on Mexican farmworkers and alcohol abuse is limited since the current literature on alcohol research is based on Mexican Americans and immigrants, many of whom reside within metropolitan areas. It would be a mistake to assume that transnational migrants engage in problem drinking for the same reasons as their U.S.-based and metropolitan counterparts. Transnational migrants differ significantly from their native and immigrant Latino counterparts. The migrants are geographically mobile; live and work in more than one country; spend months or years away from their families and social networks; and have different aspirations and views about staying in the United States. Their U.S.-based counterparts are generally settled in one region, are surrounded by their kin, and intend to remain in the country.

The Need for a Transnational Migrant Status Paradigm

Paradigms on transnational labor migration and problem drinking are a major deficiency in the social sciences. Key factors, identified in exploratory fieldwork in the United States and Mexico and overlooked in existing studies, should be considered. The model developed from these field data consists of several sets of factors, labeled by this writer as migrant status and situational, predisposing, and background factors. These factors and others to be discovered in impending analyses of field data by this writer will assist in future research endeavors by serving as areas of inquiry as well as helping in the development of a sound theoretical framework on problem drinking and transnational migration. According to the thesis behind the model, the transnational workers' "migrant status," as a foreign migrant and at times an undocumented worker, places them in living and work situations in the United States that lead to alcohol abuse. Transnational workers live with other single men (i.e., either single or married men who travel without their families) in overcrowded labor camps or apartment units, socially isolated and under peer pressure to drink (i.e., teasing and hazing, coaxing and persuading by co-workers and camp mates). These situational factors make transnational workers susceptible to alcohol and drug use for distraction and camaraderie. Predisposing factors, such as family drinking history and drinking practices in their Mexican homeland, may or may not contribute to substance abuse under these stressful situational conditions. In the model, background characteristics such as age, marital status, and education level are mediating factors that can contribute to alcohol and drug abuse or mitigate it.

The emic view of drinking among transnational migrants—that is, acceptable and unacceptable drinking and related behavior as they themselves define them—also needs to be considered in paradigm development. Alcohol studies define and measure problem drinking by the amount of alcohol consumed over a specific time period. According to this formula, there is an increased risk in alcohol-related negative behaviors after a certain number of drinks (Schulenberg et al., 1996; Weschler et al., 1998). This definition is an etic one, based on the researcher's view of problem drinking. It is not an emic, or insider's view of drinking, and does not allow for determining what is the drinking norm among the group.

Not considering the emic view of drinking, the researcher will not know whether heavy drinking is a cultural norm or a consequence of the migrants' working and living situations in the United States. Heavy drinking may be a response to these situations among migrants who were drinkers in Mexico and come from families with a history of alcohol abuse. However, not knowing whether this is indeed the case, the researcher will not be able to identify to what extent heavy drinking, as practiced by transnational farmworkers, is within cultural norms in Mexico or a violation of them. If it is not within the norm, other factors, as suggested earlier, may be responsible for heavy drinking and should be explored.

A previous study on problem drinking (Garcia, 2001a) found that each labor camp in southeastern Pennsylvania has drinking norms specific to the camp and its dwellers. These norms may be similar from óne camp to another but are not always the same. The drinking norms may moreover be similar to those found in the migrants' communities in Mexico or may differ significantly. In the camps, locally based norms prescribe times for drinking, amounts of consumption, and behaviors when drinking. When these norms are violated, the violator is dealt with according to existing social practice. For example, they are reminded of the norms, shunned, and not invited to drink with their fellow camp mates. If the improper drinking behavior continues, or progressively worsens, the abusers are asked to leave the camp.

Examining and identifying the drinking norms in the camps are important to the study of alcohol use among migrants. In some camps, the norms may call for moderation; in others, the norms allow for binge drinking. Why norms differ from camp to camp warrants examination. This research strategy yields clues related to how to formulate preventive social and drinking practices in labor camps that encourage problem drinking. To what extent problem drinking is a cultural practice or a consequence of a broader social and political context that transcends nation-state borders will also be determined.

STUDYING SUBSTANCE ABUSE AMONG TRANSNATIONAL MEXICAN FARMWORKERS

A Hard-to-Study Population

Transnational Mexican farmworkers are difficult to study (García, 2001a; García and Gondolf, in press; Palerm, 1991). This populace is not easy to locate and study using conventional research methods (García and González, 1995; Palerm, 1991). A major challenge is geographical mobility, in which the subject population migrates to various locations, is highly mobile within a given area, or resides in hidden or isolated housing, in which the farmworkers are not easily accessible (García and González, 1995; Palerm, 1991; Quintana et al., 2000). The use of conventional means, such as surveys or self-reports, may not be possible. Illiteracy, engaging in a clandestine or illegal practice, or the fear or resistance of prospective research subjects to being studied constitutes a major barrier to research in this arena.

In addition, substance abuse research among transnational farmworkers, as with other subject groups, presents myriad challenges. The problem drinker and drug addict do not believe that they have a drug problem or, if they have come to the realization that they do have one, they do everything possible to conceal it. When illegal drugs such as marijuana or cocaine are involved, abusers make every attempt to hide their use from their families, employers, authorities, and alcohol or drug use researchers. Another predicament for the researcher is that alcohol and drug abusers either dismiss or exaggerate their actual level of substance abuse.

Research Barriers

Enumeration studies of the Center for Survey Methods Research of the U.S. Census Bureau, conducted by this author and others, have identified a number of obstacles to locating and studying transnational migrants. These studies were developed in conjunction with the Ethnographic Evaluation of the Behavioral Causes of Undercount Project and the Migrant Project (see García, 1992a; García and González, 1995). The obstacles to be presented are undocumented worker status, mobility, unconventional housing and living arrangements, language and illiteracy problems, and no research participation tradition.

Undocumented worker status. Undocumented workers, also known as illegals, are individuals who enter the country illegally; that is, they cross the border into the United States without proper visas or inspection at a port of entry. These workers, out of fear of apprehension and deportation by the Bureau of Citizenship and Immigration Services, keep their immigration status to themselves and are very suspicious and distrustful of researchers or any government official who tends to ask too many sensitive questions.

Mobility. In a given year, depending on the type of crops being harvested, transnational migrants may move from one region to another seeking additional employment after only a couple weeks of work. In some regions, where crops are harvested year-round, the migrants do not travel as often. Nonetheless, as a result of migrant housing shortages, migrants in these crop industries remain highly mobile within a region. They will relocate to a range of affordable housing situations.

A consequence of this geographical mobility is that migrants are a challenge to locate and study.

Unconventional housing and living arrangements. Transnational migrants live in traditional housing, such as apartment complexes, cottages, and trailers, and in nontraditional locations, for instance, in fixed labor camps, cars, or temporary makeshift cardboard and tent camps. In traditional housing, they may be residing in irregular housing arrangements in which a group of unrelated men live dormitory style. These irregular household arrangements lead to serious overcrowding that, at times, may be a hazard. If discovered by the owner or manager of the unit, the entire group—including the one who officially rents—may be evicted. In some instances, however, landlords are aware of the overcrowding (some charging rent on an individual basis) and are not concerned about the safety of their tenants. Irrespective of the landlord's rental policy, migrants keep their living arrangements to themselves and are not forthcoming about the composition of the household in a particular unit. Research in this field indicates that they normally keep this information from strangers.

Labor camps pose another set of challenges for the researcher. Their locations, particularly those owned and operated by growers, are not always concentrated in areas where they are easily accessible. In some regions, for example, the camps are scattered on properties of different growers, hidden from public view. Locating them alone may be difficult and time-consuming. In addition, once found, gaining visitor access may be problematic, given that growers do not want strangers on their property unless given permission to enter. Some growers fear unscheduled state inspections, and others do not want labor organizers targeting their laborers.

Language and illiteracy problems. Many of the transnational migrants, especially those who are newcomers to the United States, are monolingual Spanish speakers who generally do not comprehend the English language. They also have limited or no formal education and, as a result, may be unable to read and write in their native language. If a researcher is not fluent in Spanish or knowledgeable of regional Mexican idioms, he or she will have a difficult time communicating with the subject group. In addition, overarching these literacy problems, the researcher will not be able to use a standardized questionnaire or self-report surveys.

No research participation tradition. Transnational migrants from rural backgrounds do not have a tradition of participating in surveys. Research is an abstract concept, not completely understood and, as a consequence, these subjects have a tendency of shying away from participation in studies.

U.S. Agricultural Industry, a Reluctant Collaborator

The agricultural industry should also be incorporated into studies of substance abuse among transnational Mexican farmworkers or, for that matter, any farm labor population. Growers, labor contractors, and foremen and crew chiefs often have immediate knowledge of the drinking practices of their employees. In some cases, as this author has discovered, they have dismissed some of their best workers because of drinking problems. If approached in an open, sensitive manner, growers and their associates may agree to be interviewed and occasionally grant the researcher access to work sites and grower-owned housing and encourage their workers to participate in the study. Gaining their permission in this fashion, however, is not an easy task. Growers and other agricultural employers are distrustful of researchers and skittish about participating in any capacity in research on their workers.

This crop industry is an agglomeration of businesses engaged in the production, marketing, and distribution of food, tobacco, ornamental goods, and fibers (Chibnik, 1987; Gladwin and Truman, 1989). Location, crops, farm size, labor use, and markets, to list a few criteria, distinguish the industry from one region to another. Of interest in this chapter are crop producers, commonly known as growers (Griffith and Kissam, 1995). They are not a homogeneous group—the perception often developed from the industry's public positions. Differences in the scale of their production, labor management, duration in business, and reputation are distinguishing features. Growers also adhere to a culture of their own—one that is centered around the production and marketing of crops. Informally and formally, by sharing information, equipment, and in some instances workers, they assist one another (Chibnik, 1987; García, forthcoming). Despite this cooperation, competition, conflict, and deep-seated disputes also characterize the relationships within this sector. These differences, however, are set aside when outsiders, such as union organizers, threaten the industry.

Alcohol Studies Collaboration

Growers should be recruited as key informants in alcohol studies and questioned about the drinking behavior of migrant farmworkers. Their perspective on problem drinking among these workers, together with the views of others in the community, will be helpful in gaining a holistic understanding of the drinking problem. Ideas and suggestions on how to go about developing intervention and prevention programs should also be sought in the collaboration. In their position, as insiders in the industry, they have important insights on how to go about developing and implementing needed programs. Also invaluable is the assistance of the growers in locating and gaining access to grower-owned housing and in informing and encouraging their employees to participate in research. Growers, more than anyone else, know the location of the camps and are in a position to facilitate access to their workers.

In some agricultural regions, for instance the vegetable and fruit industry in southwestern Michigan and the mushroom industry in southeastern Pennsylvania, growers, unlike employers in other industries, house their workers in labor camps on their property. In these regions and others, researchers wanting to study farmworkers at their place of residence should seek the owner's permission before entering the camps. Trespassers, or unauthorized visitors, are not welcomed on the premises, and camp residents are instructed not to answer any inquiries that they may make but to refer them to the main office. Workers fearful about contact with strangers, because of their illegal immigration status or some other reason, readily abide by their employers' instructions.

Growers, it should be stressed, are not in a position to administer surveys, self-reports, or gather data through other means for field surveys. Since they are at risk if certain information is made public, such as the hiring of undocumented or underage workers, they will not divulge it to the researcher, believing that the findings will cast them or the industry in a negative public image. In addition, with growers administering surveys, farmworkers will not be forthcoming in their response. They will be fearful that, if their employers should learn of their drug activities, such as using illegal drugs or drinking at work, they will be reprimanded, dismissed, and, in the worst case, black-listed in the industry.

Some may question the value of including growers in a critical ethnography on problem drinking among migrant farmworkers, especially in seeking their suggestions and assistance in developing and advocating for needed alcohol programs. For example, unions and labor advocacy groups argue that the agricultural industry is responsible for many of the ills facing farmworkers (American Friends Service Committee, 1997; Ferris et al., 1998; Rothenberg, 2000). However, over the years, through research in California (García, 1992a) and Pennsylvania (García, 1997, forthcoming), this writer has discovered that all growers are not alike when it comes to labor practices and workplace alcohol policies. Some growers, as discovered in the mushroom industry of southeastern Pennsylvania, believe that it makes good business sense to provide a safe working environment, pay wages above the required minimum wage, and to assist their workers to find housing, regularize their judicial immigrant status, obtain a driver's license, and establish credit locally (García, 1992a,b, forthcoming; Neu, 1988; Peterson, 1988; Pia, 1988). Instead of hiring labor contractors to manage labor, they have established human resource offices of their own. These labor practices, they have learned, create a loyal and reliable workforce and keep unions out of the industry. These same growers are also concerned about alcohol abuse among their workers and are exploring the development of alcohol prevention and intervention programs for the industry. They are well aware that worker absenteeism, poor work performance due to hangovers, and alcohol-related work injuries are costly to their businesses.

Grower Concerns About Collaborating

On the surface, it appears that it is in the grower's best interest to collaborate in alcohol studies; in fact, it is. However, as this writer has learned, two concerns limit their collaboration: distrust of academic researchers and illegal hiring practices and housing violations.

Distrust of academic researchers. In prior dealings with growers, this author has found they generally believe that researchers in the social sciences are not objective and that they conduct their studies with a liberal political agenda in mind—one that blames the agricultural industry for the social ills facing farmworkers. Researchers, according to this widely held viewpoint, paint the agricultural industry in broad strokes, and the problems of some growers are used to characterize an entire industry. Nuances in agricultural labor relations and labor management practices among employers are missed altogether in such a generalization.

Illegal hiring practices and housing violations. Employment and housing practices that violate laws or fail to meet regulations also keep growers from collaborating in farmworker studies. For example, knowingly or unknowingly, growers hire undocumented workers or underage employees. Although these practices are common in the industry, they are nonetheless illegal and punishable with heavy fines levied by a number of states. Growers may also want to keep the conditions of some of their housing units from becoming public information. The units may not meet local building regulations and, if these violations are brought to the attention of authorities, the owners will be fined. In the worst cases, if the units do not meet basic building codes, they may be razed. When this occurs, especially in areas in which housing is scarce or expensive, farmworkers leave and find employment with growers who are able to provide them with low-cost housing.

USING THE ETHNOGRAPHIC METHOD TO OVERCOME RESEARCH OBSTACLES

The Ethnographic Method and the Study of Transnational Migrants

The ethnographic method is the best research approach for examining problem drinking among transnational migrants. This research method, with a long tradition in anthropology, explores cultural beliefs and behaviors through qualitative field methods while living with the population under study (Emerson et al., 1995; LeCompte and Schensul, 1999). Social scientists may conclude that the preference is a matter of this author's academic discipline as an anthropologist. In actuality, however, ethnography is proposed over other approaches because it is ideal for exploring an understudied problem such as the one addressed in this chapter. This approach focuses on shared cultural knowledge within a group and does not assume that the researcher is aware of all the relevant questions and issues (Emerson et al., 1995; LeCompte and Schensul, 1999). Thus, it is useful for gaining an understanding of a problem that has not been examined in detail. This methodological approach provides the researcher with the flexibility to examine drinking and drug behavior in an in-depth empirical fashion, as it is discovered. The data from this kind of inquiry can then be used for developing inductive theories on substance abuse among a population that can be tested with well-grounded statistical surveys (LeCompte and Schensul, 1999).

The ethnographic approach has advantages over a survey based on a standardized questionnaire for several reasons. First of all, more structured surveys may be premature at this point, given the current dearth of knowledge on how the migrants' way of life and culture are related to their drinking activities. Structured surveys would be based on findings gathered from studies on Mexican Americans and Mexican immigrants and, as such, the questions may not reflect the migrants' reality. Second, questionnaires record "responses" to prefixed questions, often reducing these answers to numbers, seldom preserving the respondents' own words. These types of questions and the manner of recording responses to them does not allow the researcher the flexibility to explore other avenues of inquiries, which are important given the dearth of information on the subject being examined in this research project. Third, surveys based on standardized questionnaires also may not be well received by the transnational migrant population, many of whom are not accustomed to and are highly suspicious of such research procedures.

Using the ethnographic method to study problem drinking may, on the surface, appear impossible without placing the ethnographer's well-being in harm's way. However, Adler (1985) and Bourgois (1996), as ethnographers who study drug abuse issues and related illicit activity such as prostitution and drug dealing, have demonstrated that this is not the case. They lived in communities where these activities occur and successfully collected qualitative data without engaging in drug use or participating in other illegal activities. Their participation was restricted to other community activities and just "hanging out" with research subjects.

On-Site Research

Ethnographic research advocates for living on site and using qualitative research methods, such as participant observation, informal interviews, and the diagramming of genealogies or family trees (Emerson et al., 1995; LeCompte and Schensul, 1999). This approach
places the researcher in the research settings for a long period of time
and allows him or her to get close to the research subjects in a relatively unobtrusive fashion (Emerson et al., 1995; LeCompte and
Schensul, 1999). Living in a labor camp would be the ideal arrangement for the researcher who examines problem drinking among
transnational migrants, but given the shortage of living space it is not
always possible. The next best arrangement is for the researcher to reside in an apartment complex where migrants live and congregate or a
single-family house amid Mexican residents. Living on site will assist the researcher to establish rapport and trust with local residents
and promptly address fears, resistance, or suspicions that may arise
among them. Neighbors, key informants, and other community members will have a place where they can stop by to chat, have a cup of
coffee, and experience how the researcher lives, learn about activities
he or she engages in during the course of the day, and develop an understanding of the focus of the research project.

Residence in the community also places the researcher in physical
and social proximity to the daily lives of residents and their many activities. Besides implementing various research tasks, the researcher
will be able to participate in the daily routines, such as shopping and
washing clothes at the local Laundromat; attend local events, such as
community festivals; and observe everyday life. In sharing everyday
life with the residents, the researcher directly experiences how other
people live in general and also how they respond to daily challenges.

In addition, by being in contact with the researcher on a regular basis, at times daily, the research subjects and the community at large
learn for themselves about the research project. Often, it has been discovered, some transnational migrants do not clearly comprehend
why the study is being carried out until a few months into the project,
even though early on they signed consent forms in which they claim
that they in fact understand the objectives of the study and are aware
of possible risks. However, over time, they gain an understanding of
the research from the nature of the researcher's questions and his or

her field activities. Eventually, once they comprehend, research subjects and community members seek the researcher out on their own to share information that they believe is useful. Others who they think may be of assistance are also placed in direct contact. Some residents, who appreciate the efforts and concerns expressed, adopt and treat the researcher as an extended family member, visiting and extending invitations to dinner. They take a genuine interest in the researcher's well-being and work, and take it upon themselves to make sure that the research project is successful.

Using an Insider Perspective in Data Collection

Living on site to conduct research is not enough in the ethnographic method. In order for researchers to be effective in contacting and studying transnational migrants, they must be able to communicate and have an insider understanding of their culture. In terms of language, it is not sufficient knowing Spanish, particularly as it is taught at most universities or learned at home. The researcher must be able to understand and use the vernacular and idioms of the migrants. Being bicultural is also not enough for an insider perspective. Latina/o researchers, particularly immigrants and those born in the United States, innocently but the nonetheless mistakenly are under the impression that their ethnic background automatically provides them with affinity and insight. Unless the researcher was a transnational migrant, very seldom is this the case. True cultural affinity and insight into their way of life is gained only by visiting and living in their communities in Mexico and gaining an emic perspective of transnational migrants in the United States.

During the initial farmworker study which I conducted in California (García, 1992a), I quickly discovered that I, the son of a migrant, needed to learn how to speak the informants' Spanish. All segments of Mexican society and regions of the country have their own key words or phrases. These idioms are a window into the migrants' worldview, given that all thinking takes place within the construct of language (Lafayette de Mente, 1996). Visiting their homeland—as a scholar, not as a grandson, nephew, or cousin visiting relatives—I learned that migrants constitute a subculture in their own right in Mexican regions. There are unwritten values, beliefs, and norms guiding the practice of transnational migration. For example, families often decide who must make the journey north to seek work and send money back home. Often, it is young males who are chosen to make this journey. They are viewed as possessing the strength and capability to enter into the labor market in the United States and to survive the dangerous journey north.

Partnerships with Service Providers

On-site research also requires collaboration with local churches and nonprofit community organizations by seeking their views on problem drinking among transnational migrants and their ideas on how to go about developing prevention and intervention programs. Migrants and immigrants in many agricultural areas across the country compose a significant number of their parishioners and clients. Depending on the region and the crop industry, some churches and community-based service providers offer health care and other services to migrants, regardless of their legal status in the country. In reaching out to the migrant population, staff members have observed alcohol problems up close in labor camps and other residential areas. They have firsthand knowledge of heavy drinking bouts among migrants and the consequences of these episodes, among them hazing and fights and, in the worst of cases, deaths resulting from alcohol-related accidents. Some of the service providers also work with the local agricultural industry to address this and many other health problems among the farm labor force. In some regions, such as southern Chester County, Pennsylvania, for example, these organizations and local mushroom growers have teamed up to offer farmworkers inoculations against the flu, basic medical attention, and alcohol abuse counseling.

In alcohol research conducted in southeastern Pennsylvania, I partnered with two community-based service providers, La Comunidad Hispana, a health clinic, and La Misón Santa María, a Catholic mission. The directors and staff of the two, particularly the outreach workers, were familiar with the location of the migrant camps and are trusted, respected, and sought after by their residents. Both in 1993 and 2001 I provided them with information, such as census and field data, which are useful in writing grant and program proposals. Research papers on previous alcohol studies were also shared with their organizations. They imparted information about alcohol and drug abuse among local farmworkers, which is useful in developing the original research problem and subsequently reformulating it. With their assistance, the identification and mapping of labor camps, especially those hidden and located away from main roads, was readily facilitated.

One particular outreach worker in La Comunidad Hispana, employed in the research project, was instrumental in contacting, recruiting, and interviewing migrant workers. This worker—an ex-migrant himself and from the region in Mexico where the majority of these migrants are from—turned out to be an excellent key informant and field assistant. He spoke the migrants' language, using their vernacular, and truly understood their culture. This allowed effective communication with the workers and earned their trust. In fact, migrants who have left the area have contacted this individual from distant places, such as Chicago or Los Angeles, seeking advice about a medical problem or other issues. Growers, seeking assistance to address a health problem of one of their workers, trust and respect this outreach worker. Fortunately, this person had firsthand experience of how to conduct health research, maintain the anonymity of research participants, and keep information confidential. This research assistant participated in a major study titled "Accesibilidad a los Servicios de Salud para Agricultores Migrantes en Pensilvania, EUA: Un Abordaje de Evaluación Rápida," conducted by a Mexican medical doctor (Velasco Mondragon, 1993), who was examining the health conditions of the migrant population and attempting to determine their use of medical services in the area. For this project, the outreach worker located and recorded residence clusters of the migrants, interviewed a selected number of them, and learned how to record and maintain confidential information.

Qualitative Research Methods

Previous projects have led to a reconceptualization of field research strategies that are the basis for this recommendation of ethnographic methods for collecting data. These methods are basic to anthropology and have been used successfully by ethnographers to study most, if not all, of the world's cultures. The success has also included the study of transnational migrants (see Chavez, 1994; García, 1992a,b; Palerm, 1991). The ethnographic methods to be introduced have assisted me well in addressing a range of critical research obstacles associated with studying transnational migrants, as discussed earlier. They are as follows: participant observation, informal interviews, genealogical methods, and focus group interviews.

Participant observation. Participant observation is a major ethnographic field technique and should be used in valid ethnographic research projects (LeCompte and Schensul, 1999). It consists of taking part in the daily activities of the culture one is observing, describing, and analyzing (Bernard, 1995).

The researcher should make general and specific observations. For example, making general observations, this writer observed areas in the community that relate to the drinking behavior of the migrants. Visiting local drinking establishments frequented by farmworkers, such as restaurants and bars, and attending social events provides observation opportunities. The characteristics of the patrons or guests (i.e., migrant status, gender, and age) and the type, amount, and frequency of their alcohol consumption were noted.

More specific observations on the drinking behavior of migrants were made when visiting key informants at their places of residence. During the visits, participation in some of activities, such as preparing a meal or playing dominos, provided additional opportunities to observe the drinking behaviors. Specific attention to observing the living arrangements of the migrants, the number of house- and roommates, and the relationship among them was given. The drinking practices of the residents, paying attention to who drinks, what kind of alcohol is consumed, and how much alcohol is consumed per drinking episode, were noted. Activities associated with drinking, such as relaxing and conversing, playing dominos or poker, watching television or listening to music, and eating a meal, were not overlooked. They provided an idea of the context in which drinking occurs.

These observations and other research activities were made while abstaining from drinking with migrants. Abstinence follows the practices of ethnographers who have studied drug use without consuming drugs themselves (e.g., Adler, 1985; Bourgois, 1996). For the most part, most research subjects did not question why I would not drink in their presence. I suspect that given the age difference—I was twice the age of some of the younger research subjects—they did not inquire out of respect. When some of them would ask, I honestly answered that I thought it best not to drink because it would send the wrong message and look bad for an alcohol researcher to be drinking with the research subjects. Plus, while conducting research, alcohol consumption is not appropriate because it may impair important observations and related research activities. Nonetheless, they would always offer a drink, as a gesture of courtesy, especially at the beginning of the project. However, seldom did they insist or pressure me to drink, perhaps because of age or identity as a researcher, which at times they associated with that of a medical doctor.

Informal interviews. Informal interviews are based on unstructured, open-ended questions, and give the ethnographer the leeway to pursue lines of inquiry as they emerge (Bernard, 1995). This type of interviewing is conducted in conjunction with participant observation activities and, as such, is an integral part of ethnographic research (Bernard, 1995; LeCompte and Schensul, 1999).

Key informants are the main research subjects questioned using informal interviews. These research subjects inform, or teach, the ethnographer about their culture and provide detailed information about the subjects of the research (Bernard, 1995). In order to assist ethnographers effectively in this fashion, it is essential for the informants to have a clear understanding of the ethnographer's research project. They are not selected randomly from a population universe; instead, they are recruited based on their specialized knowledge and willingness to share personal information. The ethnographer recruits key informants after some time in the field and firsthand knowledge of who in the community are prospective candidates willing to help and develop contacts with other subjects (Bernard, 1995; LeCompte and Schensul, 1999).

In this research project, key informants were interviewed about their drinking behavior and the drinking behavior of migrants in general. All interviews were conducted in Spanish and in a place of the interviewees' choosing (e.g., at their residence, in a public meeting place, at the researchers' field station). They were asked why migrants drink, how much they drink, when in the course of a week they drink, and what problems arise from their drinking. Information about where and when drinking takes place among the migrant population also was sought in the interviews. In addition, the key informants were questioned about the availability of social and recreational activities at the research site and their participation in them.

The information gathered in these interviews was used to develop further questions for subjects selected as case studies.

Informal interviews were conducted with public officials, clergy, and social-service providers directly involved with the local farmworker population. These inquiries centered around farmworker health, particularly problem drinking.

Informal interviewing is also used in constructing *case studies.* Case studies are designed to individualize and represent different types of drinking practices among transnational migrants (Bernard, 1995). Case study subjects are mainly key informants. Unlike the selection of key informants, who are mainly chosen on the basis of knowledge as opposed to being representative, case study subjects are selected on the basis of both (Bernard, 1995). However, important in the selection process is their representation of the population universe.

Using informal interviews, case study subjects were questioned about their migration background, work experience, drinking history, and alcohol-related behavior. In particular, inquiries about the situational factors associated with their drinking by questioning case study subjects about their living arrangements, especially about the number of room- and housemates and their relationship with them, rendered valuable data. Examples of peer pressure to drink at their place of residence and at social gatherings were also sought. Specific attention was paid to the source of the peer pressure, how it was administered, and what were the outcomes. In addition, questions about friendships in the region were designed to further assess the degree of the subjects' social isolation. They were asked with whom, besides kin, do they visit and socialize when not working and from whom among the identified individuals do they borrow money or seek other forms of assistance. How the friendships started—and where and why they continue—were also explored in the interviews, together with whether the friends know one another and form a social network.

Genealogies. The genealogical method is comprised of procedures by which ethnographers discover and record connections of kinship, descent, and marriage using universal diagrams and symbols (Bernard, 1995). The genealogies serve to centralize and coordinate family information, provide a visual representation of a complexity of data, guide informal interviews about family history and kinship, and facilitate discussion of family problems and issues.

The genealogy of each case study subject was drawn up and used to conduct additional informal interviews. Besides assessing the number of kin of the case study subjects, genealogies and accompanying interviews were employed to collect information on predisposing factors associated with the subject's drinking. The subjects were questioned about who in the genealogy engaged or engages in binge drinking, how often, and whether any kin members had died as a result of their drinking. The negative behaviors associated with their drinking (e.g., getting into accidents or fights) were also sought for each kin member identified as engaging in binge drinking. In addition, the subjects in the case studies were asked whether they drink with kin and, if they do, with whom, how often, and under what circumstances. Moreover, the subjects were questioned about whether having local kin deterred problem drinking. If it was discovered that they indeed helped curtail this type of drinking, the subjects were asked who was important in relation to deterrence, under what circumstances, how they deter, and why.

The genealogies were also employed as a visual aid in the informal interviews and helped construct their local kinship network, if one existed. The number of kin in the network was identified in the genealogies, and the degree of contact that the subjects maintained with each kin member in the area was identified. Specifically, the subjects were asked with whom they maintained contact, how often, when, and under what circumstances. They also were questioned about their relationships to discover to what extent local relatives provide them with emotional, mutual, and economic support. These inquiries provided important information on whether the subjects have a local kinship base, how it is utilized, and the degree to which they are socially isolated.

Focus group interviews. Focus group interviews are based on unstructured and open-ended questions, which allow the researcher to explore leads as they emerge in a small group setting of no more than twelve individuals (Krueger, 1994). This research method is used in the social sciences in general (Krueger, 1994).

Focus groups were used to clarify, elaborate, and verify information gathered in the case studies. Drinking practices and situational and predisposing factors were the focus of the interviews. A set of guide questions focused on the extent and nature of negative behaviors regarding alcohol use among the workers and on contributing factors and circumstances of the drinking. Responses were probed and recorded on audiotape. Subjects for the focus group interviews were recruited through area sampling of migrant residence categories. The categories are based on living quarters, number of residents, and distance from towns. These characteristics are highly related since the kind of living quarters (dorm, cottage/trailer, or apartments) determines the number of residents living together and where the structures can be located. The large dorms, for instance, are constructed as additions to the mushroom production houses. Sufficient space for these complexes is available only some distance from the towns, and they are further blocked from being closer to the town by zone ordinances.

Facilitating Collaboration with the Agricultural Industry

Including growers in alcohol research is essential if the researcher is to obtain their knowledge of problem drinking among transnational migrants and to gather work and housing data that have a bearing on this issue. However, the two major concerns of the growers—distrust of academic researchers and illegal hiring practices and housing violations—seem insurmountable, particularly hiring practices and housing violations, but they can be effectively addressed. Researchers should understand that growers are a heterogeneous group and that some growers do understand the value of studying alcohol use among their workers. Open-minded growers, and they do exist, should be sought and their assistance obtained. If correctly approached, the researcher will be able to develop trust and rapport among them, and the growers, in turn, will assist the researcher in developing contacts with their peers.

Belaying Fears

In previous farmworker studies, there was collaboration with growers in the fashion discussed earlier. Drawing on this research, the following strategies to belay grower fears have proved effective: informing growers of research, recruiting key informants among growers, and collaborating with outreach efforts.

Informing growers of research. In an effort to belay any fears or suspicions that growers may have, the researcher should start by contacting key players in the industry and informing them of the focus of the study. Benefits for the industry should be a key issue. Growers are well aware that they, as well as their employees, have much to gain from the findings of alcohol and drug abuse studies. The results will assist them to develop needed drug abuse prevention and intervention programs for their employees that may curtail absenteeism, reduce drug abuse-related accidents at work, and, in the process, lower insurance costs and increase profits in the long run.

As a precondition to a fieldwork project in southern Chester County, for example, I met directly with local growers and informed them of the commencement date for the research. They, in turn, wrote letters of support for funding. With their recommendation, I presented the project to the Community Action Committee (CAC), a grower committee of the American Mushroom Institute. At the presentations, I introduced myself, outlined the objectives of the research, and reassured employers that their anonymity and that of their workers, should information be gathered on them, would be strictly maintained. The CAC, established nearly a decade ago, addresses, as a group, the needs of their laborers and works with local nonprofits, such as La Comunidad Hispana and the Better Alliance for Housing, to bring services to them. Improving the local public image of the mushroom industry in the region is another mission of the committee. The local populace blames the industry for the influx of Mexican immigrants and migrants in the region as well as the many challenges that a new foreign population creates for local government, school districts, and communities.

Recruiting and interviewing growers. Cultivating key informants among growers is essential in alcohol studies. It is similar to recruitment among transnational migrants; in fact, it may be easier, at least to locate them. It takes time and persistence. The researcher should start by contacting growers who are active in their communities. These individuals are involved in civic organizations, for example, as rotary club and school board members and elected officials. Public figures are accustomed to being approached and have a genuine concern about community issues. They also have influence that can open as well as close doors for the researcher in the community and the agricultural industry.

Once contact has been established, the researcher should make arrangements to informally interview the grower. Before engaging in field research, the objectives of the study should be conveyed in a clear fashion, and the need to include as many perspectives on the problem as possible should be stressed. The interviews should start with general questions about the drinking habits of farmworkers in the region. The questions should center on the drinking practices and related behavior of the workers, and include subjects such as type of alcohol consumed, quantity, and circumstances surrounding drinking episodes. Toward the end of the interview, inquiries should focus on the alcohol use and abuse of their farm employees.

When approaching and interviewing growers, the researcher should keep in mind the growers' general distrust of academic researchers. It will keep the researcher from becoming disillusioned and abandoning the study. The reception that the researcher receives, in my experience, will vary from one grower to another. Some growers will refuse to meet. Others will speak with the researcher only if they remain anonymous and the information provided is used for background purposes only. Still others will speak openly about this problem and assist in any way possible, particularly if they trust the researcher and understand the major objectives.

Collaborating in outreach efforts. When possible, and if it does not compromise their standing with farmworkers, the researcher should collaborate with the grower in outreach efforts. Some growers are attempting to meet the health needs of their workers and often work with local migrant health centers. Alcohol abuse is an important health concern being addressed by the growers. The researcher can also assist them to reach out and educate both the growers and workers about the serious consequences of this problem.

While developing initial contacts for my last alcohol study, growers placed me in touch with an ombudsman employed by the largest mushroom packing company in the region. This individual, a Honduran immigrant, is also a labor-relations consultant for the mushroom industry. He became a valuable informant and provided insights into problem drinking among mushroom workers. Visits to mushroom plants and worker activities were also made with his assistance.

This writer participated in an alcohol awareness program designed and implemented by the ombudsman. Together with a local bilingual and bicultural state trooper, alcohol awareness workshops for workers, managers, and owners educated them about the personal, social, and legal consequences of alcohol abuse. I was invited to participate in and speak at some of the workshops. Cultural differences in alcohol consumption between Mexicans and other ethnic groups in the community were among the topics discussed. This writer spoke about alcohol type, quantity, and impairment. Maintaining the human subjects protocol of the project, information about particular workers was not shared with the ombudsman or at the workshops.

CONCLUSION

Not surprisingly, few studies on substance abuse and farmworkers have focused on the growing transnational Mexican migrant labor force in the United States. Consequently, little is known about the etiology, nature, and prevalence of problem drinking among these migrants. Studying this problem among this population, as argued in this chapter, will require new paradigms and the use of the ethnographic method. The models and data-gathering techniques to be employed must be transnational migrant centric and focus on key factors on both sides of the border that contribute to problem drinking and substance abuse in general.

The paradigm proposed in this chapter, premised on critical ethnography, considers the subordinate migrant status of the transnational migrants, as foreigners and undocumented workers, and situational factors in the United States (e.g., housing arrangements, peer pressure, social isolation) that are associated with this topic. Problem drinking, often viewed as "deviant" or "pathological" conduct according to this paradigm, may actually be an adaptation, albeit a destructive one, or response to the status as migrants in the United States. Drinking appears to help many transnational migrants cope with stress associated with culture shock, social isolation, and fear and/or loneliness. The emerging ethnographic research on Mexican farmworkers indicates, furthermore, that the predominantly male migrants, as opposed to immigrants, tend to live together in the United States without family or social support. Because of stipulations in immigration laws, these farmworkers have not been able to travel and live with their families while in the United States. Their living situation makes them very susceptible to peer pressure to drink for distraction, camaraderie, and release. The judicial immigration status of farmworkers in the United States (as legal/documented or illegal/undocumented workers) may also be a compounding factor. There is no doubt that working in the United States without proper immigration documents may increase the isolation of some farmworkers, but illegality may also suppress some excessive drinking among those who fear that these behaviors might lead to deportation.

The ethnographic method, as proposed in critical ethnography, was suggested as the research approach for collecting field data on problem drinking among transnational farmworkers. A key position argued in this chapter is that in addition to the use of qualitative data-gathering techniques, ethnography requires on-site research and an insider's perspective of transnational migration. The qualitative field methods associated with this approach provide a means of gaining access to undocumented migrants who prefer to keep their whereabouts hidden from strangers and government officials, and to the somewhat protective and closed transnational migrant community in general. These field methods also provide a way to negotiate the resistance of some employers who may not want their hiring practices and their workers' living conditions to be exposed. More important, as espoused in critical anthropology, this research approach allows the subject population to participate in the study not as passive social actors to be questioned and observed but as key informants and collaborators who assist ethnographers to formulate and, at times, reformulate their line of inquiry. The research subjects or, properly stated, collaborators are both research associates and research subjects.

NOTES

1. The Central Plateau Region is a basin within the Cordilleran highlands in central Mexico. Increasing population pressure and a fragile land-tenure system in this region have contributed to a massive migration to Mexican cities, the United States, and, recently, Canada. The "core-sending states" in this vast area are Durango, Jalisco, Michoacán, Guanajuato, San Luis Potosi, Zacatecas, Tamaulipas, and Nuevo León. Peasants from these eight states have migrated and immigrated to the United States since the turn of the century (Cross and Sandos, 1981; Massey et al., 1987).

2. Since 1998, Dr. Laura González (ex-research faculty at the Centro de Investigacion en Ciencias Sociales y Administrativas, Universidad de Guanajuato, now a research scientist at the School of Social Sciences at the University of Texas at Dallas) and I have conducted ethnographic research on substance abuse, mainly alco-

hol, in Pennsylvania and Guanajuato, Mexico. This binational research on substance abuse, one of the few studies that exists, draws on the expertise of the two researchers and builds on over twenty years of ethnographic research on the peasantry in Guanajuato and their labor migration to farming regions of the Untied States (see González, 1992, 1995; García and González, forthcoming).

3. The study "Problem Drinking and Transnational Mexican Farmworkers: Exploring Predisposing Factors in Their Homeland," was funded by a 1998-1999 Academic Senate Grant from Indiana University of Pennsylvania at Indiana, Pennsylvania. Additional funding and assistance was supplied by Desarrollo Social del Municipio de Irapuato; the University of Texas at Dallas; and Instituto Tecnológico y de Estudios Superiores de Monterrey, Campus Irapuato; and the Fundación Comunitaria del Bajío, A.C., a nonprofit community organization.

4. The National Institute of Alcohol Abuse and Alcoholism funded the study, "Problem Drinking Among Migrant Mexican Farmworkers," in June 2000 (Grant Number 1 R03 AA12659-01).

REFERENCES

Adler, P. (1985). *Wheeling and dealing: An ethnography of an upper-level drug-dealing community.* New York: Columbia University Press.

American Friends Service Committee (1997). *Pennsylvania farm labor plan.* Report submitted to the Interdepartmental Council on Seasonal Farmworkers and Pennsylvania Department of Community Affairs.

Bernard, H.R. (1995). *Research methods in anthropology: Qualitative and quantitative approaches* (Second edition). Walnut Creek, CA: Altamira Press.

Bourgois, P. (1996). *In search of respect: Selling crack in el barrio.* New York: Cambridge University Press.

Chavez, L.R. (1994). The power of the imagined community: The settlement of undocumented Mexicans and Central Americans in the United States. *American Anthropologist, 96,* 52-73.

Chibnik, M. (Ed.) (1987). *Farmwork and fieldwork: American agriculture in anthropological perspective.* New York: Cornell University Press.

Clifford, J. and Marcus, G.F. (Eds.) (1986). *Writing culture: The poetics and politics of ethnography.* Los Angeles: University of California Press.

Cross, H. and J.A. Sandos (1981). *Across the border: Rural development in Mexico and recent migration to the United States.* Berkeley: Institute of Governmental Studies, University of California Press.

de la Parra, A., Terroba, G., and Medina-Mora, M.E. (1980). Prevalencia del consumo de alcohol en la Ciudad de San Luis Potosí. *Enseñanza e Investigación en Psicología, 2,* 236-245.

Emerson, R.M., Frez, R.I., and Shaw, L.L. (1995). *Writing ethnographic fieldnotes.* Chicago: The University of Chicago Press.

Fahim, H. (Ed.) (1982). *Indigenous anthropology in non-Western countries.* Durham, NC: Carolina Academic Press.

Ferris, S., Sandoval, R., and Hembree, D. (Eds.) (1998). *The fight in the fields: Cesar Chavez and the farmworkers movement.* San Diego, CA: Harcourt Press.

Galarza, E. (1977). *Farm workers and agribusiness in California: 1947-1960.* Notre Dame, IN: University of Notre Dame Press.

García, V. (1992a). "Surviving farm work: Economic strategies of Mexican and Mexican American households in an agricultural Californian community" (unpublished doctoral dissertation). Santa Barbara: University of California.

García, V. (1992b). *Results from an alternative enumeration in a Mexican and Mexican American farm worker community in California: Ethnographic evaluation of the behavioral causes of undercount* [Final Coverage Report for Joint Statistical Agreement 89-29]. Washington, DC: Center for Survey Methods Research, Bureau of the Census, Department of Commerce.

García, V. (1997). Mexican enclaves in the U.S. Northeast: Immigrant and migrant mushroom workers in southern Chester County. *JSRI Report,* Number 27. East Lansing, MI: Julian Samora Research Institute, Michigan State University.

García, V. (1998). Bringing anthropology home: Latina and Latino studies, ethnographic research, and US farm worker communities. *Occasional Paper,* Number 57. East Lansing, MI: Julian Samora Research Institute, Michigan State University.

García, V. (2001a). Exploring problem drinking among transnational Mexican farmworkers in southeastern Pennsylvania. Society for Applied Anthropology Annual Meeting, Merida, Yucatan, Mexico (March).

García, V. (2001b). Progress report, farm worker transition to farm ownership: Lessons from Mexican-origin farmers in southwestern Michigan project. Office of Outreach, U.S. Department of Agriculture, Washington, DC (August).

García, V. (forthcoming). The mushroom industry and the emergence of Mexican enclaves in southern Chester County, Pennsylvania, 1960-1990. In García, V., Gouveia, L., Rivera, J.A., and Rochín, R. (Eds.), *Rural Latino communities in the United States: Comparative regional perspectives.* East Lansing, MI: Julian Samora Research Institute, Michigan State University Press.

García V. and Gondolf, E. (in press). Transnational Mexican farmworkers and problem drinking: A review of the literature. *Contemporary Drug Problems.*

García, V. and González, L. (1995). *Finding and enumerating migrants in Mexican enclaves of the U.S. northeast: The case of southern Chester County, Pennsylvania* [Migrant Project Report]. Washington, DC: Center for Survey Methods Research, Bureau of the Census, Department of Commerce.

García, V. and González, L. (2000). Guanajuatenses and other Mexican immigrants in the United States: New communities in non-metropolitan and agricultural regions. *Occasional Paper,* Number 47. East Lansing, MI: Julian Samora Research Institute, Michigan State University.

García, V. and González, L. (2001). "Recruiting and preparing Latino students for ethnographic research in postglobal Latino immigrant communities" [session paper for annual meeting]. Society for Applied Anthropology, Merida, Mexico.

García, V. and González, L. (forthcoming). Transnational Mexican farmworkers and problem drinking: Ethnographic observations of alcohol consumption in their homeland. *Hispanic Journal of Behavioral Sciences.*

García, V., Gouveia, L., Rochin, R.I., and Rivera, J. (forthcoming). Introduction. In García, V. Gouveia, L., Rivera, J.A., and Rochín, R. (Eds.), *Rural Latino communities in the United States: Comparative regional perspectives.* East Lansing, MI: Julian Samora Research Institute, Michigan State University Press.

Gladwin, C. and Truman, K. (1989). *Food and farm: Current debates and policies.* Lanham, MD: University Press of America.

González, L. (1992). *Repuesta campesina a la revolución verde en El Bajío.* México, DF: Universidad Iberoamericana, Antropología Social, Programa Institucional de Investigación en Análisis Regional.

González, L. (1995). "El proyecto redes de migrantes guanajuatenses." Paper presented at the XIX International Congress of the Latin American Studies Association, Washington, DC.

González, L. (2001). Mexico/U.S. migration and gender relations: The Guanajuatense community in Mexico and the United States. In Kelly, R.M., Bayes, J.H., Hawkesworth, M.E., and Young, B. (Eds.), *Gender, globalization, and democratization* (pp. 75-95). New York: Rowman and Littlefield Publishers, Inc.

Griffith, D. and Kissam, E. (Eds.) (1995). *Working poor: Farmworkers in the United States.* Philadelphia: Temple University Press.

Heppel, M.L. and Amendola, S.L. (Eds.) (1992). *Immigration reform and perishable crop agriculture: Compliance or circumvention?* Lanham, MD: University Press of America; Washington, DC: Center for Immigration Studies.

Kanaaneh, M. (1997). The "anthropologicality" of indigenous anthropology. *Dialectical Anthropology, 22*(1), 1-21.

Kelly, R.M., Bayes, J.H., Hawkesworth, M.E., and Young, B. (Eds.) (2001). *Gender, globalization, and democratization.* New York: Rowman and Littlefield Publishers, Inc.

Krueger, R.A. (1994). *Focus groups: A practical guide for applied research* (Second edition). Thousand Oaks, CA: Sage Publications.

Kuper, A. and Kuper, J. (Eds.) (1996). *The social science encyclopedia.* New York: Routledge Press.

Lafayette de Mente, B. (1996). *NTC's dictionary of Mexican cultural code words.* Lincolnwood, IL: NTC Publishing Group.

LeCompte, M.D. (1994). Some notes on power, agenda, voice: A researcher's personal evolution toward critical collaborative research. In McLaren, P. and Giarelli, J. (Eds.), *Critical theory and educational research* (pp. 91-112). Albany: State University of New York Press.

LeCompte, M.D. and Schensul, J.J. (1999). *Designing and conducting ethnographic research.* Number 1: *Ethnographer's toolkit.* Walnut Creek, CA: Altamira Press.

LeCompte, M.D., Schensul, J.J., Weeks, M.R., and Singer, M. (1999). *Researcher roles and research partnerships.* Number 6: *Ethnographer's toolkit.* Walnut Creek, CA: Altamira Press.

Massey, D.S., Alarcón, R., Durand, J., and González, H. (1987). *Return to Aztlán: The social process of international migration from western Mexico.* Berkeley: University of California Press.

Medina-Mora, M.E., Rascón, L., García-Zavala, G., and Ezban, M. (1986). Patrones de consumo de alcohol y normas relacionadas con dicho consumo en una población de Michoacán, México. *Salud Mental, 9,* 87-91.

Meillassoux, C. (1981). *Maidens, meal, and money.* Cambridge: Cambridge University Press.

Mines, R., Mullenx, N., and Saca, L. (2001). The binational health survey: An in-depth study of farmworker health in Mexico and the United States. Davis, CA: California Institute for Rural Studies.

Mwaria, C. (2001). Diversity in the Context of Health and Illness. In Susser, I. and Patterson, T.C. (Eds.), *Cultural diversity in the United States.* Malden, MA: Blackwell Publishers.

Neu, P. (1988). The changing personnel climate in the mushroom industry. *Mushroom News, 36*(3), 8-9.

Ohnuki-Tierney, E. (1984). "Native" anthropologists. *American Ethnologist, 11*(3), 584-582.

Palerm, A. (1980). *Antropologia y marxismo.* Mexico, DF: CIS-INAH y Nueva Imagen.

Palerm, J.V. (1991). *Farm labor needs and farm workers in California, 1970-1989* [California Agricultural Studies 91-2]. Sacramento, CA: Employment Development Department.

Peterson, J.R. (1988). Immigration reform and the mushroom industry. *Mushroom News, 36*(3), 6-7.

Pia, M. (1988). Mushroom growing in the year 2013. *Mushroom News, 36*(12), 12-17.

Quintana, P.J.E., de Peyster, A., Hucke, R.K., and Sanudo, F.M. (2000). Surveying a hidden population: "Migrant" agricultural workers in north San Diego County, California. *Journal of Border Health, 5*(2), 3-13.

Rodriguez, C. (2001). A homegirl goes home: Black feminism and the lure of native anthropology. In McClaurin, I. (Ed.), *Black feminist anthropology: Theory, politics, praxis and poetics* (pp. 233-257). New Brunswick, NJ: Rutgers University Press.

Rosaldo, R. (1986). When natives talk back: Chicano anthropology since the late sixties. *The Renato Rosaldo Lectures, 1986.* Tucson, AZ: Mexican American Studies Research Center.

Rosaldo, R. (1997). Cultural citizenship, inequality, and multiculturalism. In Flores, W.V. and Benmayor, R. (Eds.), *Latino cultural citizenship: Claiming identity, space, and rights* (pp. 27-38). Boston: Beacon Press.

Rothenberg, D. (2000). *With these hands: The hidden world of migrant farmworkers.* Berkeley: University of California Press.

Ryang, S. (1997). Native anthropology and other problems. *Dialectical Anthropology, 22*(1), 23-49.

Salgado de Snyder, N. (1993). Family life across the border: Mexican wives left behind. *Hispanic Journal of Behavioral Sciences, 15*(3), 391-401.

Schensul, J.J. and Stern, G. (Eds.) (1985). *Collaborative research and social action. American Behavioral Scientist, 29,* 133-139.

Schulenberg, J., O'Malley, P.M., Bachman, J.G., Wadsworth, K.M., and Johnston, L.D. (1996). Getting drunk and growing up: Trajectories of frequent binge drinking during the transition to young adulthood. *Journal of Studies on Alcohol,* 57(3), 289-304.

Stringer, E.T. (1996). *Action research: A handbook for practitioners.* Thousand Oaks, CA: Sage Publications.

Thornton, R. (1998). Who owns our past? The repatriation of Native American human remains and cultural objects. In Thornton, R. (Ed.), *Studying Native America* (pp. 335-415). Madison: University of Wisconsin Press.

Van Willigen, J. (1993). *Applied anthropology: An introduction.* Westport, CT: Bergin and Garvey.

Velasco Mondragon, H.E. (1993). Accesibilidad a los servicios de salud para agricultores migrantes Mexicanos en Pensilvania, EUA: Un abordaje de evaluación rápida, un plan de trabajao.

Vélez-Ibáñez, C.G. (1996). *Border visions: Mexican cultures of the southwest United States.* Tucson, AZ: The University of Arizona Press.

Vélez-Ibáñez, C.G. (1997). "Chicano drivers of ideas in anthropology across space and place." Paper presented at the Conference of Transforming the Social Science Through Latina/o Studies, Julian Samora Research Institute, Michigan State University, East Lansing, Michigan.

Weschler, H., Austin, S.B., and Schuckit, M.A. (1998). Binge drinking: The five/four measure. *Journal of Studies on Alcohol, 59*(1), 122-124.

Whyte, W.F. (1991). *Participatory action research.* Newbury Park, CA: Sage Publications.

Wolf, E.R. (2001). *Pathways of power: Building an anthropology of the modern world.* Los Angeles: University of California Press.

Young, M. (1991). *An inside job.* Oxford, UK: Oxford Press.

Chapter 5

Community Contexts and Chicano/a Methods of Inquiry: Grounded Research and Informed Praxis

James Diego Vigil
Juan Munoz

INTRODUCTION

Chicano/a researchers from the 1960s generation charted a path of investigations focusing on Chicano/a community issues and problems. In 1969, a policy platform for the future of academic work, El Plan de Santa Barbara, elaborated on the goal of the "university serving the community." Both authors of this chapter have attempted to integrate this mission into their respective research agendas, the senior author anticipating El Plan, and the junior author refining some of its more salient directives. Vigil has examined macrohistorical issues, educational problems, and, in particular, the gang phenomenon that plagues Chicano/a youth in Los Angeles and also in southern Mexico. Munoz has focused on the examination of educational opportunities for at-risk students of color, particularly urban students placed in alternative education programs. His future research plans include investigating the role of technology in underresourced urban schools with diverse students. Both of the authors are staunch supporters of Chicano/a studies and offer the following observations on methodological strategies that have guided their work addressing persistent social problems in the Chicano/a community. With lessons learned from these early years, in combination with the mission of Chicano/a studies and research, these authors' self-reflexivity integrates a community perspective and advocates for policy formulations and changes.

Given the limited but still expanding number of researchers examining Chicano/a issues, it is imperative that increased time and energy is directed at a range of social problems that include educational attainment, workforce development, immigration and naturalization issues, neighborhood stressors, health policies, and other areas that demand sustained attention and original insights (Vigil, 1978). Moreover, research on these issues should possess an applied component and not be simply directed toward understanding a problem or issue, but rather structured with a pragmatic and applied orientation toward changing policies to alleviate or resolve social problems.

Although the majority of early research by non-Chicano/a, or outside, investigators may have created more problems than benefits for the Chicano/a barrios they purported to assist (Landes, 1965; Madsen, 1964; see Romano, 1967, and Vaca, 1970, for critiques of such work), some research by non-Chicanos/as has provided useful insights and directives for other researchers (Grebler et al., 1970; Moore, 1978, 1991; Carter, 1970). Both the productive and questionable research traditions have purposefully informed the Chicano/a research community in recognizing what to emulate and what to reject. A major position advocated in this analysis is that important contributions to community research have yet to be comprehensively explored. This is the case not only because certain issues, such as persistently high dropout rates, poverty-related health problems, overrepresentation, and rate of recidivism among Chicanos/as in the prison system, are in need of attention but also because of the lack of applied work that generates new approaches to transform public policy. Sam Rios (1978) is more emphatic on this objective and suggests that action anthropology is the most appropriate strategy for use in Chicano/a research. From this perspective, striving to serve the community through research requires authentic interaction with community "folk" to determine pressing social issues, extensive review of the literature to determine knowledge gaps and voids related to said issues, and then utilization of the information to change existing institutional responses.

THE RESEARCHER

The notion of the "insider-outsider researcher" has become more prominent among academicians since the civil rights era of the 1960s, with increasing support for the presence of invested agents, or "insiders," assisting in defining and pursuing the agenda for research. The increase of native anthropologists can be considered among the most significant developments in the discipline and application of anthropological fieldwork. These developments in anthropology, in the form of the emergence of native or organic narratives of analysis, mark the demise of anthropology as an imperialist enterprise. It recognizes the immense contribution that organic members of the studied context who are enlisted to examine their own culture provide toward further improving and authenticating the quality of fieldwork.

The researchers themselves can advance the integration of multiple perspectives into the research paradigm, including academically trained insiders. It can also be stewarded through the involvement of members of the communities who have experienced or are experiencing the social problems under consideration. With either approach, benefits accrue to the Chicano/a community. However, the contributions and perspectives of the "outsider" should not be unilaterally abandoned in favor of a strictly insider view. Rather, we see the potential for a blended or *miscegenated research* framework to offer the most promising results for studies conducted in Chicano/a communities. Ethnographers have long realized that the researcher's values and beliefs significantly influence the collection and interpretation of data. This dilemma is unavoidable. However, its negative effects can be minimized using multiple information sources. Data collection methods that afford the researcher multiple devices and perspectives through which to compile and interpret data provide a broader and deeper picture of reality (Carspecken, 1996). Nevertheless, the naive outsider and culture-bound insider interpretations should be cross-checked. Data selection and data collection methods should borrow heavily from conceptual frameworks and procedural routines from quantitative and qualitative research traditions.

QUALITATIVE VERSUS QUANTITATIVE DESIGN: AN OBSOLETE SEPARATION

Salomon (1991) proposes reconciliation between qualitative and quantitative research paradigms. He suggests that one tradition need not be superior to the other. We agree that they can work in a complementary fashion. A quantitative method produces precision, measurement, and representativeness while the qualitative method offers authenticity and depth and accommodates flux in the research context. Quantitative research requires a degree of internal control; for example, the ability to isolate foci of interest offered through stricter empirical measures.

In recent years, however, quantitative research has benefited from adopting flexible and imaginative approaches to data collection and reporting. Qualitative researchers striving to study quickly changing contexts, such as urban communities undergoing dynamic changes, first developed these procedures. Thus, quantitative research in the social sciences is currently being augmented by the use of qualitative methods; for example, studies that take place outside of laboratories. Additional qualitative procedures are becoming increasingly visible in quantitative projects that require direct observation of a situated context, respondent self-disclosure, and the presentation of data to subjects for validity checks. Indeed, the fields of qualitative and quantitative research have been merging into a mutually informing pool of ideas and useful tools to better understand human thoughts and actions. As Geertz (1973) pointed out, it is "thick description" that counts. However, the controversy over their coterminous deployment in research continues to rage.

There is considerable debate among researchers over whether qualitative and quantitative methods should be combined within a study (Bogdan and Bilken, 1992; Stainback and Stainback, 1985; Howe, 1988; Vigil, 1997). Since the 1970s the hostility between quantitative and qualitative educational researchers has dropped markedly as both groups have come to recognize the usefulness of appropriating selective features from each other's paradigmatic designs and methods. One of the fundamental criticisms of qualitative research was its indictment by traditional empiricists, who labeled it "soft data." Qualitative researchers have been accused of being overly anecdotal or descriptive rather than scientific and objective. Further, qualitative data were considered specious because the research and findings were generated from single cases taken from particular, sometimes peculiar contexts. Accordingly, data from these methods were not generalizable and could not be replicated in other contexts. Modifications in qualitative data collection procedures and protocols have altered these early criticisms.

The relatively recent advances and introduction of new research technologies such as computers, tape recorders, video cameras, and other data collection and analysis devices have become the hallmark of a new trend in qualitative research. In addition, the methods of reporting data have also undergone major adjustments, primarily owing to the influence of research from related disciplines in the social sciences, particularly psychology. Moreover, qualitative research has contributed to advancements in data collection procedures outside of controlled environments and to the formation of original theoretical explanations. For these reasons, the scientific authenticity of qualitative research has reached a new level of sophistication and accuracy.

In addition to the flexibility afforded by this approach, which includes examining and understanding unique social conditions, qualitative research is also interested in the development of new theories and descriptions of phenomena. Such in-depth research results in informed action leading to grounded policy considerations, something other researchers have failed to do in the past. The promise of qualitative methods to disaggregate the layers of activities, motives, and ideologies at work within a research context makes them an ideal match for the type of research necessary in Chicano/a neighborhoods. Appropriating this methodological approach for use in such neighborhoods has several other advantages.

First, qualitative research is grounded and freely generates more ideas to advance the production of theories that shed light on why seemingly persistent social problems are endemic to the studied site. It affords an opportunity to increase the scope of situated understanding, expand the number of critical questions considered regarding the context under examination, and suggest productive changes that stem from new insights. Further, unlike qualitatively informed projects, quantitative research is much more circumspect and decidedly less ambitious in its approach to questions of power, race, ethnicity, and gender.

For this reason, an effective research design should reflect a syncretic framework that selectively incorporates or folds in or miscegenates progressive and politically considerate theoretical and methodological tools from both qualitative and quantitative traditions in its investigation of Chicano/a communities. The topic of research in ethnic communities is discussed here in both its stable and emergent forms (Gutierrez and Stone, 1998). Examining Chicanos/as using conventional methods and singularly oriented theories may fail to uncover the dynamic and interrelated social, cultural, and political conditions that characterize this group of people. A theoretically and methodologically syncretic study of Chicano/a communities is an especially attractive approach because of its ability to link situated contexts within broader social and political consequences and historical currents while capturing recurrent and emergent events and incidents related to these considerations (Gutierrez and Stone, 1998). For these reasons, the methodology, like the theory integrated into a study of Chicanos/as, should reflect sensitivity to the histories of the individuals and the social, cultural, and political institutions of which they are a part (Bogdan and Bilken, 1992).

CONCEPTUALIZING AND IMPLEMENTING THE RESEARCH

From the inception of community-based investigations, members of the target population should be included in the development of the methodological strategies that are being proposed. There are different avenues and levels of interaction to achieve this critically important dynamic relationship. A primary goal is to form a partnership with the community or subset of the community in what is known as *advocacy/collaborative* research (Chambers, 1989; Weaver, 1985). The purpose of this methodological approach is to gather information, as noted previously, with an objective toward generating ideas and nurturing changes that assist the community residents to build from the ground up. For too long most ethnic, minority communities have been influenced, even buffeted around, by a policy science perspective (Weaver, 1985) in which outsiders determine what is needed and what is practical with respect to problems they face as a collective. It is a top-down elitist filtration process that dictates to communities rather than solicits views from the bottom up to provide the necessary social space that helps percolate solutions to problems. Key to this critical philosophy of "grounded research and informed praxis" social-issues research is the involvement of members of the community as coinvestigators. It is within this arena that the model of research advocated in this chapter differs markedly from conventional elitist models applied to ethnic communities.

The work of Munoz has investigated the experiences of students in public school alternative programs, specifically those that house significant numbers of Latino students. Anyone familiar with Chicano/a communities readily understands the unfortunate tradition of alternative education among Chicanos/as. In particular, Munoz examined an alternative school that is a single-gender (female) campus populated primarily by low-income students of color, most of whom live in the urban center of Los Angeles. Focusing on the experiences of female students in this research is of particular importance given the near absence of work examining the intersection of alternative schooling and gender. Perhaps the most recent comprehensive examination of the subject of alternative schools, such as that described in this study, was undertaken by Kelly (1993), who emphasized the conditions faced by both male and female students at a continuation high school. Other studies have considered gender in alternative programs specifically addressing literacy (Finders, 1997), identity formation (Raissiguier, 1994), and academic attrition (Fine, 1991).

The context of alternative education offers an especially inviting setting in which to broadly consider how schools and educators are responding to a growing number of students—who increasingly are members of marginalized groups—directed into nontraditional school situations. These institutions are often schools that are failing to prepare students to enjoy the luxury of multiple occupational options once they have graduated from high school. The systems of alternative education of concern are those that are designed to meet the needs of an at-risk student population. These programs include continuation high schools, independent study programs, schools for economically disadvantaged teen mothers, and education programs for adjudicated youth.

Several studies have attempted to chronicle the performance and achievement of the students in these types of schools and special programs. In one study by Fymier and Gansneder (1989) of over 22,000 students, 9,652 teachers, and 276 principals, the researchers found that between 25 and 35 percent of the students sampled were categorized, or otherwise labeled, as seriously at risk of academic failure by those educators surveyed. Although the true nature and scope of "at-riskness" remains elusive, its persistence and pervasiveness among low-income minority students is beyond doubt (Sanders, 2000).

This reexamination of alternative education was grounded in an investigative framework that considers the instructional and curricular practices present at an alternative high school in a large metropolitan school district. Both qualitative and quantitative research approaches were used to offer as rich an understanding as possible of the school culture. Although quantitative methods are less effective at providing a "thick description" (Geertz, 1998) of complex constructs such as *culture,* they are decidedly more useful in managing large data sets. Also, extensive information, certainly that obtained through qualitative procedures, can more easily be coded and inputted for statistical analysis. The high volume of data typical of case studies and the unique nature of school culture made this research an ideal candidate for a combined methodological model.

For the study described here, the school site was visited weekly for approximately six months. This study did not interrupt the routine activities of the students or teachers. Surveying students and teachers, observing in classrooms, interviewing extensively, and meeting privately with teachers, students, and administrators represents the scope of data collection procedures for the study. The data were significantly enhanced by the constant presence of a teacher, student, and a custodial staff informant, who served as sounding boards for the overall research design. The following section describes another example of grounded research and a more extensive use of the insider approach.

Joan Moore and the Chicano Pinto Research Project (hereafter CPRP) also formed a similar collaborative research team during the 1970s to investigate the roots of street gangs in barrio communities and why drug use and abuse, prison rates, job and economic issues, and other problems plagued the youth in these enclaves (Moore, 1977, 1978, 1991; Moore et al., 1979; Moore and Long, 1981). In this street-ethnographic approach older male and female members of barrio gangs in East Los Angeles were trained as community researchers to aid investigations that they themselves participated in and guided. *Pintos/as* (ex-offenders) and *tecatos/as* (ex-addicts), as part of the prison self-help movement in the 1960s (Moore, 1972, 1977), had earlier organized the League of United Citizens to Help Addicts (LUCHA). They subsequently aggressively recruited an academic, Dr. Joan Moore, to assist in implementing investigations generally addressing personal self-discovery and substantially expanding knowledge of the intricacies of barrio street gang problems. This partnership lasted for several years and resulted in landmark research on multiple dimensions of low-income barrio life. Many of the original community researchers remained with the group for all subsequent projects. For example, Robert Garcia, a member of the first clique of the White Fence barrio gang, became the invaluable executive director of the CPRP.

The senior author of this chapter has continued this legacy of a community orientation to "street ethnography" but with a different thrust. As noted previously, Moore's earlier investigations were part of an experiential learning phase of collaborative work among academics and the community. With lessons learned from these early years, in combination with the mission of Chicano/a studies and research, our work self-reflexivity integrates a community perspective and advocates for policy formulations and changes. Thus, among numerous projects developed in the past, the one focusing on street gangs has been particularly fruitful. Vigil's research quest actually began in the roles of a street worker, counselor, and high school teacher in the 1960s during the War on Poverty. Reconnecting with barrio youth perked a keen interest in literature that addressed a range of social and economic problems. Through an extensive literature review and discussions with dozens of people, it became apparent that not much information was available on the problem of street gangs in any ethnic group, much less Chicanos; the exception, of course, was the much earlier work focusing on the 1940s' *pachuco/a* (associated with a fashion of dress and Chicano youth culture) generation (Griffith, 1948; Tuck, 1956). The few works that existed were written in the late 1950s and early 1960s, and none of them addressed the historically significant gang phenomenon in Los Angeles, a city that was rapidly becoming the gang capital of the world. Upon completion of my dissertation and other projects, an investigation into Chicano/a street gangs was initiated. By 1978 I was working with Joan Moore and the CPRP. This interactive relationship eventually led to other interests and connections in this field.

A key aspect of all of these projects is that, during the initial stage, associations with gang workers either through community groups or government agencies was essential. These contacts and communications snowballed into other influential social and professional networks interested in gangs and urban youth in general. From these formal and informal interactions and discussions a whole array of ideas was generated about why gangs exist, what started them, how some youth become involved, when does it happen, and personal experiences centering on why researchers chose this field. The CPRP had already conducted research on the problems of drug use and abuse, drug rehabilitation programs, and family and job history and had compiled pioneering work on two major gangs in East Los Angeles, White Fence and El Hoyo Maravilla. I participated in most of these projects, and conducted an ethnographic study of how Victory Outreach was beginning to make inroads among street gang youth and adults (Vigil, 1982). Subsequently, these experiences of past youth work, those early literature reviews, the lessons from the CPRP, and a focus on the history of how barrio gangs were formed and why youth joined them began to emerge, which recalibrated the orientation of future projects.

Contacting former gang members from different barrios was the first task. Direct relations with a number of neighborhoods developed between the early 1980s to the present proved invaluable. This type of work was less research, as I functioned more as a gofer and functionary for what members of the community needed and wanted (i.e., basic social work), for youth and heads of households alike. Nevertheless, this period of regular interactions established a valuable rapport and gained the trust of enough people to ask for their assistance in relation to community research. There were no hidden agendas, and no ethical researcher should conduct community research with ulterior, hidden agendas. An important technique was (and is) related to patiently explaining the project proposal and sensitively answering all questions of the subject community. Those individuals who became most enthused about the surveys and interviews being planned became self-appointed research assistants, sometimes taking ownership over the project, making the professional assume the role of assistant. I just let this happen and flow. Some of the best ideas, project changes, survey redesign, and interview methods were developed from the people who had personal experience in gangs. When a researcher senses something is going wrong or someone might get offended, he or she should halt the process, discuss the issue, and explain why particular methods are being utilized. Surprisingly, when necessary, the influence of a researcher operates quite naturally and smoothly if an academic/community partnership is undertaken when the research project is envisioned and actually conducted. Among ethnographers, when the process of asking and listening is initiated in any community an expected result, and a prized experience, is to have someone from the community volunteer to become a key informant. Community members should be approached with respect and dignity, and solicited for their assistance on issues and problems that have significant impact on their lives. Furthermore, if they are involved in the thinking about and questioning these issues, adherence to this inclusive process normally results with many additional key informants. Joan Moore wrote *Homeboys* (1978) with just that type of approach and guidance: She repositioned her professional role into the conveyor of the information and insights generated by several key informants who participated in that early project.

An investigation initiated in the early 1990s summarizes the various phases of this research strategy to provide a conceptual framework of the value of community members and their contributions to the development of knowledge. In this instance, a research think tank on the East Coast was exploring the possibility of evaluating a federally funded drug intervention program in an East Los Angeles housing project. Before agreeing to accept the task, I visited the community and contacted Father Greg J. Boyle, the local parish priest, whom I had met previously. He has been a longtime champion and spokesperson for local residents, especially gang members. Through his role as a *cultural broker,* a term commonly referred to by anthropologists when making initial field contact with a person in the know and with a wide, dense social network, I was introduced to a number of key residents and contacts. Instant rapport and trust resulted from Father Boyle's involvement, thus facilitating the next phase, discussing with a select few community leaders the proposed research, intentions of use of the information, and other matters. Establishing contact with the community and involving members were two goals that were critical before the investigation was implemented. This drug evaluation effort required several months and was completed with the direct assistance of residents.

From that initial dialogue with community residents, I raised the issue of possible future applied-research opportunities and received their tacit support for those plans. Maintaining direct interactions and participation with the community continued on an informal basis. Within a year a government newsletter provided information about a pending *request for proposal* (RFP) from the Department of Health and Human Services. The focus of the research was on family dynamics and gang life. After discussions with these new cultural brokers and key respondents (note: the term "informant" had to be jettisoned for the obvious reason of what that word means in a community where police surveillance is a problem), I requested their assistance on the investigation if the project was funded. Upon receiving an affirmative answer a proposal response to the RFP was submitted and funded. For three years an investigation was conducted, shaped, and guided by an egalitarian orientation supportive of an academic and community partnership. This requires a collaborative approach aimed toward the exploration and unearthing of family life and child-rearing practices in a low-income community largely of Mexican Americans. The end product of the intensive community research was for the team to develop a series of policy recommendations that contribute to and/or start prevention and intervention programs in the community.

Research conducted between October 1992 and September 1995 was directed toward identifying and exploring the interrelationships of gang and family life in the Pico Gardens public housing project in Los Angeles, California. Pico Gardens was selected as the research site for this study in part because it is located in the heart of the East Los Angeles barrios that are characterized by deteriorating socioeconomic conditions (Moore and Vigil, 1993). It is one of three contiguous city housing projects located just east of downtown Los Angeles, which together cover 57.5 acres of "townhouse configured units," with a total "official population" of 4,762 and a "substantial 'unofficial' population" as well. Latinos constitute 85 percent of the residents and include "an unknown, but undoubtedly significant, number of individuals and families with non-legal immigration status" (Housing Authority, 1990, pp. 3-4). The principal source of income for over one-third of these projects' households consists of Aid to Families with Dependent Children (AFDC) payments, and the average reported annual income per household is $10,932 (Moore and Vigil, 1993).

The per capita arrest rates for drug-related offenses and crimes of violence among residents of these projects were much higher (40 percent and 50 percent, respectively) than the national average (Moore and Vigil, 1993). Although these arrests do not involve only gang members, it is not surprising that gang activities and conflicts have also become more prominent in these circumstances. Of the ten known street gangs active in the Pico Gardens housing project and the two other projects contiguous with it, two—Primera Flats (First Street) and Cuatro Flats (Fourth Street)—have been in existence for over forty years (Moore and Vigil, 1993). Cuatro Flats predominates in Pico Gardens. There are still *veteranos* (members of the earliest cliques) who either live in the project or regularly visit family members there.

Two conceptual frameworks have guided the investigation of gang families, and the interplay between the macro- and microlevels involved. The first entailed a macro examination of how certain factors, which have been referred to as experiencing "multiple marginality" (Vigil, 1988, 2002a; Vigil and Yun, 1998), have redundantly and cumulatively shaped some families and the youth within them to become more "choloized" (marginalized) and thus more at risk to street socialization, specifically in gangs. The second, microlevel framework dealt with social control networks, for example, families, schools, police, and church. The project focused primarily but not exclusively on the family. Family networks, especially in Latino culture, constitute the primary source of early socialization and enculturation (Moore and Pachon, 1985). In a previous study (Moore and Vigil, 1987) it was noted that four family types exist in most barrios: (1) "underclass," (2) conventional/controlled, (3) unconventional/controlled, and (4) conventional/uncontrolled.

In the first type, the underclass or *cholo* (derived from *solo,* a Spanish word for "alone" and used in Latin America to describe marginalized indigenous populations) family, it was found that family members have adopted deviant behavioral patterns and become as influential as or more influential than gang peers in shaping barrio youth. The polar opposite to this type is the second variant, the conventional/controlled family, which closely approximates what is found in stable working-class family units. The third type, the unconventional/controlled, are families that have adult members who may be involved in the gang and some deviant activities but maintain a conventional facade and conceal their deviance from the family. Finally, the fourth type, the conventional/uncontrolled family, is simply ineffectual, and there are many different variants in this category.

To generate a comprehensive profile of the variation in family types associated with gang activity and drug problems, the research methodology employed a combination of survey, interview, and observation techniques (Copeland and White, 1991). A miscegenated mix of approaches and information was utilized in carrying out these steps:

1. *Baseline sample:* A sample of thirty of the 239 units in Pico Gardens was randomly drawn for a two-hour, questionnaire-guided interview conducted with adult household principals. The instrument was constructed on the basis of field testing and focused on the social control issues of connections, engagements, involvement, and beliefs (Vigil, 2002b). Along with data from housing project management, the U.S. Census, and other sources, this survey information became the baseline for all families in the research site.

2. *Intensified observation of gang families:* Simultaneously, informal observation of family life was conducted by community researchers, and all the families exhibiting a ganging pattern were designated for further study.

3. *Gang-based selection of second sample:* A sample of all the remaining households in Pico Gardens with members belonging to local gangs was identified. Principals from these families were interviewed with the same survey instrument previously mentioned. With the gang families selected from the random sample of all family units in the projects and the gang members' families sample, the research team possessed information on all Pico Gardens families having at least one active young gang member.

4. *Focus on gang families:* After initial analysis of this extensive information, along with concerted contacts and interviews with local leaders and service providers (church, probation, school, and so on), an in-depth identification of families that exhibited an intergenerational "ganging" pattern (two or more siblings or two or more generations in the gang) was undertaken.

Adopting a broad approach to the enculturation process, this study thus combined interviews, life and family history, and observational techniques in compiling and tracing the acquisition and retention of cultural patterns and child socialization practices. Family members were encouraged to tell their "story" and from this thick description and complex mosaic, the investigators established the key sociodemographic components that constitute a "family" story leading to the clarification of what features reflect gang families. Generally, such families usually are single-parent households without social capital or extended family networks; they are almost entirely dependent on social welfare programs and suffer from emotional problems. These families were observed and interacted with for approximately a three-year period.

In sum, the ingredients for this project included a mix of quantitative and qualitative research techniques, as well as a strategy of collaboration between academic professionals (including the principal investigators), students, and community researchers. The collaborative research strategy was similar to that used in earlier efforts of coprincipal investigator Dr. Moore and her colleagues at the Chicano Pinto Research Project (Moore, 1978, 1991; Moore et al., 1979; Moore and Long, 1981). Community research trainees who were longtime residents of the research site conducted most of the formal interviewing and also served as principal sources of data based on their long experience in the community and personal knowledge of most of the residents. Data gathering began following the training of the community researchers.

The community researchers helped participate in the generation of survey questions and the design of the survey instruments, field-test interview protocols and the like, but their unparalleled strength was in the personal networks, community insights, and historical knowledge of the community. Academics could not easily make these contacts and understand the meaning behind certain behaviors and attitudes exhibited by survey respondents without the community researchers' assistance. For example, weekly debriefing meetings were held in one of the public housing offices, or at the principal investigator's home, to more thoroughly plumb the information gathered from interviews. Invariably, what household heads stated during the interviews was different from their behavior over a longer period of time—behavior that the community researchers had either witnessed or had learned about from other residents in the area. The research team had to practice a type of informational "tacking" to arrive at what, more or less, reflected accurate data.

Information derived from all of these sources was discussed regularly at research team meetings, a process that often identified the need to question particular participants further and also generated additional information pertinent to the research from the experiences of the community researchers. Both of the community researchers had firsthand knowledge of the resident gang; one had a brother in the set and the other had been an active member in an earlier set. Because of their experiences and insights as longtime members of the community familiar with the gang, initial and follow-up interviews with gang members were more easily accomplished and research team discussions filled in most of the gaps and provided a rich historical context for the family stories that were cobbled together. The exchanges each week also indicated to the academics what training and direction the community researchers needed for future data collection.

Important collateral information such as the following was also collected by the community researchers:

1. An ethnohistorical record of the five decades in which the Cuatro Flats gang has existed, based on interviews with older members and former members of the predominant gang in Pico Gardens; a less complete record of that gang's chief rivals was also created.
2. During the second year, a yearlong chronicle of all public incidents involving violence (especially gang activities) was recorded by a woman who has lived in Pico Gardens for decades and is frequently sought out by residents (including gang members) for assistance and advice in dealing with social service agencies, the police, and the housing authorities.
3. During the third year, extensive photography and videotaping was employed in both public settings and private family settings within the housing development. Professor Vigil took most of the photos, and a graduate film student at the University of Southern California was retained to videotape various events and to train the community researchers in the use of the video camera. A video documentary using some of this footage was also produced.
4. Throughout the research period, Professor Vigil, in particular, regularly discussed the research site and gang activities in the area with local police, school officials, and public and private social service providers serving the area. Father Gregory J. Boyle,

formerly the local parish priest and currently the director of a job development program attempting to address the needs of local gang youths, was particularly influential in this process.

During the third year of the study, selected senior gang members who resided outside of Pico Gardens were interviewed regarding their household and family structures, using an abbreviated form of the same questionnaire used in the surveys of resident households. A second questionnaire, primarily consisting of open-ended items involving parenting strategies and family dynamics, was used in follow-up interviews with members of many of the households from both initial samples, as well as seven additional resident families with children who had not joined the gang. All formal interviews were preceded by the researcher reading an explanation of the purpose and privacy of the research, and requiring that the person to be interviewed sign an informed consent statement in English or Spanish, as appropriate for the interviewee. Data were recorded without the names of the persons interviewed or any persons mentioned in the interviews.

PROBLEMS ENCOUNTERED DURING RESEARCH

Numerous problems affected the course of the research project. Foremost among these was the repeated outbreaks of gang-related violence and other crime, either within the housing project or conflicts in East Los Angeles with these gangs (six shooting deaths occurred in the projects or adjacent areas during the final year of the study). Police-community relations remained troubled throughout the study period but were especially acute in the weeks following the shooting of a police officer just outside the housing development boundaries in May 1994. In one episode, large numbers of police swarmed into Pico Gardens, beating and arresting several young men. One of the community research trainees was arrested while attempting to assist a neighbor by explaining to police that the man lived in the apartment next to the one where they had detained him; the trainee's wrist was injured during his arrest. Numerous other sources of tension, either personal or financial, also probably affected residents' confidence in responding to the researchers' efforts.

Perhaps because of these tensions and because residents were aware of an existing (if rarely applied) official policy of evicting resident families deemed to be "problems" (Housing Authority, 1990), most respondents in the formal interviews (which involved questionnaires and were also tape recorded when interviewees did not object) denied any and all involvement on their own part or that of any family members not only with gang activities but also with legal behaviors, such as using alcoholic beverages. Moreover, and as noted previously, they did so even though the interviewers knew otherwise and the respondents were aware of the interviewers' knowledge; indeed, during the field testing of the questionnaire, one trainee interviewed her mother, who similarly denied that she or others in the family ever used alcohol, although all did, some frequently.

The latter incident is a classic example of how crucial community researchers are to an in-depth examination of the problems and issues found in a low-income community. Throughout all phases of the research it was readily apparent that the attitudes and practices of the residents were qualitatively documented mainly because of the community researchers' local knowledge and sense of trust they had with respondents. Gradually, with regular training and feedback from experienced academics, these heretofore-inexperienced investigators improved their skills and became accomplished assistants. One major contribution was to recommend giving something back to the community. Instead of extracting knowledge and leaving, which appears to be the conventional practice in the social sciences, a reciprocal relationship was struck. Midway through the project the consultants developed a pamphlet describing the research and findings at that point, including photographs of different events. The community report was designed and printed by professionals to appear official and was distributed to all residents of the housing project. This initiative generated numerous additional opportunities for discussions with residents and other nearby families and social service providers. Seminars and workshops with local youth and family heads were followed with pizza and other refreshments that served as social lubricants. Similar feedback and give-and-take sessions among the academics and community researchers marked the research project.

CONCLUSION

Research projects that address Chicano/a communities should attempt to combine various aspects of theoretical traditions and methodological procedures. A metatheoretical framework utilizing a macromicro theoretical perspective can be immensely helpful in initiating research in urban ethnic communities. An interpretive lens of multitheoretical facets better fathoms the persistent and/or cyclical nature of certain communal practices. The goal is to gain a multidimensional understanding of the complex processes, social interactions, and concrete outcomes characteristic of different units of analysis in a community. In addition, this conceptual positioning provides the research projects the opportunity of having the community "speak for itself," and ensures that the investigation remain closer to the ground. In contrast to this more open perspective, the researcher often assumes a predetermined superordinate interpretative role. Urban research is a highly dynamic exercise embedded in social relations of production. Thus, it is important to utilize a complementary set of theoretical models to sharpen the discourse, a process that helps us understand and articulate the dynamic aspects of this condition.

Methodologically, as previously noted, investigations in Mexican-American communities will profit from eclectically enlisting a variety of methods of data collection and analysis. Data collection may include surveys and questionnaires, onsite observations, individual interviews, home visits, video- and audiotaping (if permissible), photographs, collections of community artifacts, informant portfolios, and newsprint research. Of course, serious attention must also be extended to ancillary community organizations that provide support services to individuals and their families. Such organizations include but are not limited to churches, recreation centers, schools, and public support offices.

Methods of data analysis and interpretation are perhaps more critical than the collection of information. This is true because it is through the process of interpretation that the data are given a public voice. Data which are filtered through complementary theoretical frameworks and which incorporate a variety of data collection and analysis methods provide a multidimensional understanding of key issues in the Chicano/a communities. The information gathered for any study must be protected and used solely for the purposes that were openly discussed with the participants. All data gathered should be properly coded in such a way that neither real names nor any revealing characteristics of individuals are used. The codes used to preserve confidentiality should be recorded in an aggregate, for example, numbers and letters, that refer to the date of the meeting, interviews, or taping as well as general characteristics of the participant (e.g., whether the individual is a teacher, parent, or youth).

Innumerable problems can potentially affect the course of any research project. In the case of the projects described in this chapter, foremost among the considerations of the research participants were the repeated outbreaks of gang-related violence, other crime incidents, and the general instability of the families and communities. Unlike antiseptic laboratory conditions that have become synonymous with the notion of "objective research," the context of complex societies is anything but sterile. Conditions change and research personnel must acquire both the academic insight and personal instincts to likewise adjust and interpret changes according to the contextual specificity in which they find themselves working. The purpose of intricately involving community agents as both informants and as architects of the conceptual framework and its eventual implementation is precisely to preserve and augment the research. By doing so the organic flexibility of thought and reaction already acquired and mastered by residents of the community is honored and given dignity. In this way, research is not simply informed by community members, but rather these community researchers are legitimized co-authors of the research findings, and of the recommendations that follow.

This approach recognizes community members as legitimate academic and intellectual workers. The research effort affords them an unprecedented degree of authenticity. Such respect has not been made available to projects that—as has been the case traditionally— exploit the goodwill and sincere desire of community residents. Community residents should be able to assist in programs and projects that promise to improve the quality of their lives and those to follow.

Urban settings inhabited by Chicanos/as have not received an adequate level of attention from researchers. The absence of research indicates a general indifference to a population that is often economically disadvantaged and comprised of people of color. The fact that the persistent problems confronting Chicanos/as remain in limbo raises questions as to whether conventional approaches to conduct research within these communities will yield findings that help to reduce unequal social relations. More often, conventional research appears to consign them to the lowest possible social positions. The social and political conditions faced by Chicanos/as in the larger social order may be yet further evidence of how the disadvantaged are systematically shaped and structured by the hands of others to remain in the lower echelons of the social, political, and economic realms.

REFERENCES

Bogdan, R. and Bilken, S. (1992). *Qualitative research for education: An introduction to theory and methods.* Boston, MA: Allyn and Bacon.

Carspecken, P.F. (1996). *Critical ethnography in educational research: A theoretical and practical guide.* New York: Routledge.

Carter, T. (1970). Mexican Americans: How the schools have failed them. *College Board Review,* 75 (Spring), 374-386.

Chambers, E. (1989). *Applied anthropology: A practical guide.* Prospect Heights, IL: Waveland Press.

Copeland, A.P. and K.M. White (1991). *Studying families.* Newbury Park, CA: Sage Publications.

Finders, M.J. (1997). *Just girls: Hidden literacies and life in junior high.* New York: Teachers College Press.

Fine, M. (1991). *Framing dropouts: Notes on the politics of an urban high school.* Albany, NY: SUNY Press.

Fymier, J. and Gansneder, B. (1989). The Phi Delta Kappa study of students at risk. *Phi Delta Kappa,* 71(2), 142-146.

Geertz, C. (1973). *The interpretation of culture.* New York: Basic Books.

Geertz, C. (1998). *Works and lives: The anthropologist as author.* Stanford, CA: Stanford University Press.

Grebler, L., Moore, J.W., and Guzman, R. (1970). *The Mexican American people.* New York: The Free Press.

Griffith, B. (1948). *American me.* Boston: Houghton Mifflin.

Gutierrez, K. and Stone, L. (1998). "An emerging methodology for cultural-historical perspectives on literacy learning: Synchronic and diachronic dimensions of social practice." Paper presented at the annual meeting of the American Educational Research Association.

Housing Authority of the City of Los Angeles (1990). Public Housing Drug Elimination Grant Application: Public Housing Drug Elimination Program. Application submitted to HUD, Los Angeles, California.

Howe, K.R. (1988). Against the qualitative-quantitative incompatibility thesis or dogma die hard. *Educational Researcher,* 17(8), 10-16.

Kelly, D.M. (1993). *Last chance high.* New Haven, CT: Yale University Press.

Landes, R. (1965). *Latin Americans in the Southwest*. New York: McGraw Hill.

Madsen, W. (1964). *The Mexican Americans of South Texas*. New York: Holt, Rinehart, and Winston.

Moore, J.W. (1972). LUCHA in agencyland: A Chicano self-help organization meets the establishment. *Growth and Change*: 43-50.

_____ (1977). The Chicano Pinto Research Project: A case study in collaboration. *Journal of Social Issues,* 33, 144-158.

_____ (1978). *Homeboys*. Philadelphia: Temple University Press.

_____ (1991). *Going down to the barrio*. Philadelphia: Temple University Press.

Moore, J.W. and Long, J.M. (1981). *Barrio impact of high incarceration rates*. Los Angeles: Chicano Pinto Research Project.

Moore, J.W. and Pachon, H. (1985). *Hispanics in the United States*. Englewood Cliffs, NJ: Prentice-Hall.

Moore, J.W. and Vigil, J.D. (1987). Chicano gangs: Group norms and individual factors related to adult criminality. *Aztlan,* 18(2), 27-44.

_____ (1993). Barrios in transition. In J. W. Moore and R. Pinderhughes (Eds.), *In the barrios: Latinos and the underclass debate* (pp. 27-49). New York: Russell Sage.

Moore, J.W. et al. (1979). *A model for Chicano drug use and for effective utilization of employment and training resources by barrio addicts and ex-offenders*. Los Angeles: Chicano Pinto Research Project.

Raissiguier, C. (1994). *Becoming women/becoming workers*. New York: SUNY Press.

Rios, S. (1978). Action anthropology. In Arvizu, S.F. (Ed.), *Chicano perspectives on de-colonizing anthropology* (pp. 35-48). Berkeley, CA: TQS Publications.

Romano, O.I. (1967). The anthropology and sociology of the Mexican American: The distortion of Mexican American history. *El Grito,* 2(1), 1-22.

Salomon, G. (1991). Transcending the qualitative-quantitative debate. The analytic and systemic approaches to educational research. *Educational Researcher,* 20(6), 10-18.

Sanders, M.G. (2000). *Schooling students placed at risk: Research, policy, and practice in the education of poor and minority adolescents*. Mahwah, NJ: Lawrence Erlbaum.

Stainback, S. and Stainback, W. (1985). Qualitative and quantitative methodologies: Competitive or complimentary? *Exceptional Children,* 51, 330-334.

Tuck, R. (1956). *Not with a fist: Mexican Americans in a southwest city*. New York: Harcourt Brace.

Vaca, N. (1970). The Mexican American in the social sciences: 1912-1970; Part 1: 1912-1935. *El Grito,* 3(3), 25-47.

Vigil, J.D. (1978). Marx and Chicano anthropology. In S.F. Arvizu (Ed.), *Chicano perspectives on de-colonizing anthropology* (pp. 19-34). Berkeley, CA: TQS Publications.

_____ (1982). Human revitalization: The six tasks of victory outreach. *The Drew Gateway,* 52(3), 49-59.

_____ (1988). *Barrio gangs: Street life and identity in Southern California*. Austin: University of Texas Press.

_____ (1997). *Personas Mexicanas: Chicano high schoolers in a changing Los Angeles.* Fort Worth, TX: Harcourt Brace.

_____ (2002a). *A Rainbow of Gangs: Street Cultures in the Mega-City.* Austin: University of Texas Press.

_____ (2002b). Community dynamics and the rise of street gangs. In M. Suarez-Orozco (Ed.), *Latinos! Remaking America.* Cambridge and Berkeley: Harvard University and University of California Presses.

Vigil, J.D. and Yun, S.C. (1998). Vietnamese youth gangs in the context of multiple marginality and the Los Angeles youth gang phenomenon. In K. Hazlehurst and C. Hazlehurst (Eds.), *Gangs and youth subcultures: International explorations* (pp. 117-139). New Brunswick, NJ: Transaction Publishers.

Weaver, T. (1985). Anthropology as a policy science, Part 1: A critique. *Human Organization, 44,* 97-105.

Chapter 6

Identity and Field Research in Mexico: Lessons for Research and Social Policy for U.S. Latinos

María Teresa Vázquez Castillo

INTRODUCTION

Class, ethnicity, gender, and location are some of the elements that influence positions of power relations and perspectives of social actors. Researchers, as social actors, are not the exception. The identity of a researcher is reflected in approaches to learning and knowing, but also in the way direct or indirect participants in a research project perceive the researcher. This chapter explores how the identity that participants in a research project ascribe to the researcher shapes the process and results of research. It also emphasizes the importance of location on identity and, more specifically, the identity of a Mexican/Latina researcher undertaking field research in Mexico.

In the United States the term *Latino* encompasses a wide variety of identities regardless of class, ethnicity, gender, national origin, culture, or generation. Since this term homogenizes different peoples from Latin American descent in the United States, the question arises as to what types of research agendas would advance Latino social policy. Within this context, this chapter explores my experience as a Mexican/Latina researcher undertaking field research in different regions of Mexico and reflects on differences among groups of research participants in different regions of Mexico. I extrapolate the lessons drawn from these experiences in Mexico to analyze the role of identity and to propose preliminary elements for a participatory research model for U.S. Latinos.

This chapter suggests that the term *Latino* is a generalizer of different cultural groups. It also explores how the perceived identity of the researcher interacts with the process and result of the research. A final objective is to propose elements for a participatory research approach. To answer these questions I provide a brief analysis of the interaction between identity and field research encountered during an extensive field project in Mexico. How I approached this research project is essential to an analysis of fieldwork in *ejidos*[1] in three different regions of Mexico. How I was read and interpreted by different populations in Mexico led to the intermittently blurring distinction between subject and observer, a constant back and forth toward being the "other." Finally, the lessons drawn from this field research experience in Mexico established the formulation of a participatory research approach in relation to transforming the current interpretation of the concept of *Latino,* which also has implications for Latinos in the United States.

THE IDENTITY OF A MEXICAN/LATINA
RESEARCHER IN MEXICO

A significant amount of literature centered on field research and the researcher (Denzin and Lincoln, 1994; hooks, 1990) exists from the point of view of U.S. and/or European researchers. This chapter, however, attempts to address the issue of a Mexican/Latina researcher while doing field research in Mexico. Initially, the results of my field research emerged from conventional methodological training used to design the research. The results suggest that the way I was perceived in different settings influenced access to information as well as the results of this research project. In different regions in Mexico I was perceived differently not only because of my Mexico City accent but also because I did not look like the traditional European or lighter skin Mexican researcher. This situation calls attention to the fact that the identity of the researcher is not the only element influencing the approach, design, and results of the research. Rather, the way the identity of a researcher is perceived also influences the research process. Issues of identity related to class, ethnicity, generation, location, and residence played a role in this research. Those elements are presented to explain some of the different identities ascribed to the researcher in various regions of Mexico. The objective of this explanation is to draw comparisons that indicate how the term *Latino* encompasses different identities and that research, participatory or not, should consider not only a cultural component but also questions related to class, gender, ethnicity, generation, and geographic location.

THE RESEARCH DESIGN

The research project evaluated in this chapter was not designed through a participatory approach. The violence surrounding land issues in Mexico was a consideration when deciding to use a more traditional research approach. Although the research was not participatory, during the research process the role of the researcher became that of an informant. The objective of the field research analyzed in this chapter was to determine the effects of the 1992 changes in Article 27, or *Ejido* Reforms, on *ejido* lands and on the well-being of their inhabitants. Of particular interest was the inhabitants' understanding of the transformation of Article 27 and the subsequent process of *ejido* land privatization at the local, urban, regional, and global levels. Another research interest was the comprehension of the internal and external relations of this privatizing process. Initial research included literature and theory review of *ejidos* and Article 27 in Mexico. After an analysis of the history of land policies and land-use patterns, the next phase was to visit and study *ejidos* from within, their everyday environment.

Case Studies

The major research questions focused on whether and how the application of the 1992 Article 27 was changing the *ejidos* in Mexico, including a determination of whether significant changes were taking place, how they were taking place, and the reasons that provoked those changes. Based on these questions, the case study approach was selected because it provided the capability to trace changes in *ejidos* through field research and by interviewing residents of the *ejido*. Or as Yin (1994) puts it, "in brief, the case study research allows an investigation to retain the holistic and meaningful characteristics of real-life events" (p. 3).

The *ejidos* selected represent case studies of the changes provoked by the application of Article 27 and the PROCEDE program, which is the measuring, subdividing, and titling program through which the 1992 Article 27 was to be implemented.[2] The aim was to develop three case studies that could best describe and explain what was occurring at the time the 1992 *Ejido* Reforms were in the process of being implemented. The *ejidos* selected belonged to specific regions, were devoted to specific economic activities, had a specific relation to the PROCEDE program, and all exhibited signs of transformation. Thus, they served to typify similar cases of transformation of *ejidos* in terms of land privatization. In Stake's (1995) terms, with the *ejido* as my unit of analysis, the research design was structured to "generate knowledge of the particular."

The Ejidos

Regional differences exist in Mexico and *ejidos* reflect those differences. In addition, micro- and macroplanning and social policies have been affecting *ejidos* in very different and uneven ways. With these considerations in mind, I designed a regional comparative study and for this purpose selected three *ejidos* in the western part of Mexico, but in different regions of the country: the first *ejido* in the northern, a second one in the central, and the third one in the southern region of Mexico. The *ejidos* selected for my case studies were located in the northwestern state of Sonora, the central western state of Guerrero, and the southern state of Oaxaca. In each of the states, Oaxaca, Sonora, and Guerrero, I traveled directly to the major city and visited its periphery.

The information gathered from archives and formal and informal interviews with planners, academics, local residents, and PROCEDE personnel led to the final selection of *ejidos*. In Sonora, most interviewees agreed that the border *ejido* of San Luis Rio Colorado was the case to select. San Luis Rio Colorado was the very first *ejido* that officially privatized its lands under the auspices of the 1992 Article 27 and was widely used as an "example" of successful *ejido* land privatization. In the isthmian oil region of Oaxaca most of the surrounding land in the area consists of agrarian communities and few *ejidos* exist; therefore, PROCEDE personnel suggested the Ixtaltepec *ejido,* located next to Juchitán, as a potential case. PROCEDE personnel had already measured the lands of the Ixtaltepec *ejido,* which was the first stage of the titling program. In Ixtaltepec, PROCEDE had started the measuring process, at that time without the knowledge and consent of the Indigenous population of the area. Finally, the coastal *ejido* of La Poza, on the periphery of Acapulco, Guerrero, had refused to participate in the PROCEDE program since they viewed it as fiscally damaging for the future of the *ejido* residents. Nonetheless, there were accounts that some *ejido* residents of La Poza had participated in the program on an individual basis. Thus, the three *ejidos* selected were the border *ejido* of San Luis Rio Colorado in Sonora; the coastal *ejido* of La Poza in Guerrero; and the isthmian *ejido* of Ixtaltepec in Oaxaca.

Although the selection of case studies was carried out based on the input and participation of the interviewees, I cannot claim that the research process within the *ejido* was fully participatory. The internal and external dynamics of the *ejido* are not free of conflict or contestation. Due to the explosive character of land issues and tenure in Mexico and the recent approval of Article 27, even carrying out field research was dangerous. The possibility of gathering *ejido* populations could provoke suspicions and misunderstandings among different stakeholders. Participatory action research in certain settings faces political situations that are essential for the researcher to evaluate in order to continue field research in challenging locations. *Ejidos* were this type of situation and the possibility of doing participatory research was partially constrained because of those dynamics.

Research Methods

The selection of research methods is closely linked to the nature of the research questions and the availability of data. Although extensive research exists about *ejidos,* the histories of most *ejidos* remain undocumented. On a personal note, in order to assess the current reality of the *ejido* in its internal and external relations, it was necessary to utilize a "bricolage," that is, a range of research methods that could lead to identifying those relations (Denzin and Lincoln, 1994). The multiplicity of methods used in this research is indicative of an understanding that the transformation of the *ejido* was caused by multiple elements. The objective of the fieldwork was to search, explore, and discover within each *ejido* the multiple causes of its transformation.

Consequently, in addition to the quantitative data collected from the U.S. Census and the data generated from the questionnaire applied in the *ejido,* qualitative material was gathered in the form of participant observation, ethnographic notes, and life stories of older members of the *ejidos.* These stories contributed to developing the history of the *ejidos* and tracing their transformations from the perspective of their residents.

ARRANGING FIELD RESEARCH WITHIN THE EJIDO

The field research project within the *ejido* occurred between 1995 and 1996, in the midst of the certificating and titling program (PROCEDE). A priority was interviewing *ejido* authorities. Although I had a list of the main topics to ask about the *ejido,* the interviews with the *ejido* authorities were open ended and informal, allowing them to participate freely and voice their concerns about Article 27 and the *ejido.* The research included interviews with residents of the *ejido* and participant observation. With additional time and resources, the design of survey questions would have incorporated the knowledge of *ejido* residents. Thus, lack of access to resources as well as time constraints are often obstacles to the design of integrated participatory research approaches.

In order to conduct the interviews, I lived in each *ejido* for about one month, except in La Poza, where I was advised not to stay in the *ejido* because of the violent climate created by the recent land expropriations. Obtaining permission to enter each *ejido* mandated a visit to the home of the *comisariado ejidal*[3] to introduce the project. During this visit I informed him or her about the objectives of the research and my intention of staying in the *ejido* for a period of three weeks to a month. I always addressed specific research tasks, including interviews with the residents of the *ejido.* A formal request for their approval was followed by either asking them to write a presentation letter or to announce my presence and objectives at their next *ejido* meeting.

THE INTERVIEWING PROCESS:
THE INTERVIEWED RESEARCHER

A structured interview questionnaire was designed to focus on the internal economy of the *ejido,* conversion of the land use of the *ejido,* and on changes in activities that *ejido* residents were experiencing. The key objectives were to answer questions related to the privatization and transformation of the *ejido* from within. A snowball sample was utilized to identify about twenty households per *ejido* for interviews.[4] The purpose of the structured interview was to determine the impact of the 1992 Article 27 on each selected *ejido*. I had originally planned to review the roster of *ejidatarios* (residents of an *ejido*) in each *ejido* and to randomly select twenty households. However, due to the unreliability of *ejido* records, a decision was made to undertake a home-by-home process to obtain interviews in those households that were available. The roster of the Ixtaltepec *ejido* was so obsolete that of the first eight *ejidatarios* randomly selected for interview, only one still lived in the *ejido*. In La Poza, the *comisariado ejidal* claimed not to have any roster of current or previous *ejidatarios*. Because the San Luis Río Colorado *ejido* was in the process of applying PROCEDE, their roster was updated. In this *ejido,* most interviews were conducted in the *ejido* office. Paradoxically, in each *ejido,* I became an interviewee as many of the residents did not know what PROCEDE was, thus I assumed the role of an informant about the objectives and stages of the titling program. The interviewing process was not unidirectional, as residents of the *ejido* not only asked about Article 27 but also about my role as a researcher in each *ejido.*

FIELD RESEARCH AND PERCEIVED IDENTITY
IN THE THREE EJIDOS

Ixtaltepec, Oaxaca

At a conference on indigenous women and human rights held in the state of Veracruz, two bilingual teachers of the Juchitán area invited me to do field research in Oaxaca. In conversations during the breaks of the conference they often expressed that, although I did not speak Zapoteco as they did, they did consider me an indigenous woman, same as them. Because of my phenotypic features, this was evident for them. Phrases such as "You studied, but you are still an indigenous woman," or "Just because you live in the United States doesn't mean you stopped being indigenous" were pronounced several times during these conversations. This encounter led to a trip to

Oaxaca to explore the possibility of undertaking field research. Once in Oaxaca City, I lived with a German expatriate who had resided there for several years. For this woman, who had lived in the United States for several years, it was unbelievable that I, a Mexicana, had pursued a doctoral degree and lived in the United States to accomplish this goal. If I was a "real" Mexican, she used to say, why was I living in the United States? Was I exchanging the problems of Mexico for the comfort of the United States? Apparently, the situational location of residence had converted this woman into a "real" Mexican person, while it had worked the opposite effect on me, mainly because questions of class were seldom addressed—as she lived a "reality" within one of the few expensive areas of Oaxaca City. Once again, the perceived identity played a role in this research since she was a main contact in Oaxaca City.

During the first days in Juchitán, I stayed with a family that rented rooms and had previously provided accommodations to other researchers. They were surprised that I, being a Mexican "like them," was undertaking field research in a town where researchers were primarily from the United States or from Europe. Interestingly, the family was of Lebanese descent and had become tricultural since they maintained traditions from their original culture, spoke Spanish, were a well-known family in Juchitán, and also spoke Zapoteco at home. Their identity was strongly rooted in the isthmian region. In the family there were strong supporters of the traditional parties PAN and PRI,[5] and the head of the family constantly asked about my political views. The COCEI (Coalición Obrero Campesino Estudiantil del Istmo), a leftist grassroots organization, was the predominant political force in the region, and my hostess wanted to make sure that I was not a sympathizer of the COCEI.

Different issues emerged when discussions centered on the concerns of my hostess about the national origin of a researcher. In addition, my being Mexican made them cautious about my social and political views. Although they had housed several European and U.S. researchers, it was evident that they avoided leftist researchers. Thus, early avoidance of critical questions about COCEI and the political situation in the isthmus was an issue during this visit. This situation was counteracted by the fact that the bilingual teachers who had originally invited me to Juchitán constantly expanded linkages to and knowledge about the region.

From Juchitán, I moved to the Ixtaltepec *ejido* (about forty-five minutes by bus from Juchitán), where the *comisariado ejidal* and Francisca, his wife, became my protectors. The Ixtaltepec *ejido* did not have a hotel at the time of this visit, thus they offered accommodations with the family of the *comisariado ejidal*. When the *ejido* authority learned about my objective to meet the *ejido* residents and interview them, he assigned a niece, who became my interpreter since most of the population spoke Zapoteco. They quickly viewed me as part of the family and continuously suggested that I should relocate to Ixtaltepec. They were a childless couple and my status as a single woman worried them. The *comisariado* offered some *ejido* land for sale for me to relocate to Ixtaltepec. The conversations about land and marital status provided precious insights about gender relations and access to land in the *ejido*.

Meanwhile, the bilingual teachers who had recommended this visit to the region invited me to gatherings and town parties where I met people from Juchitán and surrounding towns. I quickly became part of the scene. I generally did not have to ask, as I was constantly introduced into the community and updated about cultural meanings and manners. The indigenous identity that the *ejido* population perceived in me allowed me to be accepted, sheltered, and informed.

San Luis Río Colorado, Sonora

In Hermosillo City, accommodations were arranged with the family of an old university mate. He was from Mexico City but had relocated to Sonora. His familiarity with the region facilitated the field research. He readily introduced me to places, sources of information, and residents. Residents of Hermosillo City, as well as those of the San Luis Río Colorado *ejido* recognized me as somebody "from the south." My phenotypic characteristics and my accent situated me as a *guacha,* or somebody foreign. Conversations about discrimination against *guachos* were common. A clear distinction between people from northern and southern Mexico was constantly present as people in Sonora claimed that they were more industrious, sincere, and rational than the population in the south. Their courtesy in helping me to gather materials and arranging interviews was an indicator that although I was a *guacha,* they did not see me as a threat.

The placid context of the initial encounter was not replicated during my stay in the *ejido*. San Luis Río Colorado, being on the border area, is considered a dangerous place for single women; thus the *ejido* authorities warned me not to stay in a hotel. Instead, the treasurer of the *ejido* provided housing in her home for a couple of days. I was subsequently referred to one of the oldest female residents of the *ejido,* with whom I lived for the duration of the project in San Luis. In addition to the real or imagined risk that the border area represents, I sensed an uneasiness that could have been provoked by the internal conflict that the *ejido* was experiencing due to the process of privatization being implemented precisely at the time of my visit. This process had been difficult and had generated violent situations among the different stakeholders of the *ejido*. Consequently, although some of the personnel of PROCEDE had provided the names of the *ejido* authorities to assist in the field research, once there it was difficult to arrange meetings and interviews. Probably due to the internal divisions within the *ejido,* interviews with some of the *ejido* residents created uneasiness, while other residents wanted to talk and encouraged me to continue this research in order to "write and denounce what it is happening in the *ejido*." PROCEDE personnel warned me not to appear as an interloper and advised against visiting some areas within the *ejido,* as "something dangerous could happen." This situation could well have been the result of the nature of the region, which has a reputation as a drug enclave linked to illegal border trade networks.

The sprawling layout of San Luis, its population size, and the lack of transportation limited interviewing to the *ejido* offices where I met the *ejidatarios* and their families during the days they were receiving their certificates and titles and designating heirs of their lands. The interviews with the residents of this *ejido* seemed to be unimportant. One woman commented: "It is graceless. She just asks you about you and your family."

However, during the interviews, many of the residents of the *ejido* were interested about the reforms of Article 27 and their implications. This was the setting in which I provided more information than was gathered for the study. I responded to questions and concerns of *ejidatarios* and their families.

Since this region consists of a high percentage of transnational residents, my status as a Mexican researcher studying and living in the

United States was never questioned or criticized; rather, it was supported.

La Poza, Guerrero

The several contacts established during a prior visit to Acapulco eased introduction to several sources of information. I was fortunate in obtaining accommodations in the city, which eased the travel demands of field research. However, when I decided to move from the city to live in the *ejido,* no one offered housing. In addition, the *ejido* did not have a hotel. Conversely, the constant violent expropriations of ejido land in the area had created an explosive situation in Guerrero. Thus, residents of the *ejido* recommended against staying there because they believed no one would provide housing. This proved to be true. I asked several residents about accommodations within the *ejido* and always received negative responses. Thus, I remained in Acapulco and commuted to the *ejido* every day. The violent situation in La Poza made me question the viability of formulating a participatory approach.

Distrust reigned outside of and within this *ejido*. Newspaper articles and narratives from *ejidatarios* and academics in the area contradicted the romantic versions of public officials about the process of privatization of *ejido* land. Developers never agreed to meeting requests. In this region the position of being a "Mexican" researcher created a high degree of distrust. Some interviewees indicated that developers were suspicious that I was a journalist trying to write and denounce the violent expropriation of *ejido* land in La Poza. A resident of Acapulco stated, "Had you been a gringa, they [developers] would have given you an interview right away."

Within the *ejido,* the situation was not that different. Several land developers had deceitfully approached the *ejido* to gain inside information and, by the time of my visit, *ejido* residents distrusted any outsider. In addition, being from Mexico City, they viewed me as another potential traitor whose intentions were to discover methods to violently displace them from their lands, as had happened several times previously.

I started field research and interviews in the *ejido* and simultaneously scheduled interviews with members of the Democratic Revolution Party, or PRD, which is the main opposition party in the state of Guerrero. These interviews started opening doors within the *ejido,* but sealed the doors of developers. Ironically, *ejido* residents became more sympathetic to my presence when a resident of the *ejido* violently threw me out of her home, wrongly thinking that I was learning about the *ejido.* She felt I was working for the tourist entity that had displaced a portion of the residents. Since residents of the *ejido* encountered me daily in the community and learned about the incident, they began to know me, to talk to me, to excuse the woman who had thrown me out of her home. Some even offered a place to stay. By the end of my research, I had become friends with some of the residents of the *ejido* and with a few of the supporters of the ejido in Acapulco. I was able to stay in the *ejido* on a couple of occasions, but in general, in order to not create animosities among the residents of the *ejido,* I decided it was better to travel back and forth from Acapulco to the *ejido.*

Information from the records of the *ejido* was impossible to review because the *comisariado ejidal* "did not have them." One morning, while at the house of the *comisariado ejidal,* I was able to witness an informal sale of *ejido* land. A well-dressed woman from Acapulco City visited the *comisariado* requesting his advocacy for her acceptance as an *ejidataria* in the next *ejido* meeting. She also asked for the *comisariado's* signature to validate an *ejido* land sale she was about to finalize. The woman was not concerned about my inoffensive presence, nor was the *comisariado ejidal.* In any case, due to my situation as a visitor in the *comisariado's* house, I clearly witnessed the corrupt manner in which the *comisariado* negotiated with that woman. The *comisariado* uses persuasion and power to change the intent and focus of requests by members of the *ejido.* It is through this forum of overt power that resolutions which would benefit members of *ejidos* are continually negated.

In order to obtain further information about the fate of the privatized land of La Poza, I made an appointment with the salesperson for the development built in those lands. Access to the resort had been restricted to visitors and workers in order to prevent further protest demonstrations from affected *ejidatarios.* A wall separated the several miles of the resort and was safeguarded like a fortress. In order to obtain the appointment, I indicated that I was a well-compensated professional from Mexico City seeking a condo in that resort.

CHANGING BOUNDARIES OF MY IDENTITY
ACCORDING TO REGION

The fact of my Mexican identity did not guarantee that *ejidatarios* trusted me or allowed me into their *ejidos*. I was read and interpreted in distinct ways by different populations in Mexico. In some cases, their reading allowed me access and information to their everyday lives, and to engage in a research practice where *ejidatarios* and I learned from each other. In many cases, awareness of the political situation in each *ejido* was essential and determined their willingness to accept my role as a researcher. My perceived identity (as Mexican and as a researcher) changed according to region and in relation to the specific group of *ejidatarios* from whom data and knowledge were obtained.

What I had planned for this research project was transformed once the field activities commenced. First, letters sent to *ejido* authorities had not been answered, which affected research preparation. Presence in the *ejidos* aided in establishing positive relations with the *ejido* authorities and its residents. This situation led to restructuring the research design with a not-so-participative approach, but rather by using participant observation and ethnography.

The dynamics of these field experiences forced me to reconsider the significance of regional differences within each *ejido;* differences that had been shaped by history, geography, culture, and economic trajectory. A pressing question arose: So what if I was from Mexico? Very different kinds of Mexicans existed in a single territory and their ways of living, their land tenure arrangements, and their understanding of reality was distinct and particular to their sociopolitical situation.

Although I did not speak Zapoteco, for the bilingual teachers of Oaxaca I was considered another indigenous woman, the only difference being the place of residence and the location of intellectual development. For the *ejidatarios* in San Luis Río Colorado, I represented, as a researcher from "the south," the possibility of "denouncing" the current situation living in the *ejido*. For the coastal *ejido* of La Poza, I might well have been another *chilanga*[6] working for the tourist entities who were privatizing their lands and displacing them from their cultural and economic spaces.

The multitude of interactions with different contacts in the three states and cities influenced my research. Different social environments either permitted and facilitated access to information and to the *ejido* communities, or prevented that access. The way I was read and perceived influenced this access to *ejidos*. Both my phenotypic features and gender influenced how they perceived my social class. In addition, political views influenced their openness to guiding and giving information or resistance to access. In a way, I was constantly encountering limits as to what my identity was or was not.

While in the Ixtaltepec *ejido* I was another indigenous woman; in San Luis Río Colorado I was more an intruder, a witness to a process of ejido land privatization that was being publicized as a model privatization, but that in reality had provoked violent disagreements among the *ejidatarios*. One of the promoters of the privatization had even experienced an attempt against his life. The violence and risk were also felt in the *ejido* La Poza, where *ejidatarios* had initially distrusted my presence in the *ejido*.

The fact that some *ejidatarios* in San Luis Río Colorado wanted me to assume the role of journalist so that I could denounce the irregularities of privatization in the *ejido* reflected the lack of justice in the *ejido* and the functions and identities that *ejidatarios* wanted beyond that of a researcher. Besides a journalist, they wanted an expert on PROCEDE, as they constantly requested information about the reforms and potential implications. Access to information was not widespread in *ejidos*. The only information that *ejidatarios* had about the *Ejido* Reforms had been provided by PROCEDE personnel or by the land-measuring teams. Since *ejidatarios* requested information about the reforms, my role constantly shifted from researcher to informant since I am conversant about the amended Article 27. This role placed me in a difficult situation in La Poza *ejido,* as some of the tourist public officials viewed me as an informant rather than a traditional researcher. The trust I gained among the *ejido* residents was inversely proportional to the distrust generated among public officials and the developers interested in this area. In addition, the friendly ties developed with members of the PRD made those officials question the totality of my research activities. No matter the approach, any research activity in La Poza was difficult due to the violent environment and history of the region.

The different realities I encountered in Mexico shaped the direction of my research agenda. Furthermore, the way my identity was perceived opened or closed doors among different actors within and outside the *ejido*. I argue that these elements influenced research design and results, especially because field research was an essential aspect of the project. Although the research design was not entirely participatory in nature, there were some elements that were participatory and demanded action. For example, the selection of *ejidos* as case studies was based on recommendations provided by my informants outside the *ejido*. Inside the *ejido*, residents provided information, but also requested some kind of action and reciprocal information about Article 27 or *Ejido* Reforms, or in the form of a future denunciation of the faulty privatization process that the *ejido* was experiencing. I find that these elements encountered during field research in Mexico are relevant for research and policy design for Latinos in the United States; this is the critical topic that is addressed in the next section.

LESSONS FOR LATINO/A RESEARCH AND POLICY

This field research project in Mexico poses several questions regarding the continuous interaction between the identities of the participants and of the researcher. This continuous interaction changed constantly according to the political reality, geography, culture, and access to resources in each *ejido*. The manner in which interviewees outside and inside the *ejido* perceived me established either a constrained environment or participatory process. Within this context, a first question emerges regarding whether there is a specific participatory model to apply action research for Latinos in the United States. The question leads me to the different realities of populations in Mexican *ejidos*. They live and belong to the same country in which deep historical differences persist. The facts that they share a common language, encounter application of the macropolicy contained in Article 27, and live in the same country have not recreated a homogeneous population. If there are differences among populations within the same country, substantial cultural differences must also exist among U.S. Latinos who come from different countries.

The second question that emerges is that ethnic categorization should be included as an element in a participatory research model.

Although ethnicity plays a determinant role in the design of policy and research in the United States, other elements should be considered as well. Among U.S. Latinos there are deep differences between class, gender, race, religion, age, nationality, marital status, period of residence in the United States, and, above all, political views. Thus, the elements of rethinking a participatory model for research and social policy extend far beyond the ethnic categorization. Instead, these elements vary according to the objectives set among the participants in the research process.

In the case of the *ejidos*, I used the same strategy to approach each location. That is, I approached the *comisariado ejidal* and requested permission to be in the *ejido* to conduct field research. Ironically, the *comisariado ejidal* was a figure that in some cases was appreciated and others distrusted. Thus, the question of proposing a common strategy is challenged in relation to situations, socioeconomic factors, or leaders that attracted some residents of one *ejido* were excluded or turned away by others. A similar situation, I would argue, applies to Latinos in the United States. Not all Latinos attend the same schools, social events, and associations. In theory, participatory research offers the opportunity of democratic inclusion when research participants are asked to become part of the research agenda and the formation of social policy, but in practice our history, background, identity, and integration or lack of it establishes difference. The social environment is also important. What kind of neighborhood do we live in? Do we live in a city or in the suburbs? Are the physical and social environments conducive to participating or to fostering an exclusionary research process?

These latter questions revert to the question of place. In general terms, I assert that those working in diverse Latino communities need to first identify the places where people congregate. Churches, Latino-oriented stores, restaurants, community and neighborhood organizations, civic associations, and immigrant organizations are some of the places where the significant distinctions in Latino culture are differentiated.

The power dimensions encountered in the different *ejidos* also forced an acknowledgement of the fact that being a researcher or a policymaker of Latino origin does not guarantee that he or she will look for a participative and democratic research model or that he or she will advance a social policy agenda for the well-being of Latinos.

Lately, politics of identity have left aside the essential question of politics. Neither one should be deemphasized.

Maintaining transparency in the process of research and in identifying social policy goals has the advantage of creating the necessary trust that often inhibits filed research in numerous Latino communities. In this realm, equal access to information continues to be a key strategy. The fact that *ejido* populations did not have access to information and learned about the *Ejido* Reforms when they were already a fait accompli reasonably made them distrustful. Access to information opens avenues for an effective participatory research strategy and in the formulation of social policy.

When I was in Ixtaltepec, I needed an interpreter. Most of the population in the *ejido* spoke Zapoteco. Language, thus, was a required element for my research. In the United States, the increasingly Spanish-speaking population requires linguistic competence that forces a reconceptualization of the requirements for a researcher and for social policy assumptions once in the field. Interestingly, the latest waves of migration from Latin American countries into the United States have been composed of indigenous groups, as is the case of Mixtecos in California and Mayas in Houston. A participatory research model that could effectively lead to action would require consideration of the linguistic component according to the specific region of the subject.

The acceptance or rejection of my presence in *ejidos* was closely linked to the perception of who I was, with whom I was meeting, and who I was interviewing. Residents of the *ejido* constantly checked my identity as well as my accessibility in the *ejido*. In Ixtaltepec and San Luis Río Colorado, *ejidatarios* knew the precise place where I lived during my stay in the community. Living in the *ejido* gave *ejidatarios* more flexibility to approach me or locate me in case they wanted to enter into an extended dialogue. This availability calls attention to the advantage that the researcher and/or policymaker has when they belong to, or closely interact with, the participant community.

Two final elements I want to address are the internal and external relations surrounding *ejidos* and the application of Article 27. Those relations affected not only *ejido* populations, but they also affected me. *Ejido* residents lived and worked in that setting, but when I became a temporary resident of the *ejido,* I immersed myself in that reality and became part of the internal and external dynamics in which the *ejido* continually produced and reproduced. In the *ejido* I was the observer and the researcher, but as I also faced the potential risk of violence within the *ejido*, I became part of the "others" living in the *ejido*. This situation led to the intermittent blurring of the distinction between subject and observer, a constant back-and-forth shift toward becoming the "other." The risk attached to visiting *ejidos* and conducting field research was a situation I had to face in order to gain knowledge from those communities. Although the situation is different in the United States, risk factors are often part of the participatory research process.

In summary, although the political and social realities in the United States and in Mexico diverge, there are common elements that confront their respective populations. Mexicans are often used to seeing "foreigners" visit and live in their communities. Some of those foreigners are social scientists undertaking field research. Regularly, residents welcome them and, in a way, take care of them from a context of culturally based hospitality. When I, a Mexican researcher from a U.S. university, started dissertation field research, I encountered different dynamics that either eased fieldwork or made it difficult. These dynamics occurred not only because of who I am but also because I interacted with Mexicans from different social classes and from different regions, with different cultures and identities. My identity in Mexico, as well as in the United States, played a significant role in my research and in how I am/was perceived by the participants in this challenging research project.

CONCLUSIONS

This chapter has proposed to extrapolate the process and results of field research in Mexico and the way my identity was perceived as a researcher within the context of insulated, indigenous communities. These field research experiences document the differences and distinctions existing in Mexico as they relate to the sociopolitical conditions among U.S. Latinos. These experiences suggest that in relation to social policy for U.S. researchers it is essential to consider the deep diversity within Latino community in its totality. In illustrating this diversity, this chapter has explored the field research conducted in three *ejidos* in three different regions in Mexico. That research analyzed the constraints imposed on field research projects by either external conditions or the identity of the researcher. Finally, based on the lessons drawn from field research in Mexico, the chapter proposes ways in which methods and strategies can be transformed and applied to a participatory model for Latino social policy and research in the United States.

NOTES

1. *Ejido* is a communal land tenure system that emerged during the 1910 Revolution to carry out land reform in Mexico. *Ejidos* were inalienable, nontransferable, and nonattachable. They could not be conveyed, leased, or mortgaged, or used as collateral for loans. The 1917 Constitution allowed the expropriation of private land for redistribution purposes. In 1992, with the passage of NAFTA, *ejido* legislation changed to permit the privatization of *ejidos* and to halt land reform.

2. PROCEDE stands for Programa de Certificación de Derechos Ejidales y Titulación de Solares Urbanos. Radio and TV ads promoted it, emphasizing its "voluntary basis." To be a valid process, it required 75 percent attendance of *ejidatarios* to three required meetings.

3. *Ejidatarios* called *"comisariado ejidal"* is the president of the *ejido*.

4. Rossi et al. (1989, pp. 149-153) indicate that an initial set of appropriate stakeholders be identified through existing sources and incorporated into the field survey. Subsequently, they are also a resource in the identification of other stakeholders who they believe are knowledgeable about the subject matter. These potential stakeholders should be contacted both in relation to participating in the survey and identifying additional contacts.

5. Partido Acción Nacional or National Action Party (rightist party); Partido Revolucionario Institucional or Institutional Revolutionary Party (for a long time the official party).

6. Native from Mexico City.

REFERENCES

Denzin, N. and Lincoln, Y. (1994). *Handbook of qualitative research.* Thousand Oaks, CA, London, and New Delhi: Sage Publications.

hooks, b. (1990). *Yearning: Race, gender, and cultural politics.* Boston: South End Press.

Rossi, P., Freeman, H., and Lipsey, M. (1989). *Evaluation: A systemic approach,* Fourth edition. Newbury Park, CA: Sage Publications.

Stake, R.E. (1995). *The art of case study.* Thousands Oaks, CA: Sage Publications.

Yin, R. (1994). *Case study research: Design and methods,* Second edition. Thousand Oaks, CA, London, and New Delhi: Sage Publications.

Chapter 7

Social Scientists, Public Housing Residents, and Action Research in a Chicano Barrio in East Los Angeles

David R. Diaz

INTRODUCTION

In an era of empowerment and movement toward economic opportunity, local housing authorities are developing a range of strategies to provide public housing residents with job training and long-term career options. The goal is to provide residents with the skills necessary to compete in the regional job market, obtain permanent employment, and eventually move into conventional market-rate housing (O'Conner, 1999). This strategy presents a number of issues and problems for social policy analysts interested in research within public housing developments. In particular, this chapter argues that researchers have a direct responsibility to hire, train, and empower public housing residents during the implementation of survey-oriented research projects. This is an important goal in relation to the power of knowledge and community revitalization. The transfer of knowledge through engaging the subject community in a research partnership enriches the field survey process and contributes to local self-determination in relation to public policy. This implies negotiation, power sharing, and developing mutual relationships that inherently influence the design and implementation of social policy research.

Utilizing community-based workers is a difficult endeavor (Chanan, 1992) for a number of reasons. Researchers in minority communities have limited time frames in which to develop relations and information on existing social networks. Area residents often have direct personal knowledge of the individuals whom the researchers may be surveying, and this can create potential problems with confidentiality. The residents have limited interviewing skills, which requires intensive training and on-site supervision. Addressing language and cultural barriers that may appear prohibitive to principal investigators is an essential factor in developing this type of research team (Delgado-Gaitan, 1993). In addition, most public housing communities are plagued by high rates of violent crime, which places researchers in potentially high-risk situations (Devine and Wright, 1993). However, these issues should not preclude active pursuit of public housing residents to participate directly in social research within their immediate community.

The retention of area residents can be of significant benefit to researchers. They provide researchers with a number of fundamental technical and interpersonal challenges that invigorate the research experience and facilitate successful implementation of a project in what are considered difficult areas to conduct household surveys and focus groups (Marris, 1982). Public housing resident participation establishes a number of benefits for outside researchers. They have the inherent trust of the larger community. Area residents are better able to cope with and address crime- and gang-related incidents, which oftentimes threaten the completion of a project. They challenge the "conventional logic of research practice" of academic and private sector professionals in relation to how research should be conducted and how job training, empowerment, and hierarchical relationships evolve between team members with varying technical proficiencies (Fairweather, 1967, p. 57). In this context, participatory research is a process that magnifies the reality that "researchers are also subject to acquiring knowledge through their own experience and action" (Heron, 2001, p. 337). This development of knowledge is especially challenging in ethnic communities with entrenched, internal social networks. Lower-income neighborhoods develop strong social linkages, alliances, and support networks that evolve into factional interest groups within marginalized communities. Public housing residents often differ in the interpretation of local housing authority policies, which can create social tension among various social networks.

This analysis will focus on a case study of a comprehensive needs assessment survey conducted for the Housing Authority of the City of Los Angeles (HACLA) in 1993 and 1994. The study focused on the Pico Aliso public housing development located in East Los Angeles. The research project consisted of three main components: (1) a survey of public housing residents, (2) developing a social service directory, and (3) submitting a report of the findings to the client, HACLA. In addition, the research team made a contractual commitment to hire and train residents to supervise and implement the survey and data entry. This aspect of the project incorporated a wide range of technical, interpersonal, and pragmatic challenges to the research team. Issues included redefining our professional and technical biases; addressing problems in the field; maintaining cohesion between residents and social researchers; technical issues in terms of training, supervisory methods; and computer software; and recognizing the numerous benefits that resident researchers provided throughout the entire process. This strategy of experimental social innovation was developed to address the "unique characteristics concerning its social organization," in relation to the fact that "the investigator is often faced with creating new instruments" (Fairweather, 1967, p. 27) and in this instance different approaches to survey implementation.

The successful bid developed for this research project was a controversial proposal that forced both the members of the Resident Advisory Council (RAC) and HACLA representatives on the contract review committee to reconceptualize the project. To our knowledge no other consultant team incorporated utilizing resident researchers in their proposal. Although HACLA wanted resident participation in the project, only one proposal specified the roles and responsibilities of residents and created direct supervisorial responsibilities. The agency also advocated a strong role for residents, but they had not anticipated the levels of responsibility defined in the case study proposal. The residents on the review panel recognized the significant role and initial participation residents would assume if this proposal was selected. Two key issues were clearly defined in the bid: residents would receive more funds in terms of wages and subcontracts than the consultant team, and approximately thirty-five to forty residents would be hired and trained, and would obtain direct social research and computer training that could be transferred to the regional job market. These issues were important factors in the eventual selection of a team dominated by academic-oriented social researchers over teams dominated by professional consultants.

The community had developed a level of opposition against the proposed demolition of existing units and the housing reconstruction proposal. This HUD-funded policy created tension and increased distrust in relation to the housing authorities' motives on this issue. A major issue was the fact that a reduction in total affordable housing units would result from the project. Thus, an undetermined percentage of residents would not return to the community after the initial relocation phase. During early discussions with agency staff, the consultants refused a request to allow interviewers to present a map of the proposed redesign of the public housing development. They effectively argued that this would establish a negative impression in relation to the intent and independence of the research project. This early encounter forced agency officials to end any further consideration of manipulating this project as a mechanism to elicit support for their proposal. Some resident leaders were fearful that the survey project was solely designed to legitimate HACLA's proposal and solidify support among public housing residents. A key goal of the consultant team was to address these concerns and reinforce the fact that this was an independent research team that would not allow the agency to interfere with the integrity of either the survey design or the results.

NORMATIVE ROLE OF RESEARCHERS
WHO STUDY COMMUNITIES

Public policy researchers, through education and experience, develop certain professional biases that influence how they view clients, subjects, and themselves (Bateson, 1984; Hawkins, 1976, pp. 91-92, 98). Within the field of social policy there are differing visions of how to address this problematic professional issue. One conceptual framework argues that all researchers have biases and they need to identify them in relation to how to approach subjects (Chanan, 1992; Rosaldo, 1989). A different theoretical framework advocates the educated impartiality of social scientists by arguing that professional experience mitigates individual bias in field-related activities (Rescher, 1976, pp. 32, 41-42). Within these differing visions of practitioners, this case study interjects the significant roles provided to nonprofessional researchers, most of whom have developed internal barriers to interaction with a professional class of outside observers (Rahman,

1993). The biases of public housing residents center on trust, integrity, and practical considerations concerning how their interests would be accommodated through the duration of the project. Thus, in this instance two worldviews tacitly agreed to establish a working relationship within an intense inner-city environment.

Social researchers develop assumptions about subjects, not always flattering, which influence how they interact with novices to the field (Chanan, 1992). Specifically, the acceptance of undereducated, lower-income community residents is a nontraditional approach to the concept of independent detachment and objectivity gained from prior education and experience that the profession often assigns itself (Delgado-Gaitan, 1993). This standard of objectivity has both positive and negative connotations. In particular, the rigidity associated with professional stature and social position in relation to survey subjects inhibits focused understanding of issues and concerns of subjects (Nyden and Wiewel, 1992), potentially negating the needs of a client. What is essential for the profession is the continual revisiting of this controversial arena at the intersection of practice and relationships between subject and observer (Perkins and Wandersman, 1990). While biases can be freely admitted and endorsed, even the most progressive and sympathetic social researchers engage in one universal practice: they eventually leave the site of survey implementation, most often permanently.

Effective social research requires, at minimum, a comprehension of the community dynamics from which information is to be derived and analyzed. Prior to engaging in a particular project, the quality and type of knowledge of a specific community is directly related to the research design process (Babbie, 1973, pp. 61-62). As with most aspects of the humanities and social sciences, there is a fair amount of consistency and "sharing" of ideas, formats, development of survey instruments, and areas of inquiry. This normative practice is necessary for independent review and comparative analysis (Frankel, 1976). However, consistency in approach also contains problematic considerations that must be addressed, including the fact that social scientists can make mistakes in their approach to research (Frankel, 1976). The wealth of previous work in virtually all types of socioeconomic settings must not situate a focus on what has occurred but rather serve to define new challenges and new ways of designing models that increase the understanding of community dynamics, leading to revised approaches to conventional practice (Singer, 1994). Without engaging directly in developing a grounded understanding of a particular neighborhood, social researchers miss the opportunity to rethink how prior experience can benefit the redesign of traditional instruments to improve the quality of research.

Another consideration is how to share power in an equitable fashion in relation to the administrative control of the project. The key issue is to what extent can community residents be empowered to actively make independent decisions while remaining within the confines of valid technical approaches to survey research. This is a difficult arena of interpersonal discourse in which researchers need to cede a relevant level of power to truly engage new team members in a meaningful professional experience (Perkins and Wandersman, 1990). Empowerment implies control, yet a novice cannot be expected to perform all tasks at a normative level, this is simply too high of an expectation for any layperson. Thus, they must be properly trained and provided the technically versed methods to perform a number of duties in a proficient manner, as well as develop the confidence necessary to implement decisions concerning personnel issues, develop recommendations to improve the survey process, and provide constructive criticism within the administrative structure. Without tangible and direct administrative power vested in community researchers the whole concept of empowerment is a meaningless slogan (Fairweather, 1967).

In reality the lines of authority are blurred and commingled between social policy analysts and a new class of research interns. Principal consultants must assume responsibility for the quality, timeliness, and professionalism of the survey project to ensure that the sampling technique phase is not compromised. In addition, final decisions must contractually reside with the prime consultant firm. However, there are a number of intervention points in which direct administrative authority should be transferred directly to community residents. Through intense training, constant communication, interaction, negotiation, and defining responsibilities, public housing residents can and should be vested with a significant level of power and control over various aspects of a project.

Through power sharing, the residents were vested with the freedom to suggest changes related to their knowledge of existing social conditions and/or networks that was directly responsible for the success of the project. They have historical social information and a sense of how formalized procedures will be interpreted by the subjects of the survey. This internalized enclave consciousness should be of substantial benefit to any social policy team (Rosaldo, 1989). Practitioners need to be cognizant and open to how nontraditional information can be directly incorporated into the survey project. Specifically, the need to comprehend how this knowledge is essential in gaining the confidence of respondents to accurately answer sensitive questions (Bradburn and Sudman, 1981, p. 132). The blending of traditional and nontraditional approaches, if negotiated openly, enhances the success of the entire endeavor. The implementation phases should also reflect a level of trust and accountability in resident researchers from the inception of the project. The duality of lay and professional knowledge is an important arena of evolution within the context of new approaches of utilizing social research as job training, empowerment, and developing new voices in the public policy arena.

CONSTRUCTING RESEARCH ROLES FOR PUBLIC HOUSING RESIDENTS

Principal investigators should clearly define how to effectively train and utilize public housing residents within a realistic framework leading toward project implementation. The goal of incorporating bilingual, bicultural, nontraditional researchers requires a series of actions (Delgado-Gaitan, 1993) to ensure that a fair and open process of hiring is adopted, that adequate training and debriefing meetings are conducted throughout the duration of the project, and that problematic issues are addressed in a forum that allows residents strong influence over resolutions and revised strategies. Conversely, residents have important information that can beneficially impact the project. They need to be perceived as committed and equal partners who share the key goals of the researchers (Fairweather, 1967) and to sense that their roles are integral to the success of the project. Within this context they need to be encouraged to provide ideas that improve both the survey process and the community's reception to outside entities researching personal histories.

The issue of jobs, especially in the current economic environment, is a key programmatic strategy being implemented by housing authorities throughout the United States. Numerous agencies have implemented a range of job-training and placement programs designed specifically for lower-income communities (O'Conner, 1999). In creating employment opportunities, the experience at Pico Aliso indicates that an open, well-advertised process is essential toward generating community support and concurrence with the study by both elected and acknowledged resident leaders. Social researchers create major barriers if they are perceived as having preselected community members to be hired prior to implementing a study. What generally occurs under this scenario is that different resident factions perceive overt favoritism has been provided for specific segments of the community. The perception of unfair hiring, whether valid or not, can severely cripple the level of participation of residents in the actual survey. The relationship with residents incorporated four initial functions related to the project: (1) recruitment and hiring, (2) training of supervisors, (3) project management, and (4) conducting focus groups and pilot tests.

The methods utilized to hire public housing residents were to meet with resident leaders, designate a well-respected, local, community-based organization to assist in the recruitment process, and mail a flyer to every unit in the development. All residents were deemed eligible to apply. All applicants participated in an interview that allowed the residents to discuss their work experience and willingness to participate and explained the project, the type of position, their responsibilities, and the salary structure. In addition, all interviewees were told how many residents had applied and the number that would be hired. The interview process included a follow-up telephone call to all applicants informing them regarding whether they were hired and thanking for their participation.

This case study required three tiers of training. The most intensive involved the two supervisors with direct responsibility for virtually all on-site administrative duties of the project. Field interviewers were provided a training seminar and a debriefing after pilot tests were conducted. Data entry and survey coders were provided direct training and constant monitoring on use of computer software and the coding system.

The supervisors were provided a total of sixteen hours of training in three sessions. The training included an overview of the survey process, personnel management, addressing problems in the field, management of the survey, data documentation procedures, quality control, and how to address emergency situations.

Field interviewers participated in a one-day orientation that incorporated an overview of the project, a comprehensive review of the survey instrument, interview training, how the survey would be utilized by HACLA, and how to address a range of issues in the field. The orientation was conducted bilingually. The field interviewers were trained in two groups, one consisting of monolingual, Spanish-speaking residents and the other consisted of bilingual or English-only residents. Latino and Latina residents were strongly represented in each group.

The residents hired for data entry and survey coding were selected directly by the on-site supervisors. Training was conducted by the consultant responsible for developing the data-entry program. The training consisted of explaining how the software program functioned, how to end a session if problems arose without spoiling the existing information, how to read coded surveys, and a general orientation on computer systems. The on-site supervisors participated in this seminar. The survey coders received an overview of the survey instrument, how to code each question, how to review and edit surveys, and how to respond to questions from the data entry staff. The on-site supervisors acted as the lead staff for the coding process. One of their major responsibilities was to serve as liaisons between coders and data-entry staff.

The consultants developed a model that provided public housing residents with direct control over significant segments of the day-to-day management of the survey and project implementation. The lead consultants served the role as administrative advisor, developed administrative procedures, and supported the on-site supervisors during crisis and/or problematic situations. The goal was to truly empower residents as equal players in the process, and provide them with marketable technical and administrative skills. The two on-site supervisors were provided complete freedom to make decisions and work through issues and problems related to the study.

CRISES IN THE FIELD
AND IMPLEMENTING PROJECT ALTERNATIVES

Two issues lend insight in relation to how the resident supervisors responded to problems that occurred during the project. On two occasions, the threat of violence and incidents of violence directly impacted the process. During the initial stage of the project, immediately prior to the implementation of the focus groups, two separate shooting incidents resulted in the unfortunate death of two boys in their early teens. The entire housing development was in a high state of fear, especially during evening hours. The initial schedule of focus group meetings was canceled. The number of groups was reduced and limited to specific geographic areas within the development.

The community has three major gangs, two of which have extensive histories in East Los Angeles (Vigil, 1988), along with a number of tagger crews. A major issue was traversing different territorial zones, often a difference of only 100 yards. Reiterating the concern of the consultants, the project was delayed due to two incidents of gun violence that resulted in the tragic deaths of innocent young teens. The recommendations of the on-site supervisors saved the focus group process by redesigning the target groups according to their specific location of residence in correlation with the geography of gang territorial boundaries; the consultants were then able to facilitate highly successful sessions.

In relation to a direct threat of violence, a Cambodian field interviewer (young adult male) was challenged by gang members while walking around the projects. Gang members questioned why the individual was in their territory and clearly stated that problems would occur in the future if he returned. This incident was the first negative interaction with gang members. This situation was a major concern of the project team prior to entering into the contract. The principal consultants, fearing for this individual's safety, wanted to excuse him from the project. The on-site supervisors strongly differed from this strategy. They first identified which specific gang members made the threats and subsequently spoke with them to determine the seriousness of their verbal threats. The reality of situation was that the Cambodian had steadfastly refused to join the gang and the gang members verbally harassed him to scare him without any intention of harming him.

The supervisors explained the study to the gang members, the fact that the individual had a job and that the project was related to larger community issues. They reassured the supervisors that they would not harass anyone connected with the project nor had they intended actual harm to the field interviewer. The field interviewer was appraised of the situation; however, he continued to conduct interviews only for a brief period, then resigned. This inhibited the project for a period of time since there were only two Cambodian field interviewers during this initial period of project implementation. Another bilingual Cambodian surveyor was subsequently recruited for this aspect of the field research.

The second major crisis occurred during the coding and data-entry process. The supervisors determined that the projected need for additional data-entry clerks versus coders had proved to be an incorrect assumption by the principal consultants. In fact, the data-entry function was conducted in a rapid fashion throughout the project. The lack of coded surveys to input, due to lack of staff, was inhibiting the entire project and severely limited time the supervisors required for monitoring field interviewing and quality control. After two weeks the housing resident supervisors recommended hiring additional residents as coders. Once implemented, this eliminated the data-entry delays and increased their time for administrative and management activities. Their ability to respond to different challenges directly benefited the project on a number of occasions, which served to improve the quality of the entire project.

The on-site supervisors worked both independently and with existing organizations to develop the focus groups. This was their first important task. Their direct knowledge of the community and social relations with residents was key to the consultant team's ability to both develop the focus groups in a short time frame and respond to the shooting incidents and reschedule the groups, again within a limited time frame. This early indication of commitment and comprehension of practical issues exhibited how, if given direct authority and responsibility, public housing residents can effectively respond to a range of administrative and technical issues.

This case study is indicative of how residents can be trained and given administrative responsibility over a significant portion of social research projects. Lay field researchers need to feel vested in the process, their recommendations must be seriously considered, and their input should be solicited throughout the duration of the project (Chanan, 1992, p. 16). They must be viewed as competent and committed partners who were hired on the merits of their experience and ability.

ADDRESSING CONFLICTS, CONTRADICTIONS, AND ISSUES IN THE FIELD

In developing a comprehensive strategy to implement a major social policy research study in a public housing development that utilizes area residents, there are a number of inherent conflicts. One of the most immediate concerns is comprehending the dynamics of gang territories and the history of internecine conflicts. This tragic issue was magnified in the Pico Aliso study. This community has a substantial number of gangs for a relatively compact neighborhood, which typifies gang culture in East Los Angeles (Vigil, 1988). There were five concurrent gang conflicts through the duration of the project. Another consideration is developing specific knowledge on existing community dynamics, social networks, cultural conflicts, and personality-based group affiliations. An acute misinterpretation of the influence of social networks and cultural practice, both ethnic and neighborhood-based, will severely hinder community concurrence and participation in a particular research project. Since the 1960s there is also an inbred level of critical distance (mistrust is probably a more accurate characterization) between resident councils and housing authority officials (Piven and Cloward, 1977).

Resident motivations for both working with consultants and agreeing to participate in a research project are important considerations that social policy analysts need to integrate into the process of field research projects. The field interviewers' demand for safety and access to residents in a timely fashion also required a specific approach in allowing the surveyors to determine scheduling to ensure their retention for the duration of the project. Listening to public housing residents' recommendations served as a direct endorsement of the concept of empowerment for all members of the team.

Local community leaders, whether elected or informal, demand a pragmatic level of influence and information in relation to major government-oriented activities (Chanan, 1992, p. 147; Fairweather, 1967, p. 57). They rarely make substantive distinctions between official and nonofficial professional class "visitors" related to government-sponsored programs and policies (Piven and Cloward, 1977). Local leaders are concerned about any investigative activity conducted within their social terrain. They want to be directly knowledgeable about new proposals, they need to feel competent to discuss this type of activity with peers, and they deem it essential to maintain a role in the decision-making process in relation to important public policies impacting their community. In their view, the lack of consensus and/or support from them is grounds for vetoing a project. This level of power can manifest itself either informally (resistance to participation) or formally (opposition directed at the housing authority to cancel the project).

In this case study the comprehension of gang and socially defined territories was heightened due to the gang shootings immediately prior to project implementation. This attention to territory had a direct impact on the best on-site supervisor candidate. This individual provided highly insightful answers throughout the initial interview. However, this young adult male resided in a different gang territory. At the conclusion of the interview he was asked directly if he felt that he could safely cross First Street on a daily basis. His response was negative and that, while enrolled in college, he was perceived by the community as being loosely affiliated with one of the major gangs. For obvious safety reasons he was not hired. (All of the interviews conducted incorporated a territorial-based question.)

All field interviewers were asked to indicate their residence on a map of the development. Each interviewer was asked about areas they felt that they could not enter or did not wish to enter during the survey-implementation phase. The assignment of interviews was influenced by their responses. Scheduling of interviews was left to the discretion of the staff. This strategy provided residents direct control over working periods during which gang conflicts were not anticipated.

The barrio involved has a similar history in relation to other Chicano neighborhoods with an entrenched gang structure that exist on the Eastside of Los Angeles (Moore and Vigil, 1993). An important consideration in relation to social research conducted in high-crime communities is safe data gathering by part-time staff. This is a legitimate consideration that all principal consultants need to address. This concept of hiring and training area residents reduces the potential for problems in the field. Since they are long-term social actors within the existing social and cultural network there is a high degree of acceptance for their presence and role in a project. The field interviewers in this case study were ceded maximum flexibility and exhibited a confidence in completing their assignments. They had few inhibitions other than working beyond the early evening. Their ability to freely traverse throughout the public housing development was essential to the data-gathering process.

Conversely, the principal consultants were confronted with the potential of biased data due to use of community residents. Compact neighborhoods that exhibit long-term tenancy develop an enclave consciousness (Rosaldo, 1989). Public housing residents exchange a high level of information through direct, daily dialogue in contrast with the larger, commuter-oriented society (Piven and Cloward, 1977). This is a dilemma for social researchers committed to using resident researchers and obtaining quality data. There is a real issue whether neighbors and acquaintances will willingly share personal, and at times unfavorable, information on family dynamics. This issue was addressed on two levels, assigning interviewers to apartment units that they did not interact with and validating information by quality control methods after surveys were completed. However, this case study did not fully resolve this sensitive issue directly. All researchers will encounter interviewee resistance at some level when important family issues are investigated (Bradburn and Sudman, 1981, Chapter 5). The validity of the results of this case study indicate that in fact utilization of public housing residents as field interviewers surmounted personal barriers and relatively few problematic interview situations were reported to the supervisors.

On a different level, there are qualitative differences in the method and manner of interaction with interviewees between resident researchers and professionally trained investigators. Myriad differences exist which can hinder or facilitate success in survey research. The style of dress, the tenor and manner of presentation, eye contact, speed of questioning, and interpersonal mannerisms directly influence how subjects respond to questioning over a long period of time (Bradburn and Sudman, 1981). When an interview extends beyond thirty minutes, a relationship synergy develops between both respondent and interviewer (Bradburn and Sudman, 1981). A valuable aspect of this case study was the field interviewers' ability to transcend the normal educational and class distinction posed by professional social researchers. They exhibited a common bond to existing social conditions, style of dress, and mannerisms which eliminated most barriers normally encountered in this type of interpersonal process. This context of commonality within local culture significantly assisted broad-based community participation in the process. This ability to communicate effectively, openly and within a mutually practiced level of dialogue is an important strategy in achieving an extremely high response rate (approximately 90 percent) of the target population designated by the contract. HACLA, the official client, had a provision in the contract mandating 100 percent resident participation in the survey, which is virtually impossible to achieve in survey research. The consultants were confident that the substantial level of response would suffice in relation to this obligation.

The field interviewers were given complete flexibility in scheduling interviews. Interviewing any day of the week was permitted and the appointments could be any time before 8 p.m. The interviewers were not instructed on dress code considerations, however, they were instructed to maintain a respectful appearance and demeanor. Many wore everyday clothes in which they felt comfortable. This relative autonomy over the actual implementation process positively influenced the retention of a core group of interviewers, and it generated a highly successful system of scheduling interviews which allowed the project to meet a relatively tight time frame (caused by contractual delays and incidences of gang violence) in completing the interview phase. The time frame mandates of the project may not have been achieved without ceding authority to the residents in devising the formula for scheduling and completing weekly assignments throughout the survey implementation phase.

Within this aspect of the project, the on-site supervisors' knowledge of the sociocultural dynamics of the community proved crucial (Nyden and Wiewel, 1992). They had a common bond with the field interviewers and a sense of appropriate scheduling and time frames for optimum interaction with respondents. They asserted administrative control at an early stage of implementation. They based their judgement on both input for the field interviewers and their perception of how a flexible system would assist in completing the project. Conversely, experienced social researchers, in their normative framework, would likely have placed a number of arbitrary rules and restrictions under the guise of "quality control" (Delgado-Gaitan, 1993), for instance, demanding strict adherence to specific daytime hours for interviews or micromanaging the activities of the on-site supervisors—which quite possibly could have greatly hindered the entire project. Instead, the lead consultants focused on assuring quality control through spot checks, review of submitted interview instruments and in-field monitoring. This reduced unnecessary and cumbersome rules on the front end of the process. By focusing on the quality of completed interviews, residents were empowered to develop effective strategies and beneficially influence the entire project.

During the early stages of the project the consultants were told to meet directly with gang leaders to introduce themselves, inform them about the scope of the project, and acknowledge their influence within the community. While there were legitimate reasons to enter into this level of dialogue, these discussions did not occur within the context of this case study. A principal investigator did conduct a series of interviews with the previous president of the resident advisory council, who was a former gang leader, a year prior to the implementation of the research project. The consultant team became knowledgeable about the different gangs and the gang hierarchy from a range of sources familiar with this community. Fortunately, the strong participation of public housing residents mitigated the outsider status of the research professionals, providing gang leaders with direct, community-based avenues to become knowledgeable and familiar with the project. The entire community was informed that a comprehensive interview survey would be conducted and a few young gang aged adult males were hired as interviewers and data-entry clerks. One active gang member was hired, however he left the project relatively early during the implementation stage. Resident surveyors and the on-site supervisors apparently provided gang members with adequate access to information on the research project. Other than the one early incident of harassment, gangs had no influence on the implementation of the survey and other related activities.

MAINTAINING CONTINUITY BETWEEN
RESIDENTS AND RESEARCHERS

The previous section documents the effectiveness of respecting the knowledge and ability of public housing residents in social research settings. This section will analyze how two different cultures merged into a cohesive research team to achieve a complex and difficult social research project. The fact that the research team incorporated two distinct worldviews cannot be overemphasized within the context of this study. Both social analysts and residents approached the project with a degree of doubt, uncertainty, and social distance. A number of internal and external challenges were inherent to a strategy highly dependent on the role novice public housing residents would be required to assume at all stages of the project. The residents, quite frankly, doubted that they would be given direct administrative control and that their recommendations would be adhered to on a consistent basis. The overarching goal of both employing and empowering public housing residents required establishing effective and influential cross-communication, developing and clearly identifying mutual expectations, and soliciting the input and support of both informal and formal resident organizations. An additional challenge was bridging the distrust that exists between the public housing residents and the housing authority officials who had direct control over the contract.

During the initial meetings, when the design for project implementation was developed, the consultants determined that three criteria would be used in selecting the on-site supervisors. These individuals would be the first residents hired and would essentially establish the tenor of relationships with all other resident participants. The criteria were verbal skills, knowledge of the community, and ability to respond to problematic situations. The project supervisors would be required to communicate with all members of the team in a confident and direct manner. They implicitly had to exhibit the personal strength of character required to disagree with the lead consultants and interact effectively within a highly charged social terrain.

In the training seminars developed for the two on-site supervisors, the lead consultants constantly emphasized the importance of constant communication, the need for the supervisors to assume control over the project, that problematic situations and/or conflicts with other resident interviewers would be jointly addressed, and that the consultants would act as a support group for the supervisors. The supervisors were provided both business and residential telephone numbers, and had complete freedom to call at virtually any time. The initial training period was devised to develop a strong sense of proactive communication and mutual support. Without effective and positive communication an entire project is often placed at risk (Sclove, 1997), especially given the historical hierarchical structure of relationships between public housing residents and outside professionals. Establishing a high level of confidence with the principle consultants and maintaining an open dialogue from the earliest stages of the project was as important as the methodological design of the survey itself.

Both entities had specific expectations. The consultants assumed that the supervisors would perform in a professional manner, provide leadership to the resident interviewers, accept direction from the project manager, and ensure the integrity of the study. Although these appear to be normative objectives, the reality of the process was that the supervisors were being vested with a level of power that they had not experienced in their work history. Conversely, the supervisors demanded assurance that their reputation in the community was not to be placed in jeopardy, that the consultants would support them when they identified changes in the research process, that they would be treated with dignity and civility in all forums of discussion, that all residents would receive equal respect, and that in crisis and/or conflictive situations the consultants would play a leadership role in addressing problems without portraying a sense that the problems were due to mismanagement by the supervisors. There existed a level of disequilibrium at the inception of the project. The working relationship required a month of confidence building and gaining trust within the framework of establishing a functioning research team. The consultants were fortunate that both supervisors were willing to "trust us" during the initial stage of project implementation. They both felt confident in providing recommendations on improving the interview process and how to address the initial crisis confronting the project.

Addressing mutual expectations is a critical first phase in developing a proactive relationship with community-based staff (Delgado-Gaitan, 1993). Neither entity should assume total control over a situation, especially principal consultants who are vested with a substantial degree of power by a government client. In fact, it is the consultants who should be sensitive to the anticipation of residents placed in a new power environment, which requires a period of adjustment toward a position of authority. If the expectations of each entity are not respected, the quality of the research, participation of the community, and, ultimately, relations with the client are placed at risk. In this instance, both vantage points generated a sense of optimism that resulted in the resident supervisors addressing potential conflicts internally (which they did during informal discussions throughout the duration of the project), in a manner that provided leeway in functioning professionally within a framework of distinct power relations.

TECHNICAL CONSIDERATIONS

The project incorporated a number of technical demands common to all community-based research. In this regard, the process was normative in relation to conventional survey design, implementation, and analysis. What was different was incorporating the ideas and recommendations of the subject community into the methodology. Three areas of conventional field research activities benefited from the role of the supervisors—translations, coding, and data entry. These issues will be addressed to provide a context for the previous issues identified in this analysis. Translation of questions and accurate correlation to bilingual, bicultural community value systems is always difficult (Darder, 1991); thus, how the supervisors both evaluated the questionnaire and how they interpreted the critical comments of the interviews after the pilot test were of particular benefit to the survey design. The bilingual capabilities of the supervisors and the trust they developed with the interviewers were an indication of their beneficial influence on the project. They recommended a series of changes in the context of questions, and a few sequence shifts and adjustments in the value-rating format with particular questions. A majority of the resident recommendations were incorporated into the final survey instrument.

The two other phases of note were coding and data entry. After training the supervisors in both functions, they were given direct responsibility for implementing both processes. The consultants had overestimated the time demand for data entry and, conversely, underestimated the time demand for coding. The data analysis process became delayed due to a backlog of coded surveys. The supervisors were increasingly frustrated with the lack of progress. After a week of limited production, an informal conversation addressed this serious problem. The supervisors recommended two solutions: hiring more residents and shifting two data-entry clerks into the coding function. The consultants, recognizing their mistake, agreed with the recommendation, supporting the supervisors' initiative with authority to hire additional staff. This example of power ceding enhanced the stature of the supervisors in the community, exhibited the importance of their role, and fundamentally improved the flow of data production for the project. Once their observations were validated, the completion of the fieldwork and data entry concluded in a rapid fashion. By empowering the authority of the supervisors, they exhibited a high degree of satisfaction with their roles and a sense of confidence that influenced the other residents who participated in the study.

REPORTING THE RESULTS OF THE SURVEY

Three important issues were identified during the initial project design: (1) the role of community-based organizations and/or informal networks of power, (2) satisfying the demands of two clients, the Housing Authority and the resident leadership of the public housing development, and (3) sharing the results of the survey. An initial consideration for the project was developing the trust and confidence of the entire community. The consultants were warned not only that the role of the major community-based organization, the Resident Advisory Council (RAC), had to be incorporated into the process almost immediately but also that a number of informal networks of power existed within the resident social strata and the project may not succeed if their level of power (symbolic or tangible) was not acknowledged early in the study. The incorporation of a range of formal and informal leaders is a critical aspect of this research approach (Brush and Stabinsky, 1996). By conducting both formal and informal meetings and providing the community with comprehensive information about the goals and objectives of the research at an early stage in the process, the consultant team never encountered any meaningful opposition or public criticism of the project. The lead consultants initiated a series of meetings with the RAC and other leaders of different factions in the neighborhood. However, one interest group, three major street gangs, and smaller tagger groups that were identified as essential to establishing a safe and positive environment were bypassed by the consultant team.

The initial strategy was to meet with all interest groups, explain the focus and purpose of the study, and emphasize the critical importance of the support and participation of the community. However, after initially determining that meeting with the "shot callers" (key gang leaders) of each major gang was essential, no informal meeting was convened. The major barrier to scheduling these meetings was the series of shooting incidents previously discussed. Entering into the terrain of gang conflict, in which all movement is minutely scrutinized, could endanger the consultants, erroneously indicate favoritism toward one faction over the other, and imply an assumption by the consultants that the gangs were not interested in a "technical research project" in the midst of what appeared at the time a serious escalation of historic gang rivalries. In addition, since residents were being hired, some of whom were siblings of gang members, the integrity of the project would be protected internally by their participation. This assumption, fortunately, proved valid in the discussions with the supervisors during the study. They both indicated that the gangs were well aware of our presence and had agreed to not interfere with the study out of respect for the goals of the entire community (and obviously more concrete considerations related to surviving the recent series of shooting incidents).

Another key consideration was addressing the demands of two clients, the Housing Authority and the resident leadership of the development. HACLA was experiencing strong pressure from HUD monitors due to a series of delays related to implementation of the reconstruction grant. In fact, the agency had fallen far behind its original schedule, which placed additional pressure on the consultant team to complete the study in an expedient fashion. In relation to this time demand, the consultants simply refused to compromise the integrity of the process to problems with the initial HUD application. In fact, during one meeting HACLA staff indicated that the consultants should also serve in the role of proposal advocates, a role that we rejected since it would destroy the impartiality and objectivity of our role as independent researchers.

With regard to the residents, they demanded a fair and reasoned study that would serve as an accurate reflection of community opinion on the merits of a controversial proposal—the destruction and reconstruction of their historic community (both social and physical). The residents sensed that their perspectives had not been accurately portrayed by HACLA to HUD in relation to their concerns and criticisms, and that there was a lack of acknowledgment of opposition to the proposal, which had been expressed in the past. This arena of discrepancy between the HACLA perspective versus public housing resident concerns became readily apparent during the initial period of interest-group meetings. Thus, the most important objective of the consultants was that a strong majority of residents viewed the study as being independent and conducted with a high degree of professional integrity. In fact, this last point was critical, since some residents hired by the consultants were related to resident leaders and would convey any attempt to skew the study in favor of the Housing Authority almost immediately to their family and friends.

The final key issue focused on sharing the results of the survey. In this instance the consultants were unsuccessful in achieving full disclosure of survey results in a timely manner to the entire community. HACLA was fearful that some areas of response would reflect unfavorably on the entire reconstruction effort and could potentially dissuade HUD from final project approval. Thus, the agency assumed tight control over the last stage of the study, distribution of the final report, and the agenda for presenting the results. The agency ultimately developed a version of a "final report" for public distribution that was not inclusive of the entire study. In this scenario, a newly elected RAC, which had the support of the agency, was not assertive in demanding full access to the entire report after receiving a executive briefing presented by the consultants and agency staff. Thus, the residents were provided with a series of public meetings in which the consultants discussed specific results identified by HACLA and responded to questions accurately and honestly irregardless of the agency's position. The agency developed an executive summary for public distribution that, in their view, emphasized the positive aspects of community opinions.

In addressing the protocols and conflicts between the client, residents, and researchers a major factor is the level of power over information exerted by a public agency (Darder, 1991, p. 27). The agency, while purporting to exist for the benefit of a public good, in this instance the welfare of public housing residents, assumed a conventional role of dominance in relation to how to present information (Darder, 1991). HACLA was interested in findings that directly supported the focus of a strategy of major reconstruction, which included a significant net loss of publicly assisted housing units (over 200). The pursuit of a definitive legitimation of the proposal was the factor leading to what can be termed a "fear of information" (Darder, 1991, pp. 79-80), a factor that paralyzed the agency's civic responsibility to full disclosure of the final report in a timely manner. The actual findings indicated a conflict in opinions. A strong majority of residents were interested in Section 8 vouchers and/or discussed moving from the development; conversely, there is a historically established social network and sense of community that was important to residents in this particular development. In reality, the "fear of information" was unfounded since the results of the study were adequate justification to proceed with the proposal.

Researchers are often limited in their role when serving two clients. However, there exists a professional responsibility to acknowledge important findings to both community residents and a public agency client (Singer, 1994). In this instance, the public was informed about the findings of the study in two forums, an executive meeting with the RAC and a series of public meetings. It is the public's responsibility to engage in political negotiations to ensure full access to all aspects of a government-funded project. The RAC's inability to demand the entire report was confounding and disappointing; however, the consultants were not in a position to tell public housing residents how to develop policy positions. An authoritarian approach was counter to the entire development of resident participation in this project.

Unfortunately, whether residents assume direct responsibility for obtaining access to data does not fully address the challenge of how community-oriented research information actually reaches and impacts the lives of the subjects of a study. The integrity of the research process and the community's right to know are essential considerations for the ethical demands of survey-oriented projects involving critical public policy proposals that dramatically influence long-term public policy (Record, 1967). Researchers can assume a number of roles: public advocates, progressive political strategists, public agency apologists, compliant technicians, aloof professionals, and/or centrists interested in moderating differences between competing interest groups (Marris, 1982). How findings are reported is a critical juncture that is not always in the control of the individuals who develop data and initially interpret the information. In the public policy arena, often the access to full disclosure must be politically negotiated by local social actors, with or, at times, without the participation of the researchers. It is a difficult dilemma, since researchers may attempt to "force" a community to "recognize the importance" of their work in a postcolonial approach based on class orientation or they may, also condescendingly, assume that the community does not "deserve to know," since they make no tangible effort to force information into a public forum. The power of information is a sensitive arena, especially due to the fact that researchers are not normally directly vested in the future of the site of research. They perform one similar action: they leave and most never return.

CONCLUSION

Although the previous section explores a number of challenges to researchers involved in community-oriented studies, this case study indicates a substantial level of benefits that accrue by linking social science professionals with public housing residents. Residents can in fact be empowered with both knowledge and managerial authority to perform complicated technical tasks in a competent manner. Hiring public housing residents enriched the process of research and the quality of opinions solicited in a difficult social environment. The role of resident interviewers was critical in developing trust among respondents and gaining tremendous participation of the contracted target group (of which HACLA assumed the impossible, 100 percent participation). The two supervisors in particular crossed class, gender, and professional frontiers in an admirable fashion; they performed as well as any highly educated researcher in assuming the administrative responsibilities for project implementation. They provided leadership, insight, and corrective actions and established a cohesive team ethic for all resident participants.

A key factor in the success of this case study was the consultants' approach to effectively train residents for different roles. Early in the process they fostered open communication, created the environment to arrive at mutually negotiated solutions, and established a working relationship among equals, in the sense that all staff, consultants, and public housing residents were in the project together, irrespective of titles or experience. The level of trust and confidence invested in staff sustained the resident-led management of an intense research project.

Unresolved was the issue of reforming how "professional information" is interpreted, and how access is open and offered without public agency filters. A major reason why the community vested its trust in the study was the claim of independence (Frankel, 1976, pp. 23-24) on behalf of the consultant team, a context of objectivity that offered at least the perception of unbiased community research. The difficulty in accessing information within the framework of a public agency client in "fear of information" is a continual challenge to the ethics of research (Orlans, 1967). The client is often the ultimate arbitrator of the use of information; however, in this case study there were (and still are) multiple clients. In fact the client list should have included HUD, the city planning department, the city council office, and the surrounding community among a range of groups directly impacted by the proposal. Should the fact that most of the interest groups exhibited an acute lack of interest or ineptly attempted to gain access be considered the fault of the research team? Should the client be allowed total control over discourse concerning publicly funded information gathering? These troubling issues were a reality of a yearlong project in one of the most conflictive public housing developments in the United States. The extent of the researchers' role in "forcing" a client to provide unfettered access was (and is) both an ethical and political challenge. Ethical in relation to the concept of freedom of information, political in the context of local political negotiation and the role of a distant professional with scant long-term stakeholder status.

In relation to public housing residents and control over their future this case study offers a promising perspective. The fact that residents performed competently is an indication of their capacity for difficult, intellectual projects. The significant number of applicants is direct evidence that this sector of society is motivated to participate in the regional labor market when provided a reasonable opportunity and decent wages. Public housing resident participation is also a structural benefit to community-oriented survey research. They have the ability to provide credibility to a project and develop a community-wide trust in both the process and anticipated results. Public housing residents can manage one another, maneuver through negotiations with professional researchers, and address workplace-oriented conflicts and problems in relation to tight due dates for specific tasks. In fact, this case study is an indication for new directions in federally funded research within lower-income communities, where the subjects have been mislabeled as objects. The project is also an example of how subjects can be objective and possess the capability to balance professional subjectivity with real-life experience. This was an invaluable factor in implementing social policy research in one of the most difficult lower-income communities in our society.

REFERENCES

Babbie, E. (1973). *Survey methods research.* Belmont, CA: Wadsworth Publishing.
Bateson, N. (1984). *Data construction in social surveys.* Boston: George Allen and Unwin.
Bradburn, N. M. and Sudman, S. (1981). *Improving interview method and questionnaire design.* San Francisco: Jossey-Bass Publishers.
Brush, S. B. and Stabinsky, D. (Eds.) (1996). *Valuing local knowledge: Indigenous people and intellectual property rights.* Washington, DC: Island Press.
Chanan, G. (1992). *Out of the shadows: Local community action and the European Union.* Dublin, Ireland: Loughlinstown House, Shankill Company.
Darder, A. (1991). *Culture and power in the classroom.* New York: Bergin and Garvey.
Delgado-Gaitan, C. (1993). Researcher change and changing the researcher. *Harvard Educational Review 63*(4), 389-411.
Devine, J. A. and Wright, J. D. (1993). *The greatest of evils: Urban poverty and the underclass.* New York: Aldine de Gruyter.
Fairweather, G. W. (1967). *Methods for experimental social innovation.* New York: John Wiley.
Frankel, C. (1976). The autonomy of the social sciences. In C. Frankel (Ed.), *Controversies and decisions* (pp. 1-27). New York: Russell Sage Foundation.
Hawkins, H. (1976). The ideal of objectivity among American social sciences. In C. Frankel (Ed.), *Controversies and decisions* (pp. 89-102). New York: Russell Sage Foundation.
Heron, J. (2001). Transpersonal co-operative inquiry. In P. Reason and H. Bradbury (Eds.), *Handbook of action research* (pp. 333-339). Thousand Oaks, CA: Sage.
Marris, P. (1982). *Meaning and action.* London: Routledge and Kegan Paul.
Moore, J. and Vigil, J. D. (1993). Barrios in transition. In J. Moore and R. Pinderhughes (Eds.), *In the barrios* (pp. 27-50). New York: Russell Sage Foundation.
Nyden, P. and Wiewel, W. (1992). Collaborative research: Harnessing the tensions between researcher and practitioner. *American Sociologist 23*(4), 43-55.
O'Conner, A. (1999). Swimming against the tide: A brief history of federal policy in poor communities. In R. F. Ferguson and W. T. Dickens (Eds.), *Urban problems and community development* (pp. 77-138). Washington, DC: Brookings Institution Press.
Orlans, H. (1967). Ethical problems in the relations of research sponsors and investigators. In G. Sjoberg (Ed.), *Ethics, politics, and social research* (pp. 3-25). Cambridge, MA: Schenkman Publishing.
Perkins, D. D. and Wandersman, A. (1990). You'll have to work to overcome our suspicions. *Social Policy 21*(1), 32-41.
Piven, F. F. and Cloward, R. (1977). *A poor people's movements.* New York: Pantheon.
Rahman, M. A. (1993). *People's self development.* London: Zed Books.

Record, J. C. (1967). The research institute and the pressure group. In G. Sjoberg (Ed.), *Ethics, politics, and social research* (pp. 25-40). Cambridge, MA: Schenkman Publishing.

Rescher, N. (1976). The role of values in social science research. In C. Frankel (Ed.), *Controversies and decisions* (pp. 31-53). New York: Russell Sage Foundation.

Rosaldo, R. (1989). *Culture and truth.* Boston: Beacon Press.

Sclove, R. E. (1997). Research by the people, for the people. *Futures 29*(6), 541-549.

Singer, M. (1994). Community-centered praxis: Toward an alternative non-dominative applied anthropology. *Human Organizations 53*(4), 336-344.

Vigil, J. D. (1988). *Barrio gangs.* Austin: University of Texas Press.

SECTION III:
RESEARCH TO POLICY
AND PRACTICE—
INFLUENCING LATINO POLICY
AND PROGRAM DEVELOPMENT

Chapter 8

Community Action Research with Census Data: The Latino Coalition for a New Los Angeles, 1992-1993

David E. Hayes-Bautista

INTRODUCTION

Census data generally are considered boring lists of numbers. Yet in the immediate wake of the Los Angeles civil disturbances of 1992, a group of Latino community, political, and business leaders requested assistance in understanding the 1990 U.S. Census sufficiently to prepare a Latino agenda for rebuilding barrios and ghettos in Los Angeles. This chapter is a brief discussion of that experience in action research.

THE 1992 LOS ANGELES CIVIL DISTURBANCES

In the spring of 1991, George Holliday, a non-Hispanic white plumber testing a new video camera, stepped out onto his apartment's balcony and captured the commotion on the street below. After a high-speed chase, several non-Hispanic white Los Angeles policemen wrestled Rodney King from his car. While Holliday captured the images with his new camera, a number of policemen assaulted the prone African-American arrestee with their night sticks. Blow after blow was recorded, while King did not appear to resist.

Holliday sent the tape to a local television station, whose constant replaying of the beating created an uproar in the African-American community and throughout the region. The arresting officers were suspended, investigated, and placed on trial for the violation of

229

King's civil rights. Due to the fear that white policemen would not receive a fair trial in multicultural Los Angeles, the trial was moved to the nearly all-white community of Simi Valley, in neighboring Ventura County.

While the trial was in progress, a Korean grocer in a liquor store in South-Central Los Angeles shot and killed a teenaged African-American girl over the alleged theft of a bottle of orange juice valued at $1.98. Many in the African-American community perceived the grocer's thirty-day suspended sentence as a gross miscarriage of justice. It was hoped that the conviction of the police officers in the King case would provide some semblance of justice. The Holliday tape, played over and over, seemed to be the "smoking gun" evidence of police brutality. Thus, when the jury found the officers not guilty, a stunned South Central community poured out into the streets to share their disbelief.

In a reprise of the era of "long, hot summers," when inner-city America burned in the late 1960s, actions escalated from shouting protests at passing cars to pounding on vehicle fenders to actually stopping cars, pulling out passengers, and beating them. Stones were thrown at store windows, and crowds shouted approval when the first shops went up in flames. Los Angeles descended into civil disorder.

REBUILDING LA

The disturbances occurred during the early stages of the 1992 presidential election. Candidates trooped through the area, then-President George Bush promising federal assistance if reelected and Bill Clinton promising even more aid if elected.

Eager to capitalize on the prospects of federal largesse, Mayor Tom Bradley asked the 1984 Los Angeles Olympics czar, Peter Ueberroth, to form a committee to prepare a recovery plan for Los Angeles that would guide the expected federal spending.

Working feverishly, Mr. Ueberroth reactivated his network of contacts developed for the successful Olympic games and began to form a committee that would become known by its acronym RLA (Rebuild Los Angeles). Member after member was announced, but Latino leaders became uncomfortable with the near-total lack of Latino presence in this very important group.

The recently completed 1990 U.S. Census had confirmed that Latinos were nearly as numerous as non-Hispanic whites: 37 percent of the county was Latino and 41 percent was non-Hispanic white. African Americans were far less numerous, constituting only 11 percent of the county's population. Yet of the more than thirty-five members of the RLA, only two were Latino.

In essence, the Latino voice would not be influential in discussions related to the designation and disbursement of funds and resources, much less in long-range planning in the city. It appeared that no substantial level of the postdisturbances activity was addressing major issues within Latino barrios.

A small core of organizations established twenty years earlier, in the heyday of the Chicano movement, began to discuss this discrepancy among themselves. As they were accustomed to being on the margins of the city's political decision making, they began to form a consensus that Latinos would need to force themselves onto the public agenda.

Early in June 1992, about four weeks after the civil disturbances, an ad hoc group of the 1960s' generation met to assess the situation. They focused on the need to develop an agenda for the Latino community, not only in the rebuilding of Los Angeles but also in creating the basis for the Los Angeles of the twenty-first century.

After that first meeting I was contacted, separately and independently, by Alta Med (nonprofit health organization), TELACU (Community Economic Development Corporation), and the Mexican-American Grocers Association (MAGA), and asked to attend the next meeting. I had known these leaders personally, some for over twenty years at that point, and they were familiar with my research interests. I had been providing health information to Alta Med for over a decade and Latino demographic data to MAGA since its inception in the early 1980s. MAGA indicated that over two dozen MAGA-affiliated stores had been looted in the civil disturbances and had incurred considerable loss of merchandise. They were quite motivated to ensure that a Latino agenda be developed and implemented.

Each of the original group's attendees had invited other organizations to attend; close to two dozen groups were represented. From the discussions that ensued, it was clear that various participant members had very different perceptions of what constituted a future Latino agenda. The following section is a brief description of the major participants, which indicates the diversity of the group.

THE LATINO COALITION
FOR A NEW LOS ANGELES (LCNLA)

The membership of the LCNLA was quite varied, ranging from private-sector business groups to human services agencies and political organizations.

- Hermandad Nacional Mexicana: The last organization established by longtime community activist Bert Corona, HNM was a grassroots, immigrant-based organization providing English language and citizenship classes for those immigrants going through the amnesty process as a result of the 1986 Immigration Reform and Control Act (IRCA).
- Watts/Century Latino Council: One of the few Latino CBOs (community-based organizations) already in existence in the Watts area, its major focus was to raise awareness of Latino issues in policymakers working in economically deprived areas of South Central Los Angeles.
- Mexican American Political Association: A chapter of an organization established by Bert Corona in the 1950s, its mission is to inject Latinos into the political process.
- Latino Unity Forum: This group is a small coalition of mental health services organizations.
- Alta Med: A comprehensive health services organization providing medical, dental, rehabilitation, geriatric, and mental health services in East Los Angeles, it originally was started in the early days of the Chicano movement as El Barrio Free Clinic.
- Arroyo Vista Family Health Center: This is a smaller, comprehensive health services agency in the Lincoln Heights area of Los Angeles.
- Clínica Oscar Romero: This comprehensive health services center located in the Pico-Union area of Los Angeles serves a largely Salvadoran and Guatemalan clientele.
- El Centro Human Services: This mental health organization in East Los Angeles was founded in the early days of the Chicano movement.

- Mexican American Opportunities Foundation: One of the first federally funded Latino services and education organizations established in the 1960s as part of the War on Poverty, it focuses on Head Start services and occupational education for adults, as well as citizenship classes.
- TELACU: A community development organization, it is a legacy of the Model Cities and War on Poverty programs of the 1960s.
- Victory Outreach: This is a religion-based drug rehabilitation program, staffed by *vatos* (gang members), *pintos* (ex-convicts), and former *tecatos* (drug users).
- Political representatives: Representatives from the mayor's office, state legislators' offices, the Los Angeles City Council, and President Clinton's task force participated.
- CARECEN (Central American Resource Center): This is a human services agency focused on the Central American immigrant and refugee population in the Pico-Union area of Los Angeles.
- New Economics for Women: This recently established economic development agency focuses on issues related to inner-city women in Los Angeles.
- Mexican American Grocers Association: This is an organization of independent grocers whose clientele is largely Latino. During the civil disturbances, over thirty MAGA-member grocery stores were looted.
- Unión de Comerciantes Latinos: Sidewalk vending was a controversial matter at that time, although it was a common form of economic activity in Latino areas, especially in the major immigrant neighborhoods around Pico-Union. Harassed by police and extorted by gang members, the street vendors banded together to advocate city legislation that would allow them to sell their wares unmolested.
- Private businesses: A number of individual private businesses participated, representing different business sectors, including insurance, consulting, communications, entertainment, and retail sales.

Finding a Common Agenda

In other situations, some of these groups would have been opposed to one another's policies and programs. Yet the overwhelming sentiment was that if they did not develop a consensus on a common agenda, the Latino agenda would be simply ignored by the elites who controlled RLA's agenda. The question was how to channel their energies into a single agenda. The strategy was accomplished by two methods, one political and one analytic.

The political method was an early consensus to "agree to disagree." Early on coalition members recognized that if they had to achieve 100 percent agreement on every issue, the moment and opportunity for influence would disappear quickly. Thus they openly decided that if an issue created a split in opinion, it should be left behind so that the group could focus on the issues that all agreed on. This was, in retrospect, perhaps easiest for the private business groups and most difficult for the advocacy groups. Yet for all the difficulty, it was a principle adhered to during the life of the coalition.

Perhaps reflecting the overall community, the Latino business representatives tended to favor the Republican Party, while the community and labor leaders tended to favor the Democratic Party. At first, I was worried that the party interests would pull the group apart, especially during the election season. However, these fears turned out to be groundless: members of both parties were able to see for themselves how neither party bothered to notice Latinos and their agenda.

The analytic method was to use data analysis as a means for finding common ground. I approached the project as an exercise in adult education: I had to respect the autonomy and expertise of the "learners," while providing an opportunity for them to discover new knowledge, attitudes, and skills for themselves. I decided to use data pedagogically; I would introduce them to data on a topic, ensure that they understood the information, then let them "own" the data through debate and discussion, grafting conclusions into the emergent agenda. The coalition jointly created a data map of the Latino community, then used that common map to create the agenda.

This became a time-consuming process but not unusual for those accustomed to graduate research seminars. I was anxious for the coalition to experience some success early on.

NO LONGER A MINORITY

Fortunately, a two-year project, the California Identity Project, funded by the William and Flora Hewlett Foundation, had been completed recently, which served as a basis for much of LCNLA's analysis.

This particular project was a result of the release of my 1988 book, *The Burden of Support: Young Latinos in an Aging Society* (Hayes-Bautista et al., 1988), in which some of the first population projections indicating significant Latino population growth to the year 2030 were published. The Hewlett Foundation funded a follow-up study, the "So what?" study, that focused in depth on a range of facts related to these demographic changes, to understand their effects on daily life in California.

The core of the project was a statewide, in-person survey of 1,200 Latino heads of household interviewed during 1990, with a comparison sample of 600 non-Hispanic white heads of household surveyed by telephone with a reduced questionnaire. We probed and prodded the Latino sample with questions about their perceptions of being Latino and of being American; about their opinions on family, work, and welfare; and about patterns of work and leisure.

An important facet of this sample was that, being a probability sample, it contained nearly 70 percent immigrant respondents. Immigrants were a minute percentage in the 1980 census, while the decade from 1980 to 1990 saw a tremendous upsurge in immigration. Although the 1990 census data contained information on immigrants, most of the immigrant-specific data were not released until 1993 and 1994 (especially the public use microdata samples), and thus were not available for analysis in 1992. Since I had the data set, I had the capacity to project a preview of the 1990 census data.

Since the end of the interviewing in late 1990, my two co-principal investigators (Aida Hurtado from UC Santa Cruz and Robert Valdez, then of the UCLA School of Public Health) and I jointly drafted two monographs. They were at the printers on the night that the civil disturbances broke out. The findings were as follows:

- There had been a period of intense immigration, creating an adult Latino population that was, by 1990, predominantly immigrant.
- Immigrants, compared to U.S.-born Latinos, had lower incomes, lower educations, and less access to health care.

- Yet immigrants had behavioral characteristics that were far more positive than those of U.S.-born Latinos: higher labor force participation, stronger family formation, greater religious devotion, and more optimism about their own and their children's futures in California.
- Immigrant Latinos were no longer exclusively of Mexican origin but were, to a significant degree, from Central America as well.

Perhaps the most important finding detailed in the two monographs was theoretical. Census data from 1940 to 1980, updated with the recently developed 1990 survey data, made it evident that Latinos could not be described by the urban underclass model then used to analyze minority populations. Although it was true that during this fifty-year period Latinos had had the least education and the least income, they exhibited virtually none of the behaviors so often considered the results of low income and low education: labor force desertion, welfare dependency, disintegrated families.

In the 1990 survey, we noticed something that the 1940-1980 census data had not allowed us to examine: Latino immigrants had even less income and education than U.S.-born Latinos, yet more positive behavior, in terms of greater labor force participation, less dependence on welfare, and stronger families.

STARTING THE ACTION AGENDA: PRESS CONFERENCE

A key characteristic of the LCNLA was its intense focus on accomplishing important objectives. From the beginning, the coalition decided that it could not wait for the formalities of creating an official organization, including creating bylaws, incorporating, and establishing an administrative structure. Instead, the focus was on creating a Latino agenda in time to be part of RLA discussions.

Thus, during its lifetime, the coalition did not incorporate. It was purposely an open-ended, ad hoc group of widely divergent opinions and goals. Organizations that chose to play a leadership role simply did so, and others played roles unrelated to their own program demands and funding priorities. No one was excluded from the discussions that eventually formed a consensus, and perhaps the intense atmosphere after the civil disturbances created an environment in which there was very little conflict between groups who were more marginal to the discussions and those who seemed to be in the leadership. The line between these two groups was fluid, with positions open to constant, ongoing negotiation.

I felt it was important that the group force itself onto the public radar as soon as possible, and that waiting for a report to be finished might take too long. The fact that the Hewlett-funded monographs were now ready to be released presented an opportunity to advance the political position of the coalition.

I outlined the contents of the two monographs to the coalition members and explained that although they did not analyze the civil disturbances per se, they did offer background on Latino behavior. Although pundits from Washington were quick to characterize the residents of South Central Los Angeles by use of the urban underclass model, the monographs suggested that this would be inappropriate. An initial strategy arose from the suggestion that the coalition sponsor the release of these monographs, thereby gaining some visibility by raising questions developed from the projects.

Eager to do something, the coalition coalesced around this idea. Two Latino public relations firms offered to develop a press conference. Both firms had lists of media contacts and extensive personal networks, which they used for this event. MAGA offered its office for the announcement. Within two weeks, the coalition had its first public event: the public release of Hayes-Bautista and colleagues' *No Longer a Minority* (Los Angeles: UCLA Chicano Studies Research Center, 1992) and Hurtado and colleagues' *Redefining California* (Los Angeles: UCLA Chicano Studies Research Center, 1992).

Aggressively seeking news that might relate to the recent tragic events, the press—print and electronic, Spanish language and English—obliged with excellent attendance for the Latino press conference. Coalition members received their first taste of interaction with the press and had the satisfaction of seeing themselves on that evening's news programs and quoted in the next morning's papers. They enjoyed the experience; more important, the response to the press conference helped them sense that they had something to contribute to postdisturbance Los Angeles. It was an early feeling of success.

CREATING THE DATA MAP

At the inception of the educational process, I realized two critical demographic conclusions had remained relatively unnoticed:

1. South Central Los Angeles was predominantly Latino, not African American. The civil disturbances were played out in the local and national media as an African-American and non-Hispanic white event. As recently as 1980, that might have been the case, for Latinos were only 12 percent of the area's population then. By 1990, however, Latinos were nearly 60 percent of the area's population, but that fact was not acknowledged by most reporters.

2. The Latino population of the county had become more diverse, both geographically and in national origin. During the Chicano movement, the county's Latino population was concentrated in East Los Angeles, and most service agencies were established in what was then considered the living, beating heart of "Aztlán." In the twenty-five years since the walkouts in 1968, the Latino population grew, and it began to urbanize throughout the region, including Montebello, Monterey Park, Hacienda Heights, Santa Monica, Inglewood—and Watts, Compton, and South Central. While the population dispersed, most of the service agencies remained physically located in East Los Angeles. The Chicano leadership was not aware that their target population had moved out from "East Los." Civil wars in Central America also had added a significant non-Mexican component. In particular, Salvadorans and Guatemalans numbered over one-half million. The refugee portion of those populations had needs and interests very different from the older, U.S.-born Latino population. These groups rarely even talked to one another.

At the very least, it was important that coalition members understand how the Latino population had changed and how to properly interpret the changing Latino demographics addressed in both monographs.

ACTION RESEARCH METHODOLOGY

The Summary Tape File 3 (STF3) data from the 1990 census were just being released in the summer of 1992. This file would allow a census-tract-level analysis of the South Central area. I decided to use this as the primary data source. The coalition needed to create "census literacy" in a group of nonanalysts in order to develop a comprehensive understanding of the target populations.

Data work requires resources. The programming, analysis, writing, and editing required approximately $50,000 for a six-month project. A brief, one-page budget for the groups and a list of deliverables were proposed, and I asked the coalition how they would fund the project. I was thinking in terms of approaching a foundation or a federal agency, which would take months to reach a decision. To my surprise, the organizations decided to fund it themselves to avoid any downtime waiting for some funder's approval. Literally, they "passed the hat" around the table, and each organization offered what it felt it could afford. Some organizations donated as much as $10,000; others gave as little as $500. The fact that these organizations funded the project themselves made it imperative that the results be as useful as possible. This could not be a typical consulting job, in which very little value-added is provided; this had to be substantive enough that the agency donating $500 as well as the agency donating $10,000 would feel they had invested well.

A semiretreat late in April 1993 was designed to plan the research agenda. I "translated" the 1990 U.S. Census STF3 code book into English, to ensure that the group could understand the limitations of the census data. During a four-hour session, a number of areas of interest to the group were identified that could be examined using U.S. Census data. Of course, the Latino coalition was most interested in the data on Latino populations.

While nearly one-half million Latinos lived in South Central Los Angeles, nearly three million lived outside that area. Were Latinos in South Central different from those in East Los Angeles? Why were Latinos in the Pico-Union area seen looting but not those in East Los Angeles?

Coalition members developed their own conclusions based on the presentation of data on Latinos in three different areas:

1. Latinos in the South Central Los Angeles area, as defined by the RLA
2. Latinos in poverty census tracts outside of South Central, anywhere else in Los Angeles County
3. Latinos in nonpoverty census tracts outside of South Central

Once coalition members understood the benefits of comparing these three groups of Latinos, a nasty problem reared its head. The major drawback to the STF3 was that the data were reported for an entire census tract not for race or ethnic-specific populations. Thus, the data provided information on how many Latinos lived in a particular census tract but not on how many of them spoke English, how many of them worked, or how many of them used welfare.

Analysis of the recently released California Identity Project alerted me to the fact that Latinos had very different demographic patterns from African Americans. Yet in the census data they were aggregated together at the census tract level. We needed to distinguish between the two, yet no individual-level data were available.

This problem was solved by the use of modeling. In South Central, census tracts were identified with predominantly African-American (70 percent or more by population) and predominantly Latino (70 percent or more) populations. These were used as surrogate measures for Latino or African-American populations. Of course, the entire concept of modeling first needed to be understood and accepted by the coalition members. They grasped the concept very quickly, however, and proceeded with the project.

Every Friday morning for nearly a year the coalition members met for breakfast and data sharing. The week's chairperson—it rotated—would present the latest political developments, members would vent a little, and I would be asked to present the data. Each week I would present the information on an agreed-upon topic, make copies and overheads, then walk the members through the significance of data. Over coffee, the members would talk about their interpretations of the data. Questions would be raised, nuances pointed out, and unexplored avenues discovered. After about thirty minutes of discussion, I would summarize various questions and concerns to ensure that all issues had been addressed. Once consensus was achieved, I would have a direction for the next week's analysis. In essence, I functioned as a technical consultant to the larger group, providing the data specifics, but then fading into the background so that they could "own" the data and their interpretations.

THE AGENDA EMERGES

After weeks of meetings, an agenda gradually emerged out of what at times seemed to be the world's longest-running graduate seminar on data, research, and policy. The major points of the agenda evolved into a list of policy topics. The first part of the agenda was an illustration of how deeply the civil disturbances had affected the Latino population:

- Latinos were the main victims of crowd violence, e.g., the people who were pulled out of cars and beaten.
- One-third of those who died during the disturbances were Latino.
- Half of those arrested were Latino.
- Latinos were the owners of many of the burned and looted businesses.

Yet curiously many largely Latino areas were untouched by the violence, even though those areas were inhabited by poorly educated Latinos living and working in poverty.

The agenda's second part was a description of Latinos in Los Angeles County, to serve as a basis for policy and programs:

- The Latino population would continue to grow, becoming close to 50 percent of the county's population by 2000.
- The majority population in South Central Los Angeles was Latino, not African American.
- There were more Latinos in the county living in poverty (744,000) than the sum total of non-Hispanic whites, African Americans, and Asians (533,000) also living in poverty in the county. There were more Latinos living in poverty in South Central than African Americans in poverty there.
- Latino workers had the highest labor force participation rate of any group—higher than non-Hispanic whites, African Americans, or Asians—and the lowest labor force desertion.

- Latino adults had completed the fewest years of schooling. This, however, was largely a result of immigrants arriving with lower levels of education than U.S.-born Latinos, not the result of a lack of interest in education.
- Latinos were twice as likely as non-Hispanic whites or African Americans to form families composed of married couples with children.
- In South Central itself, Latino households were four times as likely to be composed of married couples with children as African-American households there.
- There were an estimated 1.3 million Latinos without medical insurance in the county.
- Yet Latinos showed the typical "Latino Epidemiological Paradox," including very few low-birth-weight babies, low infant mortality, low death rates, and long life expectancy.
- Latinos suffered disproportionately from basic communicable diseases that had been largely controlled in other populations: tuberculosis, shigella, giardiasis, and others.
- Latinos were severely underrepresented in the political process.
- The number of Latino-owned companies in the county grew at nearly three times the rate of overall Latino population growth.
- There were an estimated 110,000 Latino-owned firms in the county. Most were very small start-up firms.
- Latinos living in South Central were virtually indistinguishable from Latinos living in poverty areas outside South Central. Even the higher-income Latinos living in the nonpoverty areas were different from their poorer *compañeros* (associates) only in degree, with no fundamental, radically noticeable differences in behavior and social characteristics.

The third portion of the agenda was a vision of how Latinos could contribute to the rebuilding of Los Angeles:

- The growing Latino population needed to be viewed as a source of stability and economic growth.
- With modest investments in education, training, and health, the Latino workforce could become a leading workforce in the nation and the world.

- Latino businesses should be considered engines of economic recovery and invested in accordingly.
- Latino service providers and community-based agencies should be validated and empowered to provide services to the Latino population in areas that had recently become majority Latino.

Finalizing and Releasing the Agenda

Within the framework of an ad hoc coalition, not every member had been present at every weekly meeting. Therefore, to ensure the widest possible input, the coalition scheduled a one-day retreat. Once again, the participating organizations rented a conference room and provided meals, so that everyone's presence could be as complete as possible. A trained facilitator from my staff conducted the meeting while I observed and took analytic notes. Although differences remained among the groups, the consensus to "agree to disagree" held, and at the conclusion of the retreat the members were able to finalize the agenda by group consensus.

In two weeks, the draft report, complete with data, tables, and charts, was sent to all the coalition members for review and comment. Few changes were suggested, which led me to believe that the nine-month process had been successful. The coalition "owned" the data, the analysis, and the policy recommendations. In sum, they owned the entirety of the report.

At a press conference convened on the steps of the Los Angeles City Hall, the coalition shared its findings with the press and, via those media, with the county's public. A copy of the report was formally delivered to the RLA for its consideration.

THE AFTERMATH

In the aftermath, there were two distinct results. The first result was the direct policy consequence. While I would like to be able to report that the coalition's agenda took the RLA by storm, in fact it did not. A Republican governor in trouble as a result of the disturbances had found a scapegoat for the state's woes: Latinos, conceived as undocumented immigrants. The coalition did not foresee that; even as we were developing the agenda, the thanks Latinos would receive for having stabilized wide swaths of South Central was to be blindsided by Proposition 187. Yet two years after the disturbances, that turned out to be the state's major policy response, followed shortly by the abolition of affirmative action and the outlawing of bilingual education. Virtually every recommendation made by the coalition was checkmated by a demagogic gubernatorial reelection campaign.

Nevertheless, the coalition had not been an exercise in futility. In a later, similarly interactive study conducted for the United Way of Greater Los Angeles, the civil disturbances and Proposition 187 were pointed to as turning points at which Latinos were forced to find their voices and to create alternative forms of political leadership in order to oblige the state's elected leadership to respond to their demands.

The second result was more personal and professional. I had established connections with a far greater number of Latino organizations and businesses than would have been the case without the pressure-cooker of putting together the coalition report. Since our year of coalition meetings, I have continued to work with many groups—public, community, and private—to help them understand and improve their understanding of the Latino population in the region, state, and country.

Since that time, I have been asked to work with a wide variety of organizations—from Latino farmworkers to Latino movie producers—on organization-specific projects, ranging from needs assessment to strategic planning to evaluation. The basic methodology that I developed during the LCNLA process has been used many times. And as I undertake data collection and analysis, I find new insights and data sets, which I can then use for publication in the refereed, scientific journals. Since 1992, virtually all of my research has been community based, yet the findings are published in journals of academic medicine as well as being carried on television channel Noticiero 34 in Spanish during the evening news.

REFERENCES

Hayes-Bautista, D.E., Hurtado, A., Valdez, R.B., and Hernandez, A.C.R. (1992). *No longer a minority.* Los Angeles: UCLA Chicano Studies Research Center.

Hayes-Bautista, D.E., Schink,W., and Chapa, J. (1988). *The burden of support: Young Latinos in an aging society.* Palo Alto, CA: Stanford University Press.

Hurtado, A., Hayes-Bautista, D.E., Valdez, R.B., and Hernandez, A.C.R. (1992). *Redefining California: Latino social engagement in a multicultural society.* Los Angeles: UCLA Chicano Studies Research Center.

Chapter 9

Expanding Latino Community Capacity for Sustainable Programs Through Researcher-Community Partnerships

Juana Mora

INTRODUCTION

The concept of community building is part of a broader perspective of community empowerment and social change that recently has become an important component of public health initiatives across the country (Walter, 2002). Public health organizations, private foundations, and universities have formed partnerships to build the capacity of community organizations to engage in structured research and community-building activities to improve health and social conditions. Although Latino communities, particularly Mexican-American communities, have a strong history of establishing mutual aid, labor, and immigration organizations (Orozco, 1992-1993) that have provided a solid foundation for current Latino community organizations, new state and federal demands for accountability have limited the ability of Latino-based organizations to compete for federal or state support for local programming. The new accountability established by private foundations and state and federal institutes includes requirements for organizations to develop community coalitions, partnerships, and evaluation for sustained funding in education, health, and urban development. Numerous Latino community organizations and grassroots movements throughout the country have not been successful at competing for these funds because of the lack of community and organizational infrastructure to develop competitive proposals, to conduct community needs assessments and program evaluations, and to build sustainable community coalitions. Without the ability to comply with these new requirements, public health needs and concerns in Latino communities remain unaddressed. Researchers with community-based experience are instrumental in developing the capacity of these organizations in the skills needed to apply for funds to establish the needed social programs in their communities. They have an important role to play in relationship to the development of community knowledge and skills to assist organizations to become conversant and successful in the politics of funding.

The ideas and perspectives presented in this analysis are based on a twenty-year history of projects in nonprofit and county health settings as well as participation on various state and national commissions and advisory groups. In addition, ongoing research and evaluation capacity-building work with community groups has also informed this analysis. I began this work as an outreach coordinator at a local nonprofit substance abuse community center in Santa Barbara, California. Later, I became the executive director of the center. Other experiences included serving as a health planner with the Los Angeles County Health Department and appointments to the Los Angeles County and State of California Alcohol Commissions. At the federal level, I became involved in grant reviews and national demonstration program evaluations for the Substance Abuse and Mental Health Services Administration (SAMHSA), and currently I served on the Center for Substance Abuse Prevention National Advisory Council. All of these instances expanded my knowledge about the politics of community funding, how issues become articulated for priority funding, and how community groups receive funds to address these issues. Initially, I assumed that funding decisions were made based on need, merit, and the articulation of specific issues and projects. The reality is different: organizations are funded because they have the resources and technical competency to compete effectively for funds, and these organizations frequently are not those which have the knowledge or experience necessary to work effectively with low-income communities of color.

This chapter discusses the divide in local, state, federal, and private funding between those organizations which have the capacity to compete for funds and those which are not yet skilled in these arenas. The barriers to funding are identified and several options for how researchers can play a role in expanding local Latino community capacity to compete for funds for building sustainable programs in their communities are addressed.

BARRIERS TO LATINO COMMUNITY FUNDING IN THE AGE OF ACCOUNTABILITY

Changes in national and regional demographics during the 1980s and 1990s have focused public attention on the complex issues of diversity, health, education, and disparities in these and other arenas (U.S. Department of Health and Human Services, 2000; The National Alliance for Hispanic Health, 2000). Public institutions are now serving diverse populations with specific linguistic and cultural orientations that are different from the past. In some parts of the United States, former "minority" communities are now the majority. This is particularly apparent in large southwestern states such as California and Texas where Mexican-American and other Latino populations are rapidly becoming the majority. In California, for example, 33 percent of the state population is Latino (Public Policy Institute of California, 2002).

The increased visibility of Latinos and the unique health, education, and other needs of this population bring new challenges and demands to policymakers, practitioners, and community-based organizations. The challenges are formidable and range from lack of information to fragmented county and state systems that are not prepared to address the linguistic and cultural issues associated with the health and social strengths or needs of these communities. Community groups; health, education, and other experts; community researchers; and policymakers need to join forces to build new, culturally focused and collaborative approaches for addressing the major issues of concern in these communities. An important aspect of this strategy is building the organizational capacity of Latino-based programs to enhance their ability to meet these challenges and improve the health and social environments of their respective communities. Researchers, graduate students, and others can play an important role in building organizational infrastructure to enhance and improve community life.

In Latino communities there are organizations that are well established and have a long history of providing some type of service in the community. Two examples are El Centro Mental Health in Tucson, Arizona, with a twenty-five-year history of providing mental health and family services, and Avance, with a twenty-eight-year history of providing a variety of family support services to Mexican-American families in San Antonio, Texas. There are similar organizations in Los Angeles, California, and New York. In these and other communities, there are also new, emerging grassroots groups that have formed to address specific, emerging issues. For example, organizations formed in the 1980s to address the needs of newly immigrated Central American families to the United States. New organizations formed to target specific issues such as HIV and other public health concerns. In Los Angeles, there are groups coalescing to address the specific issue of Latina girls involved in gangs, while other groups focus on substance abuse, mental health, or issues of environmental safety and justice.

These newly formed organizations are primarily organic, grassroots efforts of individuals who are committed to a particular problem in the community and want to build programs to reduce these problems. They function under difficult circumstances and yet often have the trust of the community and thus have the potential to be effective in addressing social issues. Unfortunately, these organizations struggle financially because they do not have the capability to compete for funds to build their programs, sometimes lacking such basics as office space, administrative support staff, and computer equipment. Even Latino organizations that are established and have a history of service in their communities find it difficult to both meet the local needs and compete for funding, given the new funding requirements and demands.

Since the early 1980s, new health and social problems have emerged in Latino communities, creating additional challenges to community service programs. Problems associated with HIV, community violence, and unsafe neighborhoods are specific issues that require special knowledge and skill. In addition, private and public funders are now requiring an elevated level of accountability that places numerous Latino grassroots organizations at a disadvantage for these funds. Organizations which are newly forming and those which are established can benefit from a partnership with experienced researchers who can design training seminars and other strategies to develop the organizational capacity for conducting community assessments, submit competitive proposals, and increase their knowledge in program evaluation.

The types of barriers and problems that limit Latino-based community organizations from seeking and successfully bidding for funding are

- lack of knowledge of the private or public funding universe and how it operates;
- lack of connections to the individuals, networks, and systems that have information regarding funding availability and funding cycles;
- lack of strategic organizational planning and priority setting necessary to identify funding opportunities and make decisions about which grants are feasible;
- lack of internal infrastructure to seek new funding, e.g., staff or community resources to focus time and attention on funding;
- lack of internal leadership to prioritize funding resources and options; and
- lack of access to the local, state, and national data necessary to utilize in grant proposal development.

All of these barriers are significant. Without adequate knowledge to effectively utilize sociodemographic or health information and data, it is not possible to begin the process of competing for funds. Many Latino-based organizations, particularly the small and new organizations, do not have connections to individuals in public or private funding and are not familiar with the process of accessing those funds. In addition, there is often a lack of internal infrastructure, including limited staff resources, space, and technological structures to strategically plan how, where, and when to seek new funding.

Organizations in low-income communities are usually stretched to the limit, with staff members serving multiple roles and often functioning in a crisis mode. In this kind of environment, it is not possible to stop long enough to plan ahead, beyond immediate concerns. However, when community organizations do take a step back to engage in strategic planning and other capacity building activities, these actions enhance the chance of survival of the organization. In addition, investing time on capacity-building skills, including learning about the culture and politics of funding, accessing data for problem justification, and leadership development, will benefit the organization and strengthen its ability to serve the community.

Although these barriers seem insurmountable, many Latino-based organizations have the trust of the community residents, which is a major strength for implementing the development of sustainable programs and services in Latino communities.

BUILDING ORGANIZATIONAL CAPACITY: DEFINITIONS AND PROCESSES

Organizational capacity in a general sense is what makes organizations work and ensures that functioning organizations have long-term success in their communities (Chaskin et al., 2001). Agencies work when they fulfill their organizational mission and members of their respective communities actively utilize services on an ongoing basis. Organizational capacity building means "building the capacity to fulfill an organization's mission . . . to deliver a program, to expand a program, and to adapt to change" (Letts et al., 1999, p. 20). Organizational health and strength contributes to community empowerment and social development.

The concept of building organizational capacity is part of an overall orientation to community organizing and empowerment which is strength based, focusing on the identification of community and organizational assets and resources as well as needs (Minkler, 2002). Even the most disadvantaged communities have areas of strengths that can be identified and utilized to further enhance the community and improve socioeconomic conditions. Within this perspective, building capacity at the organizational level involves understanding the organizational resources, human capital, and the strengths and weaknesses of an organization in order to develop those areas that need development and enhance those that are properly functioning. Developing organizational capacity will help promote and/or sustain the well-being of the organization and those involved with the organization.

In every community there are different types of organizations with varying levels of operational management, capacity to address their mission, and connectedness with community residents. Organizations also vary in the degree to which they are connected to and part of community political and funding structures. Given the scenario of diversity of organizational structures, emerging health and social problems, and rapid growth in Latino communities, how can these entities build a researcher-community partnership that will be continuous and benefit organizations and ultimately the community?

In my experience with Latino community groups there are some important principles and practices that need to be followed in order for this type of partnership to grow and develop. An essential factor is that community and organizational leaders need to trust the fact that researchers are interested in working in partnership with them primarily for the benefit of the community. Researchers who want to build a working relationship with Latino community organizations need to build trust by showing in concrete, culturally appropriate terms that they are there not to exploit but to serve them and their needs. The types of concrete actions that have proven effective in my work are that initially, researchers need to make themselves available to community groups free of charge. They must understand that most community groups or organizations do not have the funds to pay for consultation time or initial meetings. In my experience, when a respected university researcher makes the needs of the community the priority by being available for planning meetings and so on, this sends a message to the community that the researcher is offering his or her time for the good of the community or organization. Later, when funds are available or when a successful grant is co-authored, a stipend or salary can be included for the researcher to work with the organization or project. Other trust-building strategies are volunteering to conduct staff trainings, writing or co-authoring grants for community-based organizations, or simply helping individual staff members and their children gain access to higher education. I have found that when these types of steps are taken to build trust, soon, through word of mouth, the researcher becomes known as someone to be trusted and can work in collaboration with community groups. Over time, with continuous work on a variety of projects, trust builds, and the relationship between researcher and the community organization is enriched in a mutually beneficial manner.

OTHER IMPORTANT PRINCIPLES AND PRACTICES
FOR BUILDING RESEARCHER
AND LATINO COMMUNITY PARTNERSHIPS

In a report of a collaboration between the Environmental Support Center and the Innovation Network, Inc. (Jacobs, 2001), the writers summarize nine principles of capacity building based on a study of technical assistance providers who consult with nonprofit organizations on environmental and social justice initiatives. They begin their report with the following statement: "powerful capacity-building is the result of a strong, respectful relationship between a ready and willing organization and a skilled provider working with a set of core principles" (Jacobs, 2001, p. 2). The provider in this case is the person involved in capacity building, technical assistance, or support to an organization, and trust based on a strong, respectful, and mutually supportive relationship is at the core of researcher-community partnerships in Latino communities. Other basic principles outlined in this study are as follows:

1. Every organization is capable of building its own capacity.
2. An organization must be ready for capacity building.
3. Ongoing questioning means better answers.
4. Team and peer learning are effective.
5. Capacity building should accommodate different learning styles.
6. Every organization has its own history and culture.
7. All people and all parts of an organization are interrelated.
8. Capacity building takes time.

Throughout an extensive history of working with Latino community organizations, I have found all of these principles to be relevant and they should be followed in field research settings. Every community organization, regardless of financial and/or administrative situation, is capable of building its capacity, which begins with identifying important resources and needs. The role of the researcher is to assist in that process, not to dictate what is required. Researchers have research skills such as interviewing, observation, and other data gathering that can assist in the identification of the organization's resources and needs. In the process of applying these skills to assist the organization to identify strengths and weaknesses, researchers need to understand that initially individual staff responses to their interactions may range from hostility to complete reliance on the authority and perceived position of power of the researcher. Part of the role of the researcher is to adjust his or her attitudes and perspectives when working with community groups while learning to develop a sense of colearner and coresearcher within the partnership. A researcher wanting to build partnerships with Latino community organizations needs to be open to learning from the community residents and their social environment and not enter into that environment with an attitude that is condescending or superior. In fact, a lot of humility and willingness to listen is often very useful.

Organizational capacity building is a time-consuming, invigorating, and difficult process. Part of building partnerships with Latino community groups involves adjustments on both sides. Often, these groups or staff in communities are focused on meeting immediate needs of local residents that address potentially life-threatening situations such as domestic or other forms of interpersonal violence. Their focus on immediate issues may be a barrier when considering questions about the future prospects for the organization. However, organization leaders need to understand the benefits of taking a step back from the everyday activities to reassess their short- and long-term strengths and needs. Leadership is important at this juncture, since it is the executive director or board of directors who need to make the decision to engage in capacity building, grant development, strategic planning, and other forms of capacity development. It is their responsibility to translate the importance of engaging in this process with others in the organization.

QUALITIES OF A COMPETENT RESEARCHER PARTNER

Latino community groups need to have access to researchers or community experts with specific areas of expertise and who are knowledgeable and respectful of community conditions, histories, and leadership structures. Currently, there is a significant lack of such individuals. However, in the future, as policymakers and funders direct their attention to this population, experts will respond and will want to form partnerships with Latino groups and organizations. When this occurs, Latino groups need to be able to identify the qualities of the expert individuals they want to form partnerships with and this will require the flexibility and foresight to seek experts who

- must be willing to be "learners" as well as "teachers";
- must have a network of resources (technological as well as expert) to refer to when needed;
- must be proactive and be a coparticipant in the capacity-building process;
- must be patient; and
- must have a high tolerance for change and ambiguity. (Jacobs, 2001; Carmack, 2000)

Most of these qualities are self-explanatory. In my work experience with Latino community organizations, offering technical skills, being patient, sharing that knowledge in a way that can be understood by others, and exhibiting a high tolerance for change are essential characteristics in this arena. It is also important to have the language skills to be able to facilitate trainings or meetings in English, Spanish, or both.

Latino community organizations are established by individuals or groups of individuals who are highly committed to the issues they address and to serving community needs. I have found that community leaders and workers usually have a road map or an idea of where the organization is moving and how they plan to achieve their goals. Their mission must be respected and, in fact, capacity-building tasks should enhance plans established by community residents or leaders.

BUILDING SUSTAINABLE LATINO COMMUNITY ORGANIZATIONS AND COMMUNITIES

Based on the barriers identified earlier, the types of capacity-building assistance and support needed by Latino organizations may include any or all of the following:

- Assist organizations to develop strategic organizational plans for priority setting.
- Assist organizations to identify and utilize networks and sources of funding and program support information.

- Assist organizations to develop a team of organizational and community experts who can develop grant proposals for the organization.
- Assist the organization to establish personal and technological networks with funding structures.
- Assist organizations to develop evaluation skills.
- With the staff, develop and implement a staff-training and development plan.
- Assist with leadership training and development.

Many researchers or academics are not familiar with how their education and knowledge can be useful to community groups. Academics are often trained in methods, philosophies, or paradigms that have limited relevance to community issues or problems. However, through numerous projects in community settings, I have learned that there are a multitude of skills that academics have refined through their training which can be beneficial to community groups and which can be translated and applied to a range of social needs. Some of these include analytical skills, writing, teaching, interviewing, observational skills, evaluation, basic research skills, public speaking, and computer skills. When respect and humility is combined with the application of technical assistance in community settings, fruitful partnerships with community groups develop. In the process, capacity-building strategies assist in meeting organizational needs and provide important technical competencies that remain in the community.

CONCLUSION

There currently is a major divide between those organizations which have the technical skills to compete for private and public funds and those which do not have these skills. The divide has the greatest effect on organizations in low-income communities of color, particularly Latino communities. Most often organizations that can compete for federal or state dollars are those which have resources, infrastructures, and knowledge about the politics and techniques of funding. However, these organizations may not have the cultural competency to reach those communities most in need of interventions. This situation is reaching a crisis level because as Latino populations grow and are more visible in many regions of the country, the avenues, systems, and institutions charged with addressing the needs of communities are not equipped to do so. What is required is a major revision in how funding to Latino communities is approached and managed. Some private foundations have provided leadership and are funding projects across the country designed to build community infrastructures to improve community health. However, many of these initiatives have not specifically focused on the unique capacity-development needs in Latino communities and organizations. A major effort to fund Latino community and organizational capacity development would be an important investment in this era of greater accountability and emerging community health and social problems in the largest ethnic group in the United States. Such initiatives could be utilized, adapted, and replicated throughout the country and would provide an important blueprint for building Latino community infrastructures to improve community health and social conditions.

REFERENCES

Carmack, W.R. (2000). *Planning for change: A systems model for communities and organizations.* Monograph1021, Southwest CAPT. Washington, DC: Center for Substance Abuse Prevention, Substance Abuse and Mental Health Services Administration.

Chaskin, R.J., Brown, P., Venkatesh, S., and Vidal, A. (2001). *Building community capacity.* New York: Aldine de Gruyter.

Jacobs, B. (2001). *Echoes from the field.* Washington, DC: Innovation Networks, Inc.

Letts, C.W., Ryan, W.P., and Grossman, A. (1999). *High performance non-profit organizations.* New York: John Wiley & Sons, Inc.

Minkler, M. (2002). Introduction and overview. In Minkler, M. (Ed.), *Community organizing and community building for health* (pp. 3-19). New Brunswick, NJ: Rutgers University Press.

The National Alliance for Hispanic Health (2000). *For the 21st century: The Hispanic community health agenda.* Washington, DC: The National Alliance for Hispanic Health.

Orozco, C. (1992-1993). Beyond machismo, la familia and ladies auxiliaries: A historiography of Mexican-origin women's participation in voluntary associations and politics in the United States, 1870-1990. *Renato Rosaldo lecture series, Monograph 10,* 37-77.

Public Policy Institute of California (2002). A state of diversity: Demographic trends in California's regions. *California counts population trends and profiles, 3*(5), 1-15.

U.S. Department of Health and Human Services (2000). *Healthy people 2010: Understanding and improving health.* Washington, DC: U.S. Government Printing Office.

Walter, C.L. (2002). Community building practice: A conceptual framework. In Minkler, M. (Ed.), *Community organizing and community building for health.* New Brunswick, NJ: Rutgers University Press.

Index

('i' indicates an illustration; 'n' indicates a note; 't' indicates a table)

259